Dear Brau
from
Issy
3-25-98

Fight Terrorism

The Security Connection for Family Protection

Reduce Personal Risk

ISSY BOIM
"MR. SECURITY"

Security Connection

ISBN: 0-9656939-0-2

Library of Congress Catalog Card Number: 97-65646

Printed in the United States of America

Cover Design: *Tim Fisher*

Printed by: *McNaughton & Gunn, Inc.*
                   Saline, Michigan 48176

Published by: *Safe Flyer Joint Venture Partners*

Note: Issy Boim and Safe Flyer are not engaged in the business of providing individual personal security advice. They have not made an independent evaluation or inspection of any reader's property or lifestyle and, therefore, cannot provide individual advice to a reader. Thus, the information contained herein is intended for general reference only. Readers are advised to consult with a local security expert about their particular circumstances and situations.

Issy Boim and Safe Flyer make no representation or warranties, implied or expressed, concerning the adequacy or suitability of any security prevention technique discussed herein. Nor do they make any representation regarding the successful implementation of the contents of this book.

The information contained in this book is the opinion of the author based upon many years of training and experience in the field of security services. Neither the publisher nor the editors make any claims as to the material contained herein.

Please consult with a local security expert about your particular security decisions.

World travel doesn't seem so glamorous after reading The Security Connection. My life sure seems safer though.

V.S., Fairfax, VA

What a unique book! I feel frightened and, at the same time, motivated. There is light at the end of the tunnel. Thank you.

W.F., Springfield, MO

I loved the story of the first sky marshal. Your history helped clear up misunderstandings I've had for years.

E.C., Aurora, CO

You're right — I can't depend on anyone but myself to better protect my loved ones.

S.N., Modesto, CA

I'm not a business executive, but I feel like I've been treated like one.

M.U., Pittsburgh, PA

You've made a real impact on my family; we're reading your book together.

A.P., San Diego, CA

My next door neighbor is an international traveler. When he saw the book on our coffee table, he asked to borrow it. I haven't seen it since!

T.R., Tucson, AZ

Dynamite information. It's about time someone did this.

J.S., Jacksonville, FL

What a wake-up call!

R.A., Mansfield, OH

We've been planning our European vacation for over a year. Now we're taking the book with us.

D.G., Fort Wayne, IN

Great job, Mr. Security!

G.L., Little Rock, AR

Having been victimized by travel scams in the past, I can say you've done a terrific service to my fellow travelers.

N.J., Cambridge, MA

Are you sure you're not James Bond?

H.K., Plano, TX

I've had this sinking feeling for some time that I've been on borrowed time on my travels. You confirmed it.

W.R., Waldorf, MD

We need more people like Issy Boim to help support the American Dream.

D.D., Houston, TX

TABLE OF CONTENTS

ACKNOWLEDGMENTS

This book originated from four major sources: constant travel over the last 35 years; research; consulting; and personal experience. My security work has put me in contact with all kinds of travelers in every part of the world. I listened and I observed. The people I met have had two characteristics in common whether they were business executives, celebrities, or leisure travelers:

1. They all wanted to feel more secure and be safe when they travel.

2. They all felt that the security process was too far removed from their daily lives...and they didn't know how to make personal security *"WORK FOR THEM."*

I've worked with TWA, American, Continental, Northwest and after the Lockerbie tragedy, Pan American Airlines. I've protected the lives and assets of Fortune 500 companies, as well as celebrities and foreign dignitaries. I've spent too much time working in the world's most dangerous places.

Throughout these many years of experience, I have seen the world change at an accelerating pace. All of us today face security threats we would never have imagined possible just a few decades ago.

Yes, times change, and we must change with them. It's time we all learned what we need to know to stay safe and secure. What better time to start than NOW!

This is why I am turning my attention to families across the country.

I feel very fortunate that some wonderful people took an interest in me, in my work, and in the writing of this book, **The Security Connection**. I would like to acknowledge and thank those who gave freely of their time, energy, encouragement and inspiration:

First, I want to thank my wife, Miri, for her emotional support and endless encouragement. I am thankful for her willingness to allow my work to dominate so many of our breakfast and dinner conversations, and I am exceedingly grateful for the respect she has shown for my personal goals and life's work.

I am most grateful to my AR Group Board of Directors: Rudy Fabre, whose unending confidence in me has been invaluable; Richard Wilkens, without whose support this project would not have happened; Tom Balousek, for his ongoing support; and Tim Maystrick, for his focus on how we can better serve the public.

MBA Marketing Group provided the talent, the creativity, and the productivity to make sure this became a reality.

I would also like to thank an entire team of caring people who make a 100% committment each day to provide world-wide security, including Doug Dotan, a consultant whose research contribution to this book was vital. My special thanks also go to ICTS (International Consultant Targeted Security) who have been pioneers in sharing the Israeli preventative security program with the international community.

No one writes a book alone. The ideas contained herein come from a variety of sources—some easily brought to mind, others long forgotten—and so I wish to acknowledge the contribution that others have made in my life through the unselfish sharing of their thoughts and wisdom.

People think I'm like James Bond because of the counterespionage mystique. They pay me to make sure "the bad guys" avoid them. While I'm not James Bond (I wish I had his hair!), I am always aware of lurking dangers and I *do* take my responsibilities fearlessly. Lives depend on it.

My mother taught me everyone deserves a chance to feel secure. Growing up in Israel makes you appreciate this right. So I developed a good eye for helping people and making people's lives more comfortable. I love what I do. I work hard, never tell dirty jokes, sleep with my own wife, love my family, and want to make the world a safer place. That's Issy Boim. Now let me help you and your family feel more secure.

PREFACE

"No man can terrorize a whole nation unless we are his accomplices."

—Edward R. Murrow

I believe that you can be safe, secure and significantly reduce the chances of becoming the victim of an act of terror.

Terrorism tries to ruin the American Dream. We've all worked tirelessly to make the American Dream a reality; it must always be protected as our most cherished possession.

You can better secure the American Dream from today's new threats. How? You have choices, and you should be free to act on them.

We all *must* be able to put our children in a day care center that is safe. We *must* be able to confidently go to work in a federal office building. This is all part of the American Dream.

For 35 years, I've helped build security systems that protect the lives of millions of people. During this time, I have become much more aware of how little so many people understand what security consciousness is all about. I know that there is a lot of information out there on terrorism and crime prevention...but I've always envisioned a security book that would empower and inspire your family to take better care of themselves. We're drowning in information and starving for knowledge. Let's stop being confused with all the choices, decisions and options. Let's really learn how to be security conscious.

I will clarify and simplify the security process...stripping away its mystique and revealing how you can readily implement a personal security system for you and your family.

I've observed that thinking about security brings frustration to many people.

We will show you a different way to think about security. This is a way where you feel you *can* have control. You'll actually learn *why* and *how* certain criminal acts can be prevented by fundamentally sound and easy-to-implement behavior strategies.

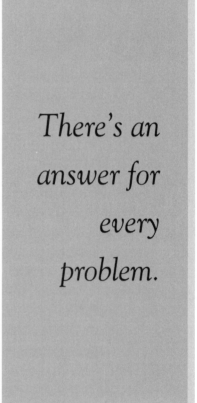

There's an answer for every problem.

You can exchange frustration and ignorance for your own personal security "system." The right system. We'll show you how to gain control and help secure your family's right to the American Dream.

Are these strategies too simple and obvious? I have been teaching this "personal security system" to large numbers of people throughout the corporate world and aviation community for years. ***Now*** I see the need to pass this information on to you and your family.

Becoming security conscious and creating a more secure future should be a joyful activity. Becoming security conscious should be an experience of achievement and success—part of the American Dream.

To me, the American Dream means to:

✔   improve my lot in life

✔   have a good job or business

✔   have security for my family

✔   do good for my community

✔   be productive, cheerful, responsible and helpful

So many people came to America–and still come–for never before dreamed of opportunities. America was built by people who gave, not just took; people who have realized this great country "lights the way" for the world to see how a better tomorrow comes from people who realize the importance of their fellow citizens. Americans strive to make this country better for everyone.

A bright future starts with creating the opportunity to secure a vision. We will not live in fear. We each have a vested interest for a better tomorrow.

It's time for us to work together to more effectively protect and secure our future. Lots of threats exist, but remember, "there's safety in numbers." We learned that in kindergarten. "Share everything, hold hands and stick together."

That's what these pages are meant to convey. That's what the American Dream is about.

Drop me a line and let me know what your thoughts are on this book. All your suggestions are welcome.

Issy Boim

INTRODUCTION

"Nothing in life is to be feared. It is only to be understood."

—Marie Curie

How did I end up writing a book for families? That's a good question!

Reflecting back, it started on July 23, 1968. On that date something happened that the world had never before witnessed. Three Palestinian guerrillas seized an El Al flight bound for Tel Aviv from Rome and diverted it to Algiers. In exchange for the lives of all on board, the guerrillas demanded the release of 1,200 political prisoners.

This event was unprecedented. Never before had the aviation community been the target of terrorism, and it became all too evident that those in charge of public safety had no security system in place to deal with this kind of crisis. It took 39 days for the hostage crisis to be resolved.

Before the Algerian hijacking, the best known hijackings were those that took place in the United States and were instigated by disgruntled Cuban-Americans who would "skyjack" a jet from Florida to Cuba. But the hijacking to Algeria was dramatically different. It was the first time skyjackers had declared they were going to kill passengers if the government, or the world community, did not give in to their demands.

Now, my own story and my future work began as a result of this event. It created a need that led me into a brand new field of work—travel security. I "woke up" abruptly to the cold, hard reality that making life more secure for masses of people was a tremendous undertaking.

Because of the pressure of that hijacking, a team of security personnel, myself included, were immediately positioned aboard aircraft, where we were situated next to the cockpit. The "high technology" gear we were given, if you can believe it, were cans of tear gas and night sticks! **They stuck a night stick in my hand and said, "Go get 'em."** The government had told us to put a stop to the threat, and though all we had were these primitive deterrents, we also had an intense desire to put a stop to any more of these reprehensible actions.

This was the official beginning of sky marshals. Though our presence made the skies a little safer, it did not solve the problem of aviation terrorism. It didn't take us long to realize that prevention first must be focused on the ground.

We will either find a way or make one.

All of this seems like such a long time ago; even, perhaps, another lifetime. Did you ever have the feeling that you've had several lifetimes within your lifetime? Just two years before that hijacking, I had been recruited from the military at the ripe old age of 22 to join the Israeli Security Services, known as the Shin Bet. It is an organization that is a cross between the CIA and the FBI and is an organization in charge of all national security, including the protection of the country's airlines. Because the main purpose of Shin Bet in the mid-1960s was to capture Soviet spies who were pervasive throughout Israel, my first security work was in counterespionage. I was charged to locate and detain Soviet spies and "escort' them to jail.

It turned out to be a short-lived job because, eighteen months later, the Six Day War erupted and life in Israel changed dramatically. Soviet spy work came to a halt and attention was turned instead to searching for potential terrorists who had been part of terrorist groups during the Six Day War. My personal life had changes as well...I had a wife, a child, and a mortgage...the dog came later, along with another child!

Then, on July 23, 1968, *life was interrupted.*

As a result of that hijacking, the Israelis improved their security measures on all El Al aircraft.

Because of the bolstered security of El Al airlines, terrorists began to change the focus of their target. Almost one year to the day after the El Al hijacking, twenty terrorists seized a TWA flight on its way from Rome to Tel Aviv and diverted it to Damascus. Syrian commandos allowed the passengers to disembark, but then attempted to blow up the plane. Again, resolution of the crisis was slow in coming. It took almost two months for all the hostages and the plane to make it back home again.

THE TRAVEL SECURITY SYSTEM

Now the question we faced as a small team of security professionals was how to design and then implement an effective security system that would allow an airline to efficiently operate, but would also avoid inconveniencing passengers.

There was no model that existed anywhere in the world, but we knew it had to be created. Out of many, many long days and nights of labor, a model was built, a blueprint for travel security. Hard work, compromises and sacrifice helped me reach my dreams. Like the German proverb says: "God gives us the nuts, but he does not crack them." There was a need; we had to fill it.

We tested our new system of ground security at the El Al airline ground station situated at London's Heathrow Airport. We knew that if we could make this concept a reality in London, it could be utilized anywhere by any airline company. Unfortunately, we also knew that once terrorists realized that they could not successfully hijack any more El Al flights, they would turn to unprotected airlines.

Too soon, this would prove to be true, as terrorists armed with firearms began to attack ground station checkpoints in Turkey, Germany and Switzerland. Sometimes you wish weren't always right—what can I tell you? The last unsecured attack took place in Rome...which ended with the killing of 16 TWA passengers inside the airport. These tragedies galvanized the European community into immediate action. Nations put pressure on those countries that were supporting terrorists, and with new security systems in place, ground attacks ceased.

THE SYSTEM EXPANDS...

This plan for our travel security system quickly grew. By now, as a private security consultant with ICTS, we programmed the security system for American Airlines throughout Europe and at their international hubs in Chicago and Dallas.

Between 1985 and 1989, American airline companies decided to improve security in their trans-Atlantic operations. They were seeking to achieve security operations that would exceed FAA requirements. I returned again to Europe to implement the security system we had put into operation with El Al. We would be called in to consult with American, TWA, Continental, Northwest and Pan Am Airlines.

The travel security system around which those operations were built is still in place today. Of course, parts of the system have been modified to meet the changing needs of the times, for as you can well imagine, terrorists, too, have become more sophisticated. Today, the basic aviation security program handles approximately 500 million passengers a year.

By the end of the 1980s, an American Fortune 500 company wanted to use the travel security concept to determine the vulnerability of their executives and aircraft when traveling internationally.

As a result of this work, it became obvious to me that the security system developed for American airline companies could also be utilized for corporate America's private aircraft. As American companies were just becoming aware of aviation preventative security, I made a decision to focus my efforts in this direction. Today, as President of Air Security in Houston, Texas, my staff and I protect the personnel and assets of Fortune 500 companies, as well as the lives of celebrities and foreign dignitaries when they travel.

NOW...THE NEXT STEP

In my experiences and observations over the past 35 years, I have found that most people...most corporations...and even most governments do not prioritize, or even really think much about travel security until:

A NATIONAL OR INTERNATIONAL TRAGEDY OCCURS

OR

THEY HAVE BEEN VICTIMIZED

Do we really need to wait until something awful happens? Or, can we change this pattern of 20/20 hindsight? As the world evolves, we must face the fact that there are new dangers that threaten our personal security. This makes it essential for all of us to learn to adapt and further our security education.

I'm saying that, while life is not an emergency, ***you need to learn and think what you would do in an emergency. No surprises!*** It the attitude: I know what to do because I've thought about it. Get the family out! Call 911. Teach the kids!

Corporate executives are busy learning how to assess travel risks. But what about you and your family?

In today's world:

+ ✈   you need to learn how to become less vulnerable...

+ ✈   if you're an American, you're a target abroad, whether you want to be ...or not...

+ ✈   you're at risk in some areas, whether you travel locally or internationally...

Family life is not structured like it was years ago. Urban alienation has put physical and emotional miles between us and our families. Thank God we can still share quality time with our families. We need all of our family members—and friends— to be safe and secure. We need to know how to be better prepared to protect them.

More than 550 million people will board jet planes in the United States in 1997. How safe will they be? How safe will *you* be? How many people will become victims of some other form of terrorism or robbery during their travels?

Can this loss be reduced?

Yes...if we make ourselves aware...if we become smart travelers. Times are changing and security education is vital if we want a safe future. This is why I wrote *The Security Connection* —so that your family can learn to live, work and travel safely.

CHAPTER 1

WE ARE VULNERABLE

"It was the best of times. It was the worst of times."

—Charles Dickens
A Tale of Two Cities

About ten or so of my friends and family members have birthdays that fall around this time of year. I guess I might be old fashioned, but I think birthdays are important days. I like to think of birthdays as inspirational days to think about what we are going to do in the future.

I've been reading about another birthday that people all over the world are beginning now to prepare to celebrate. In fact, hotels around the country are already booked for New Year's Eve 1999 to usher in our second millennium — **our 2000th birthday!** I've heard though, that you better buy your champagne now to avoid the rush!

Politicians, educators, journalists, clergy, scientists and business executives are all anticipating the continuation of the unparalleled change our civilization has experienced during the past 100 years.

What kind of birthday will we be celebrating? Just how bright is our future? What do we expect?

Many of us expect major advances in our lives, especially in the fields of science and medicine. We are an expecting group of people, aren't we? And an introspective group as well. We expect improvements in our lives — that's what the future is for. After all, look at the staggering levels of accomplishments that have transpired just in our lives and in the lives of our parents and grandparents.

But we expect violence as well...

According to an exclusive **Newsweek** poll:

➤ 48% of us say there will be more warfare than in the past 100 years;

➤ 32% say that the greatest threat to world peace over the next century will be terrorism.

Today, the further we move away from our front doors, the more we become vulnerable. Bad things happen to good people every minute of the day all over our cities, not necessarily because they are particularly targeted, although they could be, but because they may be random victims of criminals of every kind.

Take every act of terrorism as a personal affront against your space—avoid these malignant motives of others!

Extremists, cults, the mentally unstable and gangs seem to be coming at us from all directions today. Anyone who uses the Internet is now able to download the "Terrorists Handbook," and read how to build a bomb big enough to destroy an office building. Did you know that... some of the most deadly poisons known to man have been found in the possession of radicals here in the United States...or that...Iran funnels $100 million every year to the Lebanese Hezbollah guerrillas for the sponsorship of international terrorism, much of which is aimed at Americans...or that...the number of terrorist bombings and bombing attempts in the United States increased 400% over the past 10 years with tactics now emulating those used in Belfast and Beirut?

Positive lessons are not always taught in positive ways.

Although you may not realize it, your greatest enemy can be your own complacency. Complacency means to have a feeling of security while ignoring unpleasant possibilities. This is why complacency too often leads to vulnerability.

DO YOU KNOW HOW TO ACT AT GUNPOINT?

Newscasts nightly bring stories to our living rooms about acts of terror and violent crime involving guns. Do you know how to act at gunpoint? It is required learning today. A bit of forethought may avert panic and provide you with just the right response to save your own life. For example, experts tell us...

❑ If someone is threatening you with a visible weapon, take him seriously. If he says, "Don't move," assume he means just that. If he starts shooting anyway, either at you or someone else, then move! Escape or duck for cover.

❑ Your best reaction to the sound of gunfire is to drop to the ground or floor. Then get under or behind cover as soon as you can.

❑ Faced with a weapon, watch the person, not the weapon. Staring at the muzzle of a gun pointed straight at you can freeze your own reaction. Try to make and keep eye contact with the assailant, and speak calmly and reassuringly.

❑ There is no one right answer to the question of whether to comply with an armed attacker's demands. If he wants to force you to leave a public place and accompany him to a secluded place, you must rely on your own judgment of the situation. It may be wiser to refuse and take your chances if help is close by.

Will you remember this? I have found that rare is the person who takes action until after a disaster has taken place or until a loved one has become a victim. It's a matter of "closing the barn door after the horse is gone" — when it's too late to solve the problem.

- ☑ **The World Trade Center**
- ☑ **Oklahoma City**
- ☑ **TWA 800**
- ☑ **Letter bombs/car bombs**
- ☑ **Drive-by shootings**
- ☑ **Value Jet**
- ☑ **Atlanta's Olympic Park**

The media makes disasters shocking "entertainment" and their investigations provide us with fascinating stories. But I ask again: do they change us in any positive way, or do they simply serve to breed fear in us? We sit in front of our televisions watching hour after hour as the gruesome details unfold. Then, when the media interest is gone and the picture has faded from our TV sets, we go on with our lives, hoping that something terrible doesn't ever happen to us.

Two of the more popular television quiz shows were: *You Bet Your Life* and *Who Do You Trust*? Are we unnecessarily *"betting our life"* when we fail to become security conscious when we travel, even in our own cities? Who can we *trust* to improve our security?

Yes, today, threats are all around us as we approach our 2000th birthday. Americans have always faced hardships and challenges in the past. We are a group of people who are willing to face our difficulties and create new options. That work continues. Our future beckons as we strive for the vision of a secure world.

CHAPTER 2

SECURE YOUR FUTURE

"Our attitudes determine whether we experience peace or fear, whether we are well or sick, free or imprisoned."

Thomas Jefferson

One morning my secretary came in to tell me that Steven Spielberg's office was on the phone. As you most assuredly know, Steven Spielberg is one of the preeminent movie directors of our time, whose blockbuster hits include *Jurassic Park, Jaws, E.T.,* and *Raiders of the Lost Ark.*

"Mr. Spielberg wants to speak to Mr. Security," she said. I had the pleasure of meeting Mr. Spielberg's mother and stepfather years earlier when I escorted them on an extensive sightseeing tour of Israel.

It turned out that Mr. Spielberg was planning a whirlwind tour by private jet of European capitals to coincide with the international premiere of his soon-to-be-released film *Schindler's List.* For a number of security reasons, he wanted a risk assessment for each city he was planning to visit.

There is a connection here between the security needs of Steven Spielberg and your own. Truly, whether you are a business traveler or leisure traveler, you should have access to the same information as Steven Spielberg. You should have the same security information that senior executives of Fortune 500 companies are privy to...in order to insure that you and your family travel safely.

From a vantage point of having been responsible for protecting the lives of world travelers for more than 30 years, *I feel it is imperative for you to know that the security threats today are severe enough to warrant an all-out educational training effort.*

A QUESTION OF RESPONSIBILITY

Responsibility: something which is within one's power, control or management.

Taking responsibility is the key to safety and security. Because even with all the information you need, all the necessary educational training, *effective security measures depend on you.*

YOU ARE THE ONE WHO MUST BE RESPONSIBLE...

Life isn't fair...it's a bummer at times, but true. You make difficult decisions every day in your personal life and work life! What's one more—the decision to practice safety!

Do you know what I've found out over the years about being responsible? It feels good! It puts me in a healthy state of mind. I feel more worthy. The more worthy I feel, the more I want to bring good things not only into my life, but into the lives of other people.

The best way to predict the future is to create it.

Some people I know are afraid to meet their responsibilities. Some people see responsibilities as burdens that interfere with the pursuit of pleasure. Some feel that being responsible is a joyless task and only take responsibility out of guilt or fear. But throughout my life, I find that my sense of purpose and sense of accomplishment grow as I assume more responsibility.

All of us have had experiences where we were "forced" to accept new responsibilities...when we were given a promotion at work...or we had to take care of a family member...or our help was requested for a volunteer effort. Perhaps you also had moments of indecision, when you heard a voice in your head say. "Do I really want to do this?" Yet, wasn't there also another part of you that knew "it was yours to do" and that, inevitably, you would accept the responsibility?

Safety and security are yours to do...

THE NECESSITY OF BEING PREPARED!

Many of us are a hurried lot. We ask questions like, "Why does fast food take so long?"

We want...

✈ fast, pass-through security check points at airports

✈ to arrive at the airport 15 minutes before the flight departs

✈ to avoid lines at all costs

✈ the best security in the world, and

✈ effective security solutions

The question is...what security systems can we control to insure our safety? Airline security? Airport security? Government security?

We can only control...what we do...our own individual and family security.

This takes us back to "responsibility" and the fact that we can only control what, when, where and how we will be responsible.

When it comes to security, the meaning of responsibility is ***being prepared***. Being prepared increases your chance of successfully not becoming a victim. To be prepared means to make yourself ready, to know what steps to take.

> ## RESPONSIBILITY + PREPARATION =
> ## THE ABILITY TO MEET UNEXPECTED CHALLENGES

Let me tell you a story about being prepared. A colleague of mine speaks highly of a teacher who, in his youth, worked as a steam engineer. On one occasion, as he was traveling on the train, he saw that a huge truck was stopped in the middle of the tracks about four or five miles ahead. As he reached to pull the horn of the train, the head engineer stopped him and asked him instead to watch what was about to happen.

The train was going 90 miles an hour and, as it flew down the tracks toward the truck, the head engineer increased the train's speed to 120 mph. Then he opened up all the steam and all the power. Like a knife, the train cut the truck in two and continued on its journey. Neither the train nor any of the hundreds of passengers on board were hurt.

When the head engineer was asked how he thought to do such a seemingly risky thing, he said that he had a habit of thinking about what he would do if a situation like this should occur. When the situation arose, he was ready to act in the manner he had visualized in his mind.

Later, my colleague's friend learned that it was all a matter of physics; a certain weight traveling at a certain speed increases its power. So you can see that the head engineer had made himself knowledgeable and was prepared and confident to take responsibility for his actions.

How do you feel when you are prepared? Don't you feel good about yourself? **I know that when I feel prepared, I face situations with more confidence.** I feel more secure. And that's why I believe each of us is in the "security business"...securing a better future for ourselves...our families...our community...our companies...and feeling good about life!

Let's go back to Steven Spielberg and his security awareness. Here is a huge international celebrity who regularly uses security in his personal and work life. He has people, locations and technology to protect...however he took one more step. He wanted a thorough assessment of his future risks, covering all the bases. ***That's preparation!*** That's what you need to do! Follow the old Boy Scout motto: "Be prepared!"

PLACE

YOUR

PHOTO

HERE

Question: Is this the photo of a victim?

Will this person become a victim?

Answer: Get the Message?

CHAPTER 3

THE METHOD AND MADNESS OF TERRORISM

"The only thing we have to fear is fear itself."

Franklin Delano Roosevelt

I'm a news junkie...I find CNN comforting somehow. CNN makes me feel like I'm part of this "small family" of 3 billion people, and I know what's going on. Do you ever feel this way?

I remember watching CNN one afternoon as my immediate staff and I were gathered in our conference room. We were awaiting Judge Duffy's sentencing of the four conspirators convicted of the 1993 bombing of The World Trade Center in New York City. That horrible blast, as you know, killed six and injured 1,000.

The prosecution had presented the case that if the sodium cyanide in the terrorist's bomb had vaporized instead of being burned, cyanide gas would have sucked into the north tower, and *thousands* would have been killed. "That, to my mind, is what was intended," the Judge told the conspirators as he sentenced each to 240 years in prison.

And ever since that bombing, we have been under the threat of terrorism. Not that terrorism didn't exist before then, but The World Trade Center bombing was the wake-up call.

When it comes to security, the meaning of responsibility is being prepared. To prepare you for reducing your personal risk, I want you to first understand the bigger picture of terrorism. I know what you're thinking: who wants to read the "What's What about Terrorism?" Too remote, not fun! Hey—don't quit on me now! Take a break when you need to—there is even an "intermission" in this chapter. ***But read on!***

Much study, analysis, and history of terrorism has been written over the years by security experts, government officials, psychologists, journalists, and political scientists. These individuals and groups have compiled a ton of data on every aspect of the subject. My purpose, however, is not to provide you with an encyclopedia on terrorism. It is, instead, to give you a better understanding of its broadest and most damaging context so that you'll be better equipped and prepared to deal with acts of terror and crime in your own community and the places to which you travel.

In this chapter, here you'll be learning the "what, how and wherefore's" of terrorism. I know it's not a fun or easy chapter to read. I've kept that in mind as I wrote it. Remember why you're reading this book...to protect you and your family!

Terrorism. The word itself conjures up images of fear and horror. Acts of terror hold the world's attention. While it is occurring, the real-life drama is played out on our television screens, and we watch the victims...the survivors and their families...the criminals...and the heroes...and we come to know them all.

Terrorism is defined as a deliberate and systematic act of violence that is used for political ends. Terrorism uses the tactics of fear, maiming, and murder to achieve its goals. It can involve the citizens of one country or the territory of more than one country, and its violence can take many forms — buses being blown up, the capturing and murder of school children, the hijacking of vehicles, and the holding of innocent men and women as hostages.

It was terrorism that brought down Pan Am Flight 103 over Lockerbie, Scotland, taking the lives of 260 people. It was terrorism that caused those injuries and fatality that fateful night at the 1996 Olympic Games in Atlanta, and it was terrorism that took the lives of so many children in Oklahoma City.

TERRORIST ACTS SERVE TWO PURPOSES

The first purpose is to publicize the terrorist's claim or problem. Remember what P.T. Barnum used to say: "I don't care what you say about me as long as you say something." The point is, to a terrorist, bad publicity is better than no publicity at all. It is precisely because of publicity that terrorists are now high on the list of the world's most feared.

The second purpose of terrorism is to cause political change, the goal of which can be independence or revolution.

Through their own form of learned experience, terrorists now know how to play on our fears and our sense of moral outrage.

Much of what we see on the news — murders, kidnappings, executions of the innocent, ethnic cleansing — are carefully staged by terrorists to generate emotions and opinions, as well as financial and military support.

Because acts of terrorism are instantly beamed to all points of the globe through satellite communication, audiences are provided with riveting drama. When an act of terrorism occurs somewhere in the world, don't we end up watching CNN every half hour for updates? Be honest with me—which will you watch — a skyjacking in progress or reruns of *Gilligan's Island*? How many of you watched as the rescue teams desperately searched for survivors in the rubble of the Oklahoma City bombing? Or stayed up half the night searching for more news on the Olympic Park bombing? Unfortunately, terrorism plays well on television, and terrorists know this.

> There's an old saying in the newspaper business: "If it bleeds, it leads," and these days crises and disasters on TV have become *"infotainment."*

You need to understand that many terrorist groups really never expect to conquer a strong nation like America. By exploiting the media, especially television, by horrifying all of us who hypnotically stay tuned to CNN night and day, terrorists present us with the image of a powerless government. That's their goal — to make us see our government as inept and weak.

Because terrorist attacks appear to be random, we begin to question ***"How at risk are we?"*** and ***"If the government can't protect us, who can?"*** When we, the viewing audience, find these questions running around in our heads, we are unwittingly empowering the terrorists by allowing their emotional manipulation of us.

You're not manipulated, you say? You—the one who is always on the run? You run to work...to school...to the mall...to the doctor...the hairdresser's and the airport. Too busy to stop, look and listen. Well—Stop! Look! Listen! Avoid the chance of putting yourself in the path of an act of terror. "Busyness" can equal manipulating and sabotaging yourself!

What have we learned so far about terrorism and media exposure?

1.   It provides benefits to terrorists.

2.   It reaches its target audience and is able to communicate its message worldwide.

3.   Because of our society's interest in broadcasting drama and our viewing habits, using television to broadcast terror is a low-cost, high-result proposition.

4.   Because of all of the above, we should expect that terrorism will continue to be a threat to Americans, especially American travelers.

As we analyze our human history, terrorism has always existed in some form. We call it **"man's inhumanity to man."** Like it or not, once it was discovered that terrorists could gain strength and influence by attacking defenseless victims, it "legitimized" terrorism in the minds of the more mentally unstable and evil groups.

Let's talk about the war on terrorism. Before I explain things like government policy, who are the bad guys and how they operate, it's important to make a statement. Yes, you do need to know all of this information; without it, you'll be less prepared and therefore more vulnerable. However...the war on terrorism is won by each of us, every day, as we become more conscious of the world around us...*no matter where we are.*

Each time you become more alert and notice something suspicious and possibly dangerous that you may not have paid attention to before, you are winning the war on terrorism. For example:

Self-Protection:

- When entering a shop or office – especially a bank – size up what is going on inside before letting the door close behind you. You wouldn't be the first person to walk innocently into a robbery in progress and become one of its victims; or

- Learn to carry your wallet in a front pants pocket rather than in a back pocket or a jacket pocket. Get in the habit of stuffing your hand in on top of it when in a dense crowd; or

- When attending conferences in other cities, take off your name tag when you leave the meeting. Such a tag labels you a visitor to the area and hence a potential victim.

Here is my point: The federal government, the airline companies and the law enforcement community all have roles to play and responsibilities to take in fighting this menace of terrorism in our modern world. But our role and personal responsibility is just as important as theirs. We are all "pieces of the puzzle."

...and the puzzle isn't complete until all the parts are in place!

We can win this war—if we decide we really want to. It's our decision.

...Now let's get on with the information I promised!

Airlines and travelers are targets for what is really an attack on the United States. While government efforts have not and will not completely eliminate terrorism, you should be aware of US counter terrorist policies.

US policy follows three general rules:

➔ **First**: it makes no deals with terrorists and does not submit to blackmail. We have found over the years that this policy works.

➔ **Second**: it treats terrorists as criminals, pursuing them aggressively, and applying the rule of law.

➔ **Third**: it brings maximum pressure on states that sponsor and support terrorists by imposing economic, diplomatic, and political sanctions and by urging other states to do likewise.

Nations around the world are working together increasingly to fight terrorism through law enforcement cooperation. Several governments have recently turned over major terrorists to US authorities for prosecution, including the reputed mastermind of The World Trade Center bombing, Ramzi Ahmed Yousef. Some of Yousef's suspected gang members also were apprehended by other governments and extradited or rendered to US authorities.

You and I also need to work together to stop acts of terror. Let's "make a big deal" out of something that looks suspicious—and not "let it go." Let's approach the situation quietly and not panic. Let's dig down and trust our intuition. Maybe we're right. If we are...both of our lives are safe.

WHO ARE THE BAD GUYS?

You will not be comforted to know that throughout the world today, there are literally hundreds of ethnic, nationalist, and religious, as well as political organizations that resort to terrorism...but the US Department of State lists approximately 35 to 40 as those that are of major concern.

Which terrorist groups are most likely to strike at Americans and American interests at home and abroad?

1. ***Fanatic fundamentalists...who are by far the most sophisticated and dangerous.*** They are supported by governments who tolerate and engage in international terrorism. It is widely recognized that state support for terrorist groups enhances their capabilities and makes law enforcement efforts to counter terrorism more difficult.

   The United States currently lists the following countries as state supporters of terrorism:

   ❏ CUBA   ❏ NORTH KOREA

   ❏ IRAN   ❏ SUDAN

   ❏ IRAQ   ❏ SYRIA

   ❏ LIBYA

   In addition to fulfilling the desires of their patrons, these terrorist groups also have their own agendas. They act independently as well as on orders from their state sponsors. For the above-mentioned countries, terrorist groups are like armies; their acts are cost effective, and when things go wrong, deniable.

2. ***Radicalized and frustrated Americans of single-interest movements*** who believe the only way to gain attention for their cause is to commit terrorist acts inside their own country. This group includes, among others, left-wing and right-wing radicals and racists.

3. ***Unstable individuals.***
   There is also a common thread among terrorists. They are fanatics. Fanatics are those whose minds are closed and cannot see beyond the scope of their own limited vision. Don't kid yourself...there's no way to communicate with a fanatic.

Take the case of Ramzi Yousef, the man who was involved in the New York City bombing. He escaped to the Far East, Pakistan, Afghanistan, and then to the Philippines. At the time of his capture, it was discovered that he was preparing a tremendous assault against the United States and the free world, which ranged from assassinating the Pope to placing bombs on 12 American carriers. No way that guy was going to change—no way.

THE ACTS OF MADMEN

The terrorist grabs the world's attention by:

hijacking

kidnapping or executing

bombing

April 18, 1983: a delivery van filled with explosives is driven to the front of the US Embassy in Beirut. When it detonates, it flattens most of the building, killing 17 Americans and 46 others. The Reagan Administration later learns that Iran and Syria had ordered the attack.

October 23, 1983: a Mercedes truck roars right past the US Marine guard and into the center of a building that houses most of the Marine Battalion Landing Team near Beirut International Airport. This suicide mission kills 241 Marines; the worst single surprise attack on US forces since Pearl Harbor, December 7, 1941.

December 21, 1988: Five and one-half years after the Beirut bombing, the shortest day of the calendar year becomes the longest day in American aviation history, forever to be remembered as "Lockerbie." It was 6 p.m. when Pan Am Flight 103, which had originated in Frankfurt, Germany, pushes back from the gate at Heathrow Airport with 243 passengers aboard and a crew of 16. The plane also carries about 20 tons of cargo, including 43 bags of US Military mail.

At 6:25 p.m., enroute to New York City, the plane levels off at 31,000 feet. At 7:17 p.m. the aircraft explodes over Lockerbie, Scotland, and disappears from control tower radar screens. All of the passengers and crew are killed, along with 11 other people on the ground.

In recent years, terrorist bombings are becoming more common. From 1969 to 1983, 220 terrorist bombings worldwide have killed 463 people and injured almost 3,000. In the decade that followed, nearly 11,000 explosive bombing incidents occurred in the US alone.

Nobody can make you feel inferior without your permission.

February 26, 1993: a close-knit group of Muslim fundamentalists import bomb-making manuals. A bomb is built and packed into a rented Ryder van, then driven into the parking garage of The World Trade Center in New York City. The conspirators detonate the whole package, killing six people, wounding 1,000 and sending tens of thousands of workers down darkened stairwells onto the streets below. Reverberations from the noontime explosion brings the threat of international terrorism right to our front door. The explosion ends up costing $510 million in property damage.

April 19, 1995: the most vicious terrorist bombing on US soil occurs when a nine-story federal building, situated in Oklahoma City, is torn from its foundation by the blast of a bomb. The building, which houses 15 federal agencies, three non-federal offices, and a day care center is home to more than 500 employees. This blast causes the partial collapse of the building, killing 167 people and injuring almost 600 others.

These events have been recorded as the most dramatic and horrific chapters in the history of terrorism in the 20th Century against the United States and its citizens. Maybe you don't think about these events anymore, but the victims' families will never forget them.

THE PLAYERS OF DEATH

Iran continues to be the world's most active supporter of international terrorism. According to the Department of State's *Global Patterns of Terrorism*, "...although Tehran tried to project a moderate image in the West, it continues to maintain its support and financing of groups that pose a threat to US citizens."

Unlike territorial wars, Iran's war is referred to as a *jihad* or "holy war." To the Muslim fundamentalists of Iran, America is the enemy of Islam. In their eyes, Western culture undermines the philosophy of the Koran. Therefore, their war is a rightous one, and the use of terrorism is justified to ensure their place in eternity.

In the 1970s, Palestinian terrorists were being educated and trained in South Yemen in the Middle East. By 1981, fanatic Muslims had established, in northern Tehran, the first Iranian terrorist camp. Additionally after the Soviets' retreat from Afghanistan, guerrilla training camps became a center of terrorist training supported by the Iranians. Then in 1982, in Lebanon, the most organized and dangerous of all terrorist groups was founded — Hezbollah — which is run by highly trained politicians who carry out the political and religious goals of Iran.

Avoid asking questions... avoid making decisions... avoid being happy...

It was Hezbollah that was responsible for the 1983 bombing of the US Military barracks in Beirut, the hijacking of TWA flights, the kidnapping of Western hostages in Beirut, and the car bombing of the Israeli Embassy that killed 56 people in Buenos Aires, Argentina.

WHAT YOU NEED TO KNOW TO STAY SAFE

How does this information translate into advice for you?

1. Play down your image as an American when you travel internationally.

2. In addition to Cuba, Iran, Iraq, Libya, North Korea, the Sudan, and Syria, you also will want to avoid the following countries that engage in terrorist activities:

❑ Turkey	❑ Algeria
❑ Ecuador	❑ Nigeria
❑ Russia	❑ Cambodia
❑ Peru	❑ Morocco
❑ Columbia	❑ Pakistan
❑ Sri Lanka	❑ Egypt
❑ India	

Like I always say: if you *have* just returned from one of these places—it is the only thing to do if you find yourself there!

3. You'll need reliable, up-to-date security **intelligence** reports when you travel. We'll help provide them for you.

HOW TERRORISTS PLAN THEIR ATTACKS

Intermission!

At this point, you may be feeling a bit overwhelmed! Take a break — walk the dog, do some isometrics, hug your kids. Then come back — I'll wait for you.

Back so soon? Good. One more section I want you to understand...

How does a terrorist think? How does he plan an attack? Consider the following points as you begin your training in security awareness.

Point #1

An adversary will attempt to damage your life, your property, or your reputation. He wants to achieve maximum success with minimum effort and minimum risk—exactly how you and I approach our work!

Therefore, the terrorist will try:

✓   to invest the least possible in human resources, as well as other resources...

✓   to expose himself to as little contact as possible with his target–YOU–and with his target's defenses...your security "system"...

✓   to make sure that he has appropriate retreat and escape routes...

Point #2

An adversary's success depends on selecting a target that:

✓   it is easy to get at...

✓   allows for the best method of attack.

An adversary will take advantage of being in the right place at the right time. **And, of course, you'll be in the wrong place at the wrong time.** For example, a thief will be aware of opportunities that arise that make it optimum for him to grab a purse or steal a briefcase. Any plans and decisions made by him are probably made in haste. His chance for success relies on so many factors...such as the target fighting back or shouting or the police may spot the incident in progress.

Your adversary's main objective is to escape as quickly as possible. To reduce his risk of failure, he is likely to take some extreme action. He may be armed with a gun. He may shoot you or try to injure you in some way to prevent you from interfering with his objective.

In the case of a pre-planned action, it requires that an adversary spend time researching and gathering information before attempting any action. This type of crime may involve a usually highly skilled individual or a team.

THE ANATOMY OF A CRIME

Let's create a scenario. A terrorist has decided to blow up a passenger jet. I'll warn you now; it's grizzly. You say, "I don't want to read it!" Let me remind you—terrorists do not act haphazardly. Or halfheartedly. They are focused and committed.

Remember...terrorism doesn't just happen aboard a plane or in some foreign country. It can appear in many forms and in many places—wherever you may travel. I know "terrorism" is a scary word, but sometimes the world can be a very scary place.

Horse sense is having good, stable knowledge.

First: the terrorist is most likely to choose a specific flight, and he will select a method that will, once again, achieve maximum results with minimum investment. He has learned that the greatest amount of damage to an airplane is caused by attacking it while in the air.

Second: to create a successful plan of attack, the terrorist will need to know the target's weak points. He must collect information that will cover:

✈ **Routine of the crew, the passengers, and the aircraft...**

✈ **Aircraft data...**

- type of plane and frequency of plane usage and customary flight
- location of airfield and parking
- level of security
- how and by whom the aircraft is serviced

✈ **The physical environment...**

- hiding places and approaches
- buildings commanding a view and in range of takeoff

This information can be collected by various methods, including:

✈ planting a worker in the organization against which the attack is being planned...

✈ finding a collaborator (any employee who has access to the aircraft) who may be "persuaded" to cooperate through the use of bribery, blackmail or threat...

✈ extracting information from someone close to the target without that person being aware of the purpose...

✈ surveillance and the utilization of listening devices...

Once all of the required information has been collected, the planning stage is initiated. A specific program of action is developed and will cover and include:

1. Timing...day or night, weather conditions...

2. Choosing a method of action...physical attack, kidnapping, attacks on relatives, threats, blackmail...

3. The resources that will be needed...weapons; firearms; explosives; hiding places; cars; communication devices; documentation...

4. Choosing the personnel...

5. Utilizing the target's schedules...

6. An analysis of what may occur in any given situation...

7. Retreat plans...escape routes, means of travel, hiding places, safe shelters, documentation, diversions and deceptions...

Instructions are then given to each person involved in executing the attack, and exercises and drills are carried out to ensure success.

> **The ability of a terrorist to carry out an attack is related proportionately to the target's state of preparedness: awareness of security issues, vigilance, avoidance of routines, and lack of complacency.**

Whether it's a terrorist or a common thief, it is their job to know your weakness. But you don't have to be weak or victimized by your lack of knowledge. ***You can be prepared...you can be vigilant...you can increase your awareness and eliminate your own sense of complacency***. You've read about terrorism...Now become security smart! Our goal is to give you practical and easily understood guidelines that you can use to protect yourself while traveling and operating in possible hostile environments, both locally and internationally.

MR. SECURITY SAYS........

Remember......

➢   Media exposure provides the desired benefit for the terrorist: communication of a message world-wide.

➢   The most likely groups to strike at Americans and American interests at home and abroad are: fanatic fundamentalist groups, American extremist groups and unstable individuals.

➢   The United States lists the following countries as state supporters of terrorism:

Cuba	Iraq	North Korea	Syria
Iran	Libya	Sudan	

➢   The "war on terrorism" is won by all of us doing our part...becoming security conscious no matter where we are.

CHAPTER 4

CRIME AND THE RISKS YOU FACE

"Whether you think you can or think you can't, you're right."

Henry Ford

A businessman needed $1 million to close his deal. He went to church to pray for the money. The guy next to him, by chance, was kneeling and praying for $50. The businessman opened his wallet and handed him the $50. The guy about fainted! The businessman closed his eyes and prayed, "Lord, now that I have your attention..."

OK! Now that I have your attention about how vulnerable we are in today's world...while the subject of terrorism brings to mind guards with guns, kidnapping and espionage, the average person will more likely face another kind of risk, the personal risk of crime. We all know by now that violence and crime can occur at any time, any where — at the local fast food store, in the work place, in our own homes. But all of us can take basic steps to reduce the risk of becoming a victim.

The funny thing is most of us already take these steps whether we're conscious of them or not. We don't drive through crime-ridden neighborhoods. We don't walk through isolated areas of our cities at night, and we warn our children about the danger of talking to strangers. But there are also certain safeguards of which we may not be aware...that should be adhered to when we're on the road, walking or driving, no matter if it's a business trip or a pleasurable outing.

You can be *"ripped-off"* anywhere in the world, but nowhere like here. Did you know that the United States is the first country to have more than one million people in jail...yet there are more criminals on the streets than there are incarcerated?

Most violence, no matter where, is the result of robberies and drug-related crime. Violent crime, especially in urban areas, is very real and should be taken very seriously. And so you know, too, that anyone can be vulnerable to crime wherever he goes, whether it be in:

- ◆ cities
- ◆ the countryside
- ◆ museums
- ◆ churches

- ◆ on the streets
- ◆ in vehicles
- ◆ even in "secure" places

LOSING THE HOME COURT ADVANTAGE

Criminal elements target those who are vulnerable, or unaware; the ones who are not paying attention. Because we are aware of the crime that exists in our own country, **we tend to be more alert to danger on our own home ground**. I'll bet if I take you and stick you on foreign soil, it can be as if your good sense gets thrown out the window. When we are visiting a foreign country, we tend to believe that it is a safer place than home. After all, we're on vacation; we want to relax and have a good time...not worry about crime. But because crime is a worldwide phenomena, the criminals are there waiting for the opportunity to take advantage of those who are vulnerable.

Overseas, travelers are primary targets because of their unfamiliarity with the local environment, as well as the fact that they usually carry cash. It is essential that a person becomes educated about the crime situation in the country of his destination. Then he will know what particular types of crime are prevalent in which area and what sections of the city or town to avoid.

To help you become more aware of what you need to know, this book contains valuable security information pertaining to about 40 domestic and international cities; information which is designed to make your travel more pleasurable and less worrisome.

The book also contains many chapters of preventative behavior tips — things for you to learn and put to use that will help thwart criminal activities that are normally associated with:

A winner sees the answer in every problem; a loser just sees the problem.

- ✈ tourist activities—***shopping!***

- ✈ business travel—***airport scams***!

- ✈ hotel security procedures—***check-in!***

- ✈ transportation security—***fake accidents!***

- ✈ family travel—***tour guide hustles!***

In these chapters you will learn more about how obvious your habits are to criminals. For example: Criminals know that most American tourists will stop and get out of their car if they perceive an accident has occurred. Therefore, many criminals will stage phony accidents. Be aware!

Interesting isn't it?

All travelers are ideal targets for a variety of crimes. For example, the threat of street crime is heightened when you, as a traveler, exhibit signs of fatigue or disorientation, especially when you first arrive at your hotel, or when you begin a sightseeing tour, or when you are rushed or harried on a shopping excursion. Also, keep in mind that the more lively and crowded the street scene, the more likely you are to suffer separation from your wallet or watch.

In watching people travel for over 30 years, I can definitely say this:

TOURISTS ARE PREDICTABLE!

They stay in the same areas.

They do the same things.

They go to the same places.

Tourists make ideal targets for crooks because they carry so much cash, and everyone knows where they keep their valuables—hotel rooms, cars, readily available luggage. Re-think your circumstances! Life doesn't have to be a "soap opera." Don't be surprised—anything can happen, *good or bad*.

Common criminals can be pickpockets, con men, as well as con women and con kids, professionals, and junkies. These people work at their occupation. I'll say it again, they know your habits—everything from what you will do when you check into your hotel, to where you keep your valuables, and the easiest way to get at them. **Protect yourself—even when you go to sleep!** Really! When spending the night in a hotel or motel room, here at home or overseas, a little ingenuity goes a long way to help you sleep more securely.

❏ If the mechanism permits, leave your room key in the lock after locking yourself in at night. The hook end of a coat hanger, threaded though the key and hang over the knob, will help hold it in place.

❏ The hanger-over-the-knob trick works as an alarm, too, if you hang a ring of keys or another clattery device over it so that the door cannot be opened without disturbing the hanger.

❏ The back of a chair jammed under the knob will make forced entry more difficult. If there is no carpet to help hold the legs, place them in the heels of a pair of men's shoes, toes pointed toward the door.

❏ After locking up, hang a small, empty desk drawer or nightstand drawer over the upper corner of the door frame so that the door will dislodge it when opened. If the door opens out, hang the drawer over the doorknob, and the frame will make it fall when the door is opened.

❏ Add more racket by setting a couple of empty glasses in the drawer.

SAFE AT HOME...WITH YOUR PHONE

Self protection includes strategies to reduce your vulnerability inside your home as well.

For example...intruders can get into your home by means of the telephone. You should be aware of different methods of stopping unwanted attention, especially if you live alone. Security specialists recommend:

❏ Be cautious about your out-going message on your answering machine. Of course, you won't say "We are not home..." but "We can't come to the phone..."

Consider the following tactics for your phone book listing:

❏ List your last name with first and middle initials only.

❏ List name but not address.

❏ Add the name of an imaginary roomate or husband to the listing.

To deal with unwanted calls:

❏ Simply cut off caller with, "I'm not interested," and hang up.

❏ Don't be fooled by disarming techniques like, "Steve gave me your number," unless you really believe it to be true. Even then, this may just be the prelude of an obscene call.

❏   If you are the least bit suspicious about a call, pretend you are talking to a male companion: "Excuse me – honey, will you please turn down the television."

❏   Hang up at once on obscene calls or the ones that deliver only silence. Don't keep asking, "Who is this?" Your uneasiness may be giving the caller exactly the thrill he is after.

❏   The loud whistle into the mouthpiece still works.

❏   Call the telephone business office if you are harassed repeatedly. The people there are usually very supportive of their customers in situations like this, and they will tell you what to do. If it becomes necessary to call for police intervention, you will be able to demonstrate that you have already taken appropriate measures.

With so much happening, even on the streets closest to home, it is time to make yourself aware of how you can protect yourself and your family. When you walk out your front door, you become a traveler, whether it be local or long distance. All travelers...grocery shoppers or frequent flyers... have the right to be safe.

CHAPTER 5

TRAVEL SECURITY & YOU

"Learning about yourself will be a process you will never want to end once you have experienced its rewards."

Jeanne Segal, *Living Beyond Fear*

The only thing that doesn't change is the fact of change. Right now, we're in the midst of the most explosive change our society has ever known. An old man born 95 years ago has seen the end of the pioneer society and he saw World War I as the war to end all wars. He lived through the Roaring 20's, the Great Depression and World War II. He went from horse and buggy to car to plane to witnessing space travel. He's seen the communications revolution, and explosion in knowledge and technology. From near to far, he saw the rise and fall of the Soviet Empire. As this tumultuous century draws to a close, even the rate of change accelerates.

To keep up-to-date with change, we must learn, study and ask questions. When it comes to being up-to-date with security, we must learn to ask questions like...Does this street look safe? Do these people look OK?

Am I in the wrong place? Forget the cost of admission—get the hell out of there!!! We ask questions, we find answers and solutions. I asked a question in 1968: how can there be a security system that would truly work? And from asking questions, after almost 30 years of improvements, it is this system that we now bring to you. It is known as the "Travel Security System."

TRAVEL SECURITY SYSTEM

The Travel Security System is currently being used to protect passengers on international flights, and by corporations, foreign dignitaries, and celebrities who operate their own aircraft.

I have divided the presentation of this system into four parts:

1. The Introduction.

2. The Security Formula: $T \times V = R$. Don't worry, you'll learn it!

3. A model of security circles.

4. Methods of preventative behavior that can be applied in any travel situation, whether you travel one mile or 5,000 miles:

    - **avoid routines!**

    - **be aware and alert!**

    - **keep a low profile!**

    - **restrict access to information!**

PART ONE - THE INTRODUCTION

Risk is part of everything we do. When we get up in the morning and drive to work, we take risks. We take risks by ignoring medical warnings about overeating or smoking or drinking too much. Risk is the result of our vulnerability to a threat...How much harm can come to us? If you can identify a potential threat, then you can assess your vulnerability to that threat. If you know how vulnerable you may be, then you can take steps to reduce your vulnerability. To take risks is to ignore threats and your vulnerability to them.

Here's my question to you:

Why is it, when we travel, we leave our common sense behind and risk our personal safety? **Why are we vulnerable?**

I ask this because, after 35 years in the travel security business, here are my observations about my fellow travelers:

❖ We routinely travel between our US cities without the necessary knowledge and information about the threats specifically associated with those cities.

❖ We envision cities in foreign countries as safer than the crime-ridden urban areas of the United States when, in so many places, the opposite is true.

❖ When we are overseas, in what we perceive to be secure environments, we tend to "let down our guard" and become rather apathetic toward security concerns. This kind of attitude can be hazardous, considering that most American travelers are not familiar with their destination's local language, problems, or security conditions.

❖ The US State Department has noted that foreign intelligence agencies and criminals view Americans as easy targets because of our desire to make friends. Americans tend to think that, though governments may differ, "people are people..." and so the friendly person with whom they are speaking could not possibly have ulterior motives. Every security professional will tell you to be wary of the stranger, especially in a strange country, who easily strikes up a conversation with you.

RISK: THE DEGREE OF PROBABILITY
FOR INJURY, DAMAGE OR LOSS

✓   Travel threats are subject to change.

✓   Travel threats depend on regional and global factors.

Because no security program is capable of or has the resources for dealing with the entire range of identified threats, you will learn to take **calculated risks**. In other words, you will decide which threats are of lower priority than others and which ones you must be prepared to respond to immediately. You will learn how to target your efforts.

> *The mind is like a parachute; it works best when open.*

For example, a business trip to Moscow requires a different and more extensive security effort than a family vacation to Toronto and Niagara Falls. Obviously, you will need to determine what to focus on in each travel scenario by analyzing the risks involved.

Practice your "inner strength" in any case. **Be security conscious! It seems overly simplistic...and it is!** Take a minute and remind yourself of what's important—you and your family!

You must be able to analyze the degree to which you are at risk.

Some travel risks are minor and should not hinder your travel plans. Some are more dangerous and you should seriously plan for them. The goal is to give you practical and easily understood guidelines that you can use to protect yourself while traveling and operating in potentially hostile environments, both foreign and domestic.

REMEMBER:

☞ Be mentally alert when you travel!

☞ Use your common sense!

☞ Avoid underestimating and overestimating possible threats!

☞ Don't be paranoid!

THINK!

That's right. To learn how to be prepared is related to learning how to think.

Thinking is a matter of

✓ observing!

✓ analyzing!

✓ relating!

✓ understanding!

✓ solving problems!

If an individual is aware of security issues, thinks about them, and complies with the rules of preventative behavior...things to do to prevent being vulnerable to threats...a high level of personal security will be assured.

Remember, we're learning how to put you—the target — in a more advantageous position than a potential adversary!

Your potential adversary has:

➤ a clear advantage

➤ the initiative

➤ the element of surprise

Right? By learning security strategies or rules of preventative behavior, a traveler can reduce vulnerability. Reducing vulnerability reduces risk and limits the opportunity for an unfortunate event to occur. Failing to learn makes it easier for an adversary to identify you as a "soft target" and encourages him to execute an attack. My Uncle David told me that nobody want to be a soft target. He also told me that I was a "good egg in the long run...but who likes runny eggs?!

All of what I am saying applies to sophisticated terrorist attacks as well as those conducted by the common criminal. Precautions against criminal action in foreign lands are not particularly different from those applied in our own country. Anyone can more effectively respond to potential threats if he or she is aware of their vulnerability. By merely demonstrating that you are attentive, you can avert a common crime or a serious incident, such as kidnapping.

Security is indeed a battle of wits. Make sure you use yours!

PART TWO

THE FORMULA: T x V = R

The key to your security awareness can be summed up in a simple equation:

T (*threat*) x **V** (*vulnerability*) = **R** (*risk*)

In determining the risk factor for any location, you need to be able to identify the potential threats, assess your vulnerability to these threats, and then evaluate the potential risk.

In simple terms, here is how the process works:

Phase One - Threat Identification

First, you must examine certain threats that can exist in a particular country or city. For example:

- ⊃ crime...
- ⊃ health threats...
- ⊃ political instability...
- ⊃ organized crime...
- ⊃ industrial espionage...
- ⊃ specific threats...
- ⊃ socio-economic problems...
- ⊃ corruption...

Next, you identify these factors and evaluate them on a scale from 1 to 8, with 1 representing the lowest threat, and 8 the highest. These are threats that we do not control.

Phase Two - Vulnerability

We add up the threat assessments for all eight threats to find out the level of your vulnerability.

Phase Three

If the total equals:

> **0-16** you're in a low-risk situation
> **17-32** caution is advised
> **33-48** concern is warranted
> **49-64** you're at very high risk

The risk rating tells you the degree of threat for any particular destination. Got it? Are you willing to do it? You better be! Sure...you've got to think about this...sure...it's a challenge. When you look at life and its many challenges as a *test*, or a *series of tests*, you begin to see each issue as an opportunity to grow and a chance to roll with the punches. **What's a more important challenge than your personal security?**

PART THREE - SECURITY CIRCLES

Here is another way of understanding the nature of preventing risks. It is an analogy of concentric circles — circles that are set one inside of the other.

The innermost circle contains the target...you. The rings emanating from the target are the various levels of security and protection. The circles consist of various preventative actions that can cause the adversary difficulty and possibly cause him to abandon his scheme. **In other words, the circles are ways in which you can be protected.**

No one action can solve a complex security problem...and a single circle has weak points. Therefore, a number of circles are used in order to provide maximum security protection for the target.

Look at it this way:

A doctor prescribes a number of measures to help a patient who is suffering from heart disease. The doctor may suggest medicine, a diet change, exercise, stress reduction, and no smoking to further reduce the risk to the patient. However, the patient may choose to adhere to only one or a few of the recommendations.

The number of preventative actions prescribed by the doctor will depend on whether the patient is in a high-risk or low-risk category. The same is true with your security needs. If you're in a low-risk area, the number of circles needed to protect you will be less than if you're traveling in a high-risk area.

The reason for exercising preventative behavior is to make it difficult for a potential adversary to collect information for an attack, plan it, and execute it. Ease of planning, ease of attack, minimal risks, and optimal probability of success are basic adversarial principles. Frustrating these principles encourages an adversary to select a target other than YOU!

What four strategies are essential to your travel safety?

1.   Avoid routines

2.   Be aware and alert

3. *Maintain a low profile*

4. *Restrict access to information*

Experience has shown that neglecting these four "preventative behavior rules" makes it relatively easy for an adversary to identify weak points in your security "system."

THE IMPORTANCE OF DETERRENTS

Deterrents are security measures that will prevent your adversary from carrying out an attack on you. These are signals that send a message to your attacker to go find a different, easier target.

A deterrent is successful when it:

- Causes the adversary to perceive the security system as threatening

- Reduces confidence about achieving the objectives successfully

- Makes it difficult for the adversary to gather information prior to acting

- Makes access to the target difficult

- Complicates an adversary's method of attack

- Causes the adversary to invest more resources than he would want

- Increases an adversary's personal risk

In all the crime books we've read and the movies we've seen, the adversary always plans his activities leading up to the attack based upon the target's **routine behavior.** The less routines followed by the target, the more difficult it will be for the adversary to plan.

People have been kidnapped while they were following a certain routine pattern. It's difficult *not* to follow a routine. Think about how many routines you follow every day and every week. If someone was watching you, how easy would it be to predict your actions? When my company takes on a new client, we see that they almost inevitably fly to the same city with a schedule which is fixed and repetitive and always take the same taxi route and travel to the same hotel. If an adversary wants to attack, he will use their routine the planning of his operation. If we don't have a behavioral pattern he can follow, he'll seek out another potential victim.

At Air Security in Houston, our Research and Intelligence Department constantly uncovers frightening examples of how acting in a routine manner can be a person's worst enemy. We just read about how an unknown terrorist apparently had studied the routine of a US Consulate in Karachi. Two consulate workers were killed when the van, on its usual route, was overtaken and fired upon by two gunmen wielding AK-47s.

What's most important is to be **aware** and **alert**. In the absence of an actual threat we tend to lose our vigilance. So, first and foremost, we have to be security-minded: **Stay focused: don't take chances…the present moment** is where you are! Always! Not what happened last week or last year. Not what may or may not happen tomorrow. If you see something strange or out of the ordinary, don't say, "It must be my imagination." Perceive the situation as a potential threat.

> In every terrorist or criminal event that has ever been analyzed, there were always found a number of indications that would have spelled out an attack but no one bothered to notice. Sometimes the writing is on the wall; we look, but we do not see.

This is the true story of Hassan Salan, an El Al representative in Sweden who lived in Stockholm. Opposite his home was a bakery shop. Every morning, as his wife left home to go to work, she noticed two bakers standing outside the shop watching her. After a couple of days she told her husband that she didn't know why, but every time she left the house she saw these bakers standing outside watching her. Her husband answered, "That's nonsense. The bakers are just getting a breath of fresh air outside." "Yes," she replied, "but even when it's raining and cold they are outside watching me. If I enter the house or go out of the house, they still stand and watch. But when I go and come back, they're gone."

She was sure that she was a target. Hesitating no more, she called the authorities to check out the situation. It turned out that on that very same day a terrorist (who was later captured) told the authorities that there was a plan to kidnap the El Al representative and his wife but the plan was called off at the last minute because other terrorist plots in Sweden were uncovered.

The adversary has the advantage because he takes the initiative. The only time that we have an advantage over the adversary is when he is in the planning stages, because now we can dictate to the adversary how he will behave.

If we are routine in our behavior, it will be easy for the adversary to corner us and very difficult for us to detect him. But, if we are aware of our surroundings and break our routine, at the critical moment we will expose him. It's like when we discover somebody is following us and we look to see.

PAY ATTENTION TO DETAIL

➤ Do you regularly see the same people relaxing in the hotel lobby or coffee shop, or loitering outside?

➤ Do you feel uncomfortable because someone has asked you for information about your schedule?

➤ Do you see the same car parked in the same place with a driver in it?

➤ Don't be afraid to report your suspicions to security officers or the police. Let them check it out! Don't worry about seeming paranoid. Paying attention to detail creates a new skill which you will find will not only help to keep you safe but it will bring you dividends in your daily life.

KEEPING A LOW PROFILE

For those of you who are business executives, minimize media attention and restrict access to information. It is vital, not only for your peace of mind but also for your safety. If you're not a business executive, you still need to keep a low profile. **DON'T STAND OUT!!**

Some rules for the road to help you avoid standing out:

- ❏ Sometimes foreign money doesn't seem real to us. Be careful not to flash wads of it or treat it nonchalantly, any more than you would U.S. greenbacks.

- ❏ Don't divulge personal information to strangers anywhere. That includes Americans you encounter abroad.

- ❏ Remember, the more you look like a tourist, the more the locals will think you are "loaded."

- ❏ Pickpockets in most foreign countries make American pickpockets look like amateurs. Be extra careful in jostling crowds.

- ❏ Be discreet about cameras and electronic gear; carry them inside jackets or pockets, not flung over a shoulder.

- ❏ Spread your money, credit cards and I.D. over several pockets, purses or money belts.

- ❏ Never leave jewelry and expensive gear in view in your room, even when you are present...and take them with you when you leave.

Those of you who own your own aircraft or fly in corporate jets, know that this mode of travel can be to your advantage. Unlike commercial airlines, which are faced with high visibility, publicized schedules, and are expected to follow routines, the advantage to private travel is knowing that very few people have to be apprised of your itinerary.

For all of you who travel to "risky" cities, for whatever reason, to increase your safety margin, be careful in letting the hotel staff or even your office know your schedule in advance.

For business travelers, in many places in the world where anti-corporate feelings exist, it is always best to conduct quiet negotiations and maintain a low profile. Many who have tried to venture into foreign markets have encountered protests or have found themselves on the receiving end of terrorist attacks.

I've got a lot more specific security "tips" for you about how to shop, where not to go, how to go sightseeing, etc. — all of these strategies contain the principles of *preventative behavior*.

Now you have the basics of what I call "your personal security system." There are security fundamentals in this chapter, as well as many examples to illustrate those principles.

Learning to be security conscious starts with seeing its importance. ***If personal security is NOT important to you, forget it!*** Personal security is being open to discover new alternatives to prevent becoming a victim. It's time to let go...to rethink your circumstances and see security where you didn't see it before. "Normally, we do not so much look at things as overlook them." ***Focus!***

MR. SECURITY SAYS........

Remember......

➤ **FOUR STRATEGIES ESSENTIAL TO TRAVEL SAFETY:**

    1. AVOID ROUTINES

    2. BE AWARE AND ALERT

    3. MAINTAIN A LOW PROFILE

    4. RESTRICT ACCESS TO INFORMATION

CHAPTER 6

PRE-TRIP PLANNING

"Experience is not what happens to a man. It is what a man does with what happens to him."

— Aldous Huxley

I was on a flight from New York to Houston. It was at the end of a hectic week of business, and I was looking forward to a peaceful flight and an enjoyable weekend with the family.

After 30 minutes of relative quiet, a commotion started. I turned around to see ... there was a problem with a French speaking family.

One of the flight attendants who could understand French was quickly on the scene. It turned out that this family...two parents, two kids, and grandma...was visiting the United States. They had spent three days in New York before leaving for Houston to meet cousins living in Texas. Apparently, the parents forgot to recheck grandma's luggage before leaving their New York hotel room. Her passport, medical records, and some travelers checks were left behind.

By now you've read—and know—that **people gain a great sense of security by knowing they are prepared for potential crises.** That's what *The Security Connection* is about—and gaining a sense of security by knowing how to reduce the likelihood of being involved in a crisis, whether in Houston or in Paris. This kind of security awareness is the real pre-trip planning!

Go back to that French family on the plane. Have you ever left home on a trip only to discover on arrival at your destination that you neglected to bring an important document—something that could put an end to a potentially productive trip?

Make two lists: The obvious items you must have, and the not-so-obvious items that make your trip easier.

The obvious include:

- ❒ Passport.
- ❒ Visa (if necessary).
- ❒ Tickets.
- ❒ Travelers checks (preferable over cash—see later notes).
- ❒ Hotel addresses and confirmation numbers.
- ❒ Rental car confirmation number.
- ❒ ID.
- ❒ Driver's license.
- ❒ Maps, directions to hotel, appointments.
- ❒ CITYWATCH reports—security information about the area.
- ❒ Business itinerary.
- ❒ Needed medicine.

❒   Required medical records.

❒   Business papers.

❒   Insurance information.

❒   All your luggage.

Your "other list" includes such items as:

❒   Extra pair of eyeglasses, plus your prescription.

❒   Electrical converter and plug adapters (overseas trips).

We're looking at this from a security perspective: ***The more hassle-free your trip is, the more security conscious you'll be ... less diversions!***

Our advice on cash, as I mentioned above, is just this: Don't take chances carrying large amounts of cash when you travel. **Use travelers checks.** Do not take "extra" credit cards, either. One is enough—assuming your credit limit is sufficient. **Leave all unnecessary credit cards and expensive jewelry at home.**

GET A HEALTHY START
ON YOUR TRIP

If you are planning to take any prescription drugs on your trip, check with your doctor. If you are traveling abroad, check with the embassies of the countries you are visiting to ensure you do not violate foreign laws.

Many travelers have been innocently arrested for possession of drugs not considered to be narcotic in the United States, but that are illegal in other countries. You can ask your doctor for a certificate attesting to your need to make customs processing easier. Note, however, that this may not be enough authorization to transport drugs into some foreign countries.

It's impossible to get unless you begin.

Always leave medicines in original labeled containers. Ask your pharmacists for the generic name of any prescribed drug in case you need to refill the prescription. Brand names differ in other countries.

If you are allergic to certain medication, insect or snake bites, wear a medical alert bracelet and carry a similar warning in your wallet.

If you become injured or seriously ill abroad, a U.S. consular officer can help you find a physician. He or she can arrange the transfer of funds from your family or friends in the United States to pay for your treatment.

Carry a summary of your medical records. Be sure to include past illnesses and blood type.

THE PACKAGE DEAL

Planning for your trip means planning for the good and the bad. It's a package deal. I sat next to a woman on an airplane flight to London. The woman had a very large, gorgeous, ten-caret diamond ring. I commented on the beautiful diamond. She said was The Schwartz Diamond…and that with the largest diamonds, comes a curse. I asked, "What's the curse?" She said, "Mr. Schwartz. It's a package deal!"

Pre-trip security precautions always include having your affairs in order, leaving a file of important documents at home, especially when you are traveling overseas.

Why? Security involves reducing risks. Many travelers do not want to think about disaster. But if one does occur and you do not make it back from a trip, legal and other documents should be accessible to the appropriate person. You reduce the risk of an insecure future for your family by failing to be prepared in this manner. Make certain all your important papers are up to date.

Many hostages have expressed regret that their affairs were not left in better order for their families. That is why we recommend that you discuss and plan with your family what should be done in the case of any **emergency.**

Your collection of important papers might include:

❐ Will.

❐ Birth and marriage certificates.

❐ Guardianship or adoption papers for children.

❐ Power of attorney for spouse or relative.

❐ Deeds, mortgages, stocks and bonds, car titles.

❐ Insurance papers—car, home, life, personal effects, medical.

❐ Tax records.

❐ Proof of termination of previous marriage(s) and/or child support/ alimony agreements.

❐ Proof of membership in any organization or union that entitles the estate to any benefits.

USEFUL INFORMATION

An Information List might include:

❐ U.S. and local driver's license numbers.

❐ Insurance policy numbers and names of carriers.

❐ Social Security numbers.

❐ Credit card numbers.

❐ Bank account numbers and addresses.

❐ Passport numbers.

❐ Duplicate passport pictures in case passport needs to be replaced due to loss.

❐ Travelers check numbers and issuing bank.

❐ Medical and dental information, distinguishing marks and scars, and medicine and eyeglass prescriptions.

❐ Assets and debts.

- ❐ Names and addresses of business and professional contacts.

- ❐ Updated inventory of household and personal possessions with pictures/videos.

- ❐ Employment records for each family member; resumes, references, commendations.

Now you're organized and ready to go. Good! Let's make sure that your papers and baggage get there. There's nothing more frustrating than getting to an airport only to discover that your bags have been sent to another city – or even worse, luggage never-never land. Airlines handle thousands of pieces of luggage each day, and for the most part, it goes where it's supposed to go.

With a little effort on your part, you can increase the odds of your bags making it not only to the right city...but to your hotel room as well.

- ❐ Remove all old flight tags. This will prevent confusion about the destination. Check to make sure the flight tag on the bag is the right one.

- ❐ Avoid overly expensive luggage. It attracts thieves.

- ❐ To further avoid theft, pick up your bags as soon as possible. The longer it sits in the claim area, the better the chances of it being stolen.

- ❐ Never, ever leave bags unattended. Thieves move fast.

Finally, your pre-trip preparation involves knowing and keeping abreast of current events in your destination cities. Know what is going on in the country as well as world events that could affect that country.

"He who makes frequent inquiries about the road does not go astray."

PREPARATION IS THE KEY TO SUCCESSFUL TRAVEL.

ANOTHER TOP 10: PREPARATION TIPS

And, finally, travelers should also consider the following, which will assist and possibly protect you during the actual journey:

- ✔ Put a plain cover on your passport.
- ✔ Use hard, lockable luggage.
- ✔ Be sure luggage tags contain your name, phone number, and full street address; that information is concealed from casual observation; and that company logos are not displayed on luggage. Verify baggage claim checks before and after flight.
- ✔ Obtain small amount of local currency, if possible.
- ✔ Be aware of airline safety records when booking vacation trips while overseas; do not include company name in reservation.
- ✔ Use soft luggage instead of a briefcase so hijackers will not perceive you as a business traveler (i.e. valuable hostage).
- ✔ If the hotel where you plan to stay has a computer service in your room, you can use office computers when you arrive. Avoid carrying a PC if possible.
- ✔ Memorize your passport number.
- ✔ Stay away from unattended luggage.
- ✔ On foreign carriers, avoid speaking English as much as possible. Do not discuss business or travel plans, even to traveling companions.

BE PREPARED!

TRAVEL SMART!

HAVE A SAFE TRIP!

MR. SECURITY SAYS........

Remember......

➤   Good preparation creates less travel hassles and distractions; it therefore reduces risk.

➤   Avoid carrying large amounts of cash. Avoid carrying unnecessary credit cards and wearing expensive jewelry.

➤   Check with your doctor and embassy when taking prescription drugs abroad.

➤   Have your personal and business affairs in order at home before traveling abroad.

➤   Keep abreast of current events in your destination cities.

CHAPTER 7

FAMILY TRAVEL SCAMS

"The best time to go to Disney World, if you want to avoid huge crowds, is 1962."

Dave Barry

My wife and I feel very fortunate to have been able to take our children on many travels, especially when they were younger and we would visit Australia and Europe. To me, travel is important. It broadens our view of the world and enriches are lives. That's my motivation.

Kids — and families — travel more today than ever before: 512,000,000 domestic boardings are projected for 1997! I know children who have their own frequent flyer cards and regularly rack up free tickets! Ours has always been a nation on the move, and we're seldom deterred by violence and crime.

However, as you undoubtedly know from your own "adventures," many of us, at times, have experienced the old saying, "The family who travels together, unravels together!" It's funny and true. I recall many vivid memories of when my wife and I would travel with our young children to Disney World, where we would spend "about forty percent of our disposable income."

With travel comes responsibility. When it comes to travel security, children need to be given instruction, education, and varying degrees of responsibility for their safety. Parents should explain the reasons for security and give their kids necessary information in such a way that it fits the child's age and maturity level. Even rehearsing behaviors with your children is a good idea.

After all, since we teach our children how to care for themselves at home, at school and in the neighborhood, we can certainly impart travel security guidelines to them as an extension of that teaching. What's most important here is that we teach our kids without creating fear in them.

INVOLVING KIDS IN THE TRAVEL PROCESS

Kids like to be included when travel plans are being discussed. It is a perfect time for talking about security and how to keep the family safe. If you have your child's interest and attention from the start, the more likely your security measures will be adopted and the greater the measure of success. The likelihood of avoiding potential threats increases the more kids are willing to cooperate with your security plans.

If, for example, you and your family are planning to travel to a particular country in the world, make sure you research the country together. Today, the Internet has terrific information and graphics about places throughout the globe. Review the geography, the distances, language(s) spoken; teach your children about the uniqueness of every culture.

Everything starts in the home

The basics of security for kids are the basics you teach them at home. Here is a list of things that my wife and I taught our kids, and that you can do to begin teaching your kids security awareness before you leave on your trip and during the time you are traveling.

1. Always stay in sight of your parent or guardian. Don't wander off alone, and avoid talking with strangers.

2. Have your kids memorize the name of the hotel where they are staying. Before you take them on an outing, make sure you instruct them as to what to do if they should get lost.

3. It is important to establish firm ground rules for your children's behavior. **As a technique for helping them to understand security awareness before they travel,** assign them security-related tasks at home — such as, locking doors and windows. Your attitude and ability to project the importance of taking responsibility and the confidence you show in their abilities is crucial.

4. Give your children a sense of participation in the actual planning process. Include in your travel itinerary their input on ideas for improved family security. There were several summers when my wife and I would take our youngest child and his friend on vacation. We all would collaborate on what we wanted to do the following day, then we laid down ground rules for behavior and security into the planned activity.

My wife and I have tried to teach the children to let us know if what they see or feel is "not right" — and I've learned to trust their observations. We've taught them to report to us if anyone asks about our whereabouts; for example, if they see the same person in the same location on a repetitive basis.

We also make sure the kids have an "emergency plan"...

This includes:

✈ When and how to call the front desk of the hotel

✈ Airport instructions if they become separated from us

✈ What to do in case of an accident to us

✈ Phone numbers

GETTING YOUR MESSAGE ACROSS BY...HOOK OR BY CROOK

When arriving in a foreign city, you can use vocabulary flash cards to help kids memorize certain important expressions in the local language... police, help, etc. This, of course, infers that **you** will have already learned these phrases. Did you forget that you can't ask your kids to do something you aren't willing to do? This also may give you and your spouse the opportunity to put into practice the estimated 1,000 hours of French or Spanish you took in high school! You don't have to be a linguist to pick up some key expressions in the local language. Handy pocket-size language guides are also useful to bring along.

Communication Secrets From International Experts:

In the United States, you can crook your finger to beckon someone. In the Far East, that's a major insult.

If someone doesn't speak your language, be wary of resorting to gestures or hand signals to get your message across. You may find out the hard way that hand signals are not universal in meaning.

Consider the almost reflexive "OK" signal so common among Americans, the thumb and forefinger touching to make a circle. To us, its meaning may range from "I agree" to "Congratulations" to "Go ahead." And in most of the rest of the world, the connotation is very much the same as here.

However:

- To the Japanese, the gesture makes a circle, and a circle is a positive symbol. But in some situations, the "OK" sign signifies money.

- In Brazil, the sign is regarded as insulting and vulgar.

- In southern France, it means "worthless" or "zero."

- In most of the countries of the former Soviet Union and in Greece, our "OK" sign is regarded as impolite or obscene.

UNDERSTANDING CULTURAL DIFFERENCES

"When you travel, remember that a foreign country is not designed to make you comfortable. It is designed to make its own people comfortable."

Crossing cultural barriers take work, and it's easy to fall prey to cultural stereotyping and generalizations.

- Teach your children that when they travel to a foreign country they are guests in that country.

- Where appropriate, explain that the dress code is very important.

- Remind them that standards of right and wrong may be different from what they have been taught.

- Familiarize yourself first with local customs.

More Communication Secrets ......

➤ While Americans may crook the index finger to beckon anyone from a child to a taxi to a colleague, in other countries the effect may not be the same. To most Middle and Far Easterners, it is insulting to be beckoned with the fingers. Instead, turn palm down and wave the fingers or the whole had. The same goes in Portugal, Spain and Latin America.

➤ In Europe, crossed fingers most commonly mean "good luck" or "protection." In Paraguay, crossed fingers may be offensive.

➤ Almost everywhere in the world, the "thumbs up" sign indicates approval – except in Australia, where it is considered rude.

➤ In Europe, signal "good-bye" by raising the hand and wagging the fingers in unison. Waving back and forth as we do in America means "no" in Europe, while in Peru it means "Come here."

➤ Waving the hand close to someones face is a serious insult in Greece and Nigeria, and it should never be done to flag a waiter or cabdriver.

➤ In Finland, arms folded indicate pride or arrogance. In Fiji, the same posture shows disrespect.

➤ In Bulgaria, shaking the head means yes; a nod means no!

> *If you think education is expensive, try ignorance.*
>
> *Derek Bok*

Failing to do your cultural homework beforehand, and failing to learn key vocabulary and phrases will, at the very least, produce wasted time and energy, complications, and unpleasantness in your trip. At worst, you will expose yourself to unnecessary risk.

DOING THOSE THINGS YOU DO

You and your family do things on vacation that turn whatever hairs I have left prematurely gray!

➤ You dress strangely!

➤ You carry lots of money!

➤ You go where all tourists go and do what all tourists do!

➤ Your routines are predictable!

➤ You probably overeat (and maybe drink)!

➤ You drive an easy-to-spot rental car!

➤ You're easy to find!

> *Don't stick out! Leave your Hawaiian shirt at home. Please don't gawk like a tourist...and tell your son not to brag about his $120 Air Jordan shoes. Better yet, leave the shoes at home. Don't talk so loudly. Stop carrying enough cameras to make you look like a pawn shop.*

SIGHTSEEING AND SAFETY

Sightseeing is truly what traveling is all about. It is learning to appreciate the beauty of foreign cultures. It really doesn't matter how long your sightseeing excursion will be, you and your family's security is still of paramount concern. You must stay alert. I know that's not always easy to do, especially with family distractions.

In order to reduce your family's risk, *common sense* is the key. You see, there's a balance between complete ignorance of security matters and security paranoia. So watch what's going on around you. Pay attention to your intuition. Obviously, you and your family need to be careful when you're sightseeing.

If you're going to be in an urban area, limit your sightseeing to the daylight hours. Walk down the middle of the sidewalk. Watch out for blind alleys, shrubbery, etc., and cross the street to avoid suspicious looking people.

HOW TO STAY HEALTHY AND ALIVE

The following advice is what every person who travels should know by heart:

✓ Stick to known routes. Tell your security concerns to the hotel staff. Make certain you have an in-depth city map.

✓ Stay clear of graffiti stricken areas.

✓ Avoid the temptation to explore or find shortcuts that might, instead, lead you into dangerous areas.

✓ If you find yourself in a dangerous area and are robbed, never chase the perpetrators to recover property.

THOSE MEAN STREETS...

The driver of a car, trying to find a shorter route to his destination, turned down a dead-end street in the troubled Cypress Park area of Los Angeles and was fired upon by gang members. The attack resulted in the death of a two year old child who was a passenger in the car.

A Virginia family, visiting the St. Louis Cemetery, was robbed. The adult daughter and her mother pursued the thieves on foot while the father followed in the family van. One of the assailants turned and opened fire, killing the daughter.

OK, I know some of you don't want to hear these kinds of stories. Don't be surprised...**anything can happen, good or bad.**

In some cases, an area itself may not be safe but the road to get there is. Coconut Grove, south of downtown Miami, is one of the most popular restaurant and nightclub districts in Dade County. The central Grove area is safe and heavily trafficked. It also has a visible police presence. However, according to city policy, several of the routes to the Grove are highly unsafe and plagues with drug dealing. Area residents who frequent Coconut Grove are aware of the safer access routes, but most tourists are not.

To combat this problem and similar ones, the Greater Miami Convention and Visitor's Bureau distributes a tourist road map called, "Follow the Sun," which highlights primary thoroughfares from Miami International Airport to some of the most popular destinations in the region. The "Follow the Sun" logo has been affixed to highway signs to further help drivers find their way.

> Police officials in major cities affirm that theft from autos is the most common crime in central business districts. People commonly leave computers, briefcases, shopping bags, and other goods in plain view inviting smash-and-grab robbers. It is better to place baggage and goods out of sight and in the trunk of your car. Better yet, rather than driving around with any luggage in the car, travelers should first go to their hotel. If the room isn't ready, the hotel can provide a safe, secure place for your bags.

Travel is fatal to prejudice, bigotry and human mindlessness.

...AND STREET SMARTS

- Pay attention to safety havens — police stations, hotels, public buildings, churches. Make sure you let someone know where you are going and when you will be back.

- Avoid fumbling with a map on an unfamiliar street. Plan ahead so that you'll know what route to take. Keep your eye on landmarks. And, by the way, tell your kids not to "broadcast" the family's sightseeing plans in public. Why take the chance of being followed or of returning to a burglarized hotel room?

FATIGUE

Know your physical limits and recognize the physical limits of your children. Some people look like and walk like "victims waiting to happen" — without any confidence or self-assurance.

DRESS APPROPRIATELY

Let's talk about your clothes and your accessories. Dress comfortably — low profile, loose-fitting clothes. Carry your purse close to your body with flap opening in toward you. Wind the strap around your shoulder or wrist. If you're carrying extra layers of clothes, use them to cover your handbag. **And, no matter where you are, don't put your purse down on the seat next to you! Wallets should be carried in secure pockets — which means not in the back.** Clothing with pockets that zip, button or have velcro pockets are preferable.

STREET HUSTLERS

PICKPOCKETS are one of the biggest problems you'll face in a city. Some regular vacationers protect their money with rubber bands or safety pins. Shoes and boots are excellent hiding places. Avoid carrying more cash than you need. Don't keep all your cash and credit cards in the same wallet. **Use Traveler's Checks.**

Avoid talking to strangers. Don't allow anyone to stop you or crowd around you or your children. Watch out for street gangs in certain areas (including bands of gypsies, or children who will surround you). In South American countries street kids also may approach a prospective robbery victim and ask for the time or a light for a cigarette. If the answer comes to them in English, a gang will then surround the target and rob him or her.

Be aware of anyone touching you for any reason; someone losing their balance, or accidentally spilling something on you. It may seem harmless at the time, but be aware, most thieves are swift and cunning.

Scam Alert!...

You're walking through an airport with your family in tow when suddenly a man eating a hot dog bumps into you and spills mustard on your clothes. He immediately begins to apologize and tries to clean up the spot. You say, "No, that's alright. Never mind." He walks away. Your mind and emotions are in a whirl.

"Look at this mess on my shirt. How am I going to clean it up? Have they started boarding for our flight? Where are the kids? Whew! They're playing hide-and-seek in the waiting area. Of all times for this to happen!"

You finally calm down, get your kids and proceed with your family to the ticket counter for your boarding passes. The attendant asks you for a picture I.D. You reach for your wallet and discover...IT'S GONE!

SAY CHEESE!

Here is some advice for the entire family about your photographic efforts:

☀ Watch out for picture-taking set-ups. This can be a diversionary tactic used by pickpockets.

☀ It's very prudent to use a small pocket camera that can be carried in your jacket or purse.

☀ Never put your camera down. You'll greatly increase the odds against not having that camera when you go home.

☀ Determine what's off-limits to photograph. Tourists have been detained because they were innocently taking pictures of buildings or street scenes when they were, in fact, filming clandestine military operations. In Muslim countries, taking photos of sacred shrines are prohibited. Before you click, become familiar with what you may or may not photograph. Be careful also of taking pictures of people who do not want to be photographed.

☀ Watch out for "pseudo" guides and hustlers at airports, train stations, and scenic sites who are primed for American-made and, therefore, custom-made victims.

DON'T LOOK LIKE A VICTIM

An appearance of self-confidence, a brisk business-like stride and a sense of purpose impart more protection than most people imagine. **Some people just look like victims.**

- Appear to know where you're going. Get clear directions beforehand, but if you are lost and need directions, approach a police officer, store clerk or service station attendant.

- Walk with a companion whenever possible. Experts say you can reduce your chances of being attacked by 70 percent by walking with one other person...and by 90 percent if you are in a group of three.

- Look purposeful, as though you have something to accomplish and plan to be on your way. If one or more persons block your path, focus your eyes beyond them and make it clear you do not have time to stop.

- Be conscious of what is going on around you. But understand that odd behavior in public may be a diversionary tactic to direct attention away from a pickpocket or mugger. Hold your belongings more securely and move away from the commotion, not toward it.

- Keep some quarters on your person. A telephone booth can be a temporary refuge if you sit on the floor with your feet against the door while awaiting police.

WHAT'S TRAVEL WITHOUT SHOPPING?

"Veni, vedi, Visa, ...we came, we saw, we went shopping! Right?

Shopping...the number one activity for travelers young and old! Here are your security shopping tips.

- My friends at Customs have told me many times about Americans returning home with alleged "works of art" that they were told were duty free. The surprise hits when people come through Customs and, not only is a duty imposed, but there's usually a very high price to be paid. You need to know how Custom's evaluates art—specifically glass, ceramics and tapestries.

Shopping, money and thieves go together. If you act carelessly when you put away your wallet or your purse, you create an opportunity for a thief to relieve you of your valuables. Not adhering to the instructions about "unattended purses and wallets in back pockets" — even for a minute — can result in a successful crime. In addition, be discreet about showing your money. Again... keep a low profile — try not to advertise the contents of your wallet.

Remember when I said, "keep your hands free?" *You can't very well do that if your arms are full of packages, can you?*

More Family Tips for Travel Abroad:

- Register with the US Embassy or a similar facility. Notify them of your name, hotel or address while visiting, plus planned departure date.

- Stolen US Passports are a valuable commodity in many places. Carry passports on your person in a secure manner.

- Keep telephone numbers and addresses of the US Embassy, local emergency services, police, and personal contacts with you at all times. Learn how to use local public and private telephones. Always carry the correct change or tokens to make a call from a pay phone.

- Learn key foreign phrases that might be necessary in an emergency, such as "I need help," "Please find me the police," and "Where is the nearest hospital?"

- Carry on your person important medical information. In the event of an injury or illness, medical personnel will need to be aware of certain information such as blood type, allergies, illnesses, special medications. Carry copies of current prescriptions.

> Hopefully, in your travels, you and your family will never become victims of crime. But...because there are no guarantees in life, you can take basic common sense steps to reduce your risks. There is a great psychological value in the entire family knowing that you are prepared. Confidence and preparation are very powerful deterrents to crime.

The struggle to make the world a safe place for children is the most important struggle in the world today. I believe that you and I share the view that the love for our families can knock down all the obstacles the world sets before us.

This chapter is dedicated to you and your family with my love and respect. *The Security Connection* is for you, your spouse, your kids and your relatives. Whether a journey takes you across town or across the globe, there are ways to protect yourself and the ones you love from becoming victims of terrorism.

I *must* now focus my attention on families...because of the terrible things that are happening here in the United States and throughout the world. The American family needs to recognize **THE NEW LOSS OF INNOCENCE IN AMERICA.**

How the world has changed...and how unfortunate that terrorism has reached our shores. We all must be prepared for these changing times...so we can then claim: "It will be the best of times and not the worst of times", as Mr. Dickens would say.

MR. SECURITY SAYS........

Remember......

➤ When it comes to travel security, children need to be given instruction, education, and varying degrees of responsibility for their safety.

➤ Failing to do your cultural homework beforehand can expose your family to unnecessary risk.

➤ Stick to known routes; stay clear of graffiti-stricken areas; avoid shortcuts.

➤ Learn the favorite tactics of street hustlers and pickpockets.

➤ Shopping, money, and thieves go together — take common sense precautions.

CHAPTER 8

THE HIGH RISK OF BUSINESS TRAVEL

"Toto, I don't think we're in Kansas anymore."

Dorothy, from The Wizard of Oz

Having spent my share of time over the years in corporate boardrooms meeting with some of the "biggest names" in the business world, one thing I can safely say about these executives is that ***they thrive on risk!*** Closing sales...making deals...doing things never before tried. Risk taking is a part of their make-up and a part of what makes them so successful.

Why do I meet with these executives?

I am there because when it comes to security, a risk taking mentality can lead a person down paths where they suddenly find themselves the object of criminal or terrorist actions. That's why business travel is perhaps the most dangerous form of travel. Executives on business excursions routinely put themselves at risk from terrorist or criminal threats and actions.

Why is business travel so dangerous?

⇨ When companies have business dealings abroad, it raises their visibility, their vulnerabilities, and subsequently their risks.

⇨ Americans are favorite targets of terrorists and criminals. Simply representing an American company makes you a target.

⇨ Business travelers must fly to certain locations when no other options exist. These locations may inherently contain security hazards.

⇨ Deadlines put pressure on travel schedules which eliminates options of when to fly. Heavily populated flying periods or bad weather conditions cannot be avoided.

⇨ Business travelers are catered to by service industries — hotels, restaurants, stores. Criminals are aware of this.

Traveling executives are vulnerable on almost every continent.

IN MOSCOW...

Recently a businessman was severely beaten by armed robbers after he took an unofficial taxi from Domodedova Airport in Moscow. Because there was such a wait for official taxis, the traveler decided to take a ride with a private individual who may or may not have been a licensed taxi driver. The victim said that the driver looked reputable and was driving a clean white Volvo. The driver offered the traveler a price three times lower than the going cab fare for the journey; the driver explained, "I'm going to that part of the city anyway."

Shortly after leaving the airport, the driver stopped and picked up three well dressed, middle aged men who were waiting at the roadside. Because it was raining, the driver said he felt obligated to pick the men up, and the traveler agreed. The three men entered the car and almost immediately demanded that the traveler play cards with them. At this point, the traveler became suspicious, so he asked the driver to pull over so he would not "spoil the card game" of the other three men.

Immediately one of the card players produced a pistol and told the driver they would kill him if he stopped. The traveler was robbed and then severely pistol-whipped. The cab stopped and the traveler was thrown out onto the road with only the clothes on his back. It seemed highly likely the driver was in complicity with the criminals, although the four made an effort to keep this hidden.

IN NIGERIA...

A group of American businessmen, evaluating investment opportunities, arranged from their hotel room by telephone a meeting with a reputable local company that offered to have a car pick them up. Twenty minutes before the scheduled time, front desk personnel called to say their car had arrived. The Americans were driven away by a well dressed man who claimed to be from their host company. They were taken to a dark road, roughed up and robbed of several thousand dollars and their personal possessions. Whether the tip to the robbers came from someone in the business or at the hotel is unknown. However, it is possible that the Americans' telephone conversation was monitored by the switchboard staff and used as a lead for the robbery gang.

IN BELGIUM...

An executive flew to Brussels to meet with a large corporation. After sleeping through the morning on the day of his arrival, he left his hotel for the afternoon, returning only in the evening. At his meeting the next day, he noticed that executives of the corporation had copies of documents he had kept secured in his hotel room but which obviously had been secreted out.

We all know that since the end of the Cold War there has been an explosion of business travel worldwide. Employers searching for new opportunities for their companies are visiting far-off countries they might not even have heard of a decade ago. ***You know the saying: "business is a good game—lots of competition and a minimum of rules. You keep score with the money." Unfortunately, business is also exposing itself to unprecedented risks.***

With so many new overseas markets opening up, the number of robberies, kidnappings and other crimes against US business people continues to rise.

Even though the risks of business travel are increasingly becoming known, in this era of corporate downsizing, security is one of the first areas to suffer from the budget axe. ***This means that the responsibility for travel safety may fall back on you.***

I'm concerned about your welfare.

Whether your company has security policies for you or whether your travel safety is left entirely in your hands, let's examine some of the weak links that can contribute to a security breakdown.

Weak link example #1

There's an executive who believes in coordinating travel arrangements himself.

What does he do?

♦   He faxes his itinerary haphazardly around the world to local subsidiaries.

♦   Hotel reservations are made in the company's name.

♦   Transportation arrangements are made through the local luxury hotel.

This executive's destination country is a high-risk location for kidnapping, especially abductions that take place while the victim is traveling in a hired vehicle. A local security source confirms that hotel drivers may be connected to criminal rings. Security control is weak because the background of the hotel driver is unknown.

> *Getting rid of habits is like peeling an onion …it must be done one layer at a time.*

This example illustrates the importance of making all hotel and other reservations in an inconspicuous manner without using the company's name. Personnel involved in itinerary scheduling should be kept to a minimum "need-to-know" level.

We have now moved from the Industrial Age to the Information Age and security awareness must keep up with the changing times. It is often difficult to retain control of faxes that are sent internationally.

Such documents may accidentally fall into the wrong hands, and local agents may not be security conscious. You can guard against problems by using secure fax machines when possible, and by making sure that a designated recipient is waiting on the other end when the fax is sent.

Weak Link Example #2

An executive is arriving via commercial carrier to a South American city. A limousine has been arranged to pick him up and drive him to the hotel. Unfortunately, his flight is three hours late, and the limousine has returned to its headquarters. Since it is late at night and the executive is traveling with another man, they decide to solve the problem themselves by asking for assistance at the airport.

An airport employee arranges for a taxi to pick them up. The taxi driver, however, is collaborating with a local criminal gang. The businessmen are driven to an isolated area and robbed at gunpoint.

♦ Because in many countries law enforcement officials collaborate with criminals, a call to the police department may simply provide the adversary with assistance.

♦ Kidnappings of executives during the past two years has spotlighted the fact that a business person must take a personal role in learning how to protect himself or herself. It is essential to know how to effectively respond to unexpected situations...to understand the importance of varying routines...to notice any changes in the local environment...and to become acutely aware of any surveillance activity going on around you.

Corporations cannot let their guard down! Corporations must assess the potential for all over the world. Conduct a potential risk analysis of areas that you travel to frequently...Meet today's changing security challenge!

LOCAL DOES NOT NECESSARILY MEAN SAFER

There is a hustle going on today that is being used to steal laptop computers at airports all across the country.

This is how it works: An unsuspecting traveler …could it be you?…is carrying a laptop and is about to enter the metal detector security area. Two people position themselves in front of the unsuspecting traveler. They stall until the person places the laptop computer on the conveyor belt. Then the first subject moves through the metal detector easily. The second subject sets off the detector and begins a slow process of emptying his pockets, removing jewelry, etc. While this is happening, the first subject takes the laptop as soon as it appears on the conveyor belt and moves quickly away. When the traveler finally gets through the metal detector, the laptop is gone. The subject that picked it up heads further into the gate area and disappears among the crowd. Sometimes a third subject will take a hand-off from the first subject and the computer will be out of the restricted area even before the victim …could it be you?…knows it is gone.

OK—now you know about this scam. What steps will you take now?

How about this: Avoid being in a line when entering through the metal detector. When that's not possible, delay putting your laptop on the conveyor belt until you are sure that you will be the next person through the metal detector. As you move through the metal detector, keep your eyes on the conveyor belt and watch for your laptop to come through, as well as watching those who are picking up belongings in front of you.

To prevent the loss of proprietary information your company should mandate that employees may not place any confidential information on a laptop. Loss of proprietary information cost companies **$20 billion** last year!

WHEN YOU CAN'T TELL THE GOOD GUYS FROM THE BAD GUYS

In some countries government officials are an integral part of the criminal scene. Corruption is rampant in many places in the world.

From the coast of Africa...

In Nigeria, for example, it is common for government officials, soldiers and police officers to solicit or demand bribes from foreigners.

Business scams in Nigeria are also rampant, and the industry has grown into an international syndicate involving prominent government officials. Scams generally lure targets with contracts which frequently invoke a particular authority, or ministry, or office of the Nigerian government, and even may cite the support of a Nigerian government official by name.

...to South of the Border

When traveling to many of the Central and South American countries you may be faced with officials soliciting bribes. In Venezuela, officials at the Caracas International Airport are famous for it. I know a business executive of a large US corporation who was approached by a Caracas airport customs agent and asked to give $20 as a bribe. When the executive refused, he was taken to a room at the airport where he was detained for six hours before being released.

COMMON SENSE PRECAUTIONS FOR BUSINESS TRAVELERS

First, let's review how you will prepare for your trip. **Responsibility + preparation = the ability to meet unexpected challenges**. When you are prepared, you feel better about yourself. You feel more in control, less stressful. We recommend:

★ In addition to making sure your affairs are in order before you leave home, discuss with your family what they would do in case an emergency did occur.

★ Family members need to know that your travel information must remain confidential. Your messages can be forwarded to you. Keep your family informed if you make any changes in your travel plans.

★ **Be very cautious** about discussing personal matters, your itinerary or program, and avoid publicity.

★ Do not advertise your executive status; do not place a logo or business name on your luggage; dress appropriately not flashy; wear a cheap watch and no jewelry.

★ If you believe you may be a **high-risk target,** hire protection to travel with you, or take in-depth security training classes in anti-terrorist procedures.

★ If possible, avoid traveling alone.

★ Do not carry alcohol with you or pack it in your luggage. Do not carry unmarked prescription drugs.

★ **Divide your money** in half and keep it in separate places.

★ Carry family photos in your wallet, not club membership-type cards.

★ Travel light.

★ Be aware of "volatile" reading material...Playboy, political magazines, etc. Leave them at home!

★ **Find out the local laws and then obey them!**

★ Set up meetings yourself so that you can control the time and place.

Once you arrive at your destination:

★ Register with the US Embassy as soon as you arrive.

★ Know your "safe havens"...police stations, hotels, hospitals, etc.

★ Stay inside after dark.

★ **Keep your hotel door locked** at all times. Do not leave any personal or business documents in your hotel room. Make copies of all important papers.

★ Refuse unexpected packages.

★ Meet all visitors in the lobby.

★ **Refrain from photographing** police or military personnel or installations near border areas.

★ Deal only with authorized agents when exchanging money or buying airline tickets.

★ If any of your possessions are lost or stolen, immediately notify all appropriate authorities. Keep all reports for insurance claims, as well as for your own "defense," if necessary. Notify the American Embassy if you lose your passport.

★ Avoid well known restaurants frequented by wealthy tourists.

★ In public places, sit away from the entrance so you cannot be seen through the front window or front door.

★ **Pay attention** to see if you are being watched.

★ Be on guard for con games.

Had enough precautions? How about a poem?

> *A chapter full of sparkling tips about security and winning...*
>
> *Certainly is appreciated if the end is close to the beginning!*

THE TWO TYPES OF TRAVELERS

During the past 35 years, I've seen and protected millions of travelers all over the world. It is easy to distinguish a corporate traveler from the leisure traveler — and not just because of the person's attire. There are major differences between the two, differences that require mental alertness and awareness on both sides of the traveling fence.

Examine the differences and think about the security risks posed for each group. If you were an adversary, would you recognize the patterns that would influence your strategy?

CORPORATE	LEISURE
• Alone/with a business group	• Alone/with a touring group
• Exposed to industrial espionage	• Not exposed to industrial espionage
• More attractive attire	• Less attractive attire
• Repetitive visits to same location	• Random one-time visits
• Represents a company/organization	• Does not represent a company/ organization
• Others involved in planned agenda	• No others involved in planned agenda
• Accommodation - Business Center	• Accommodation - Tourist Center

FLYING ON CORPORATE AIRCRAFT

For those of you who work for companies that own their own aircraft, we suggest you pass along this information to your corporate security and flight departments. If you fly commercially and do not work for a company that has its own aircraft, give the information to those who can utilize it.

Whether you fly corporate or commercially, you might be surprised to know that the demand for corporate jets is on the rise. Business jet sales actually soared 23% last year (no pun intended) surpassing the $2 million mark! Companies of all sizes today own, lease or charter business aircraft. Even before TWA's tragic Flight 800, travel security had been a chief concern for many companies. With new international markets available, traveling by private jet is increasing among executives who are seeking business opportunities.

THE MOST VULNERABLE TARGETS

Corporate or private aircraft passengers are attractive targets for terrorism. They may be well know and/or wealthy business people, senior executives of companies, political figures, or high profile celebrities. Frequently, their activities are the focus of widespread media attention. Aircraft crews, simply by association, are equally as vulnerable.

Attacks are perpetrated for a variety of reasons ranging from personal motives such as competition, jealousy, hate and vengeance to ideological, political and religious. The safety and security of passengers and crew has frequently been jeopardized by political extremists. When traveling, these conditions cannot be ignored.

The aircraft, the passengers and the crew are difficult targets to protect. Why? Information about these targets can come from a number of sources and is fairly easy to obtain. It is difficult to restrict access to this information and to maintain secrecy.

BULLETIN! BULLETIN! Getting there and back safely is your mission. Everything else can be fixed, projects completed, phone calls made. "Security first!"

POTENTIAL THREATS TO THE AIRCRAFT, PASSENGERS AND CREW:

1. **Anonymous messages**

    Conveyed either before take-off or while in-flight, they may be about a bomb planted on board or may concern some form of sabotage to the aircraft.

2. **Sabotage**

    Sabotage involves the following:

    a. Deliberate damage (which could result in a crash) to one or more of the aircraft systems.

    b. Destruction of the aircraft and related equipment.

    c. The planting of an explosive charge on the aircraft.

3. Taking hostage(s) for bargaining or other purposes

4. **Arson**

5. Theft of aircraft or spare parts

Theft of parts of parked aircraft is a common phenomenon. It is used for the purpose of causing financial harm or to obtain the parts. Such thefts generally occur at airports that have poor security and where spare parts inventory is not supervised.

6. Light arms/missile assaults

7. Damage to name and reputation

Perpetrators exploit information about aircraft routes, schedules and slack security measures at airports. Discovery of hidden cargo could seriously damage the name and reputation of an aircraft owner, as well as the crew who could be deemed responsible for the illegal activity.

8. **Theft** of commercial information/classified documents

Someone may enter the aircraft in the absence of passengers, crew or other supervision to obtain materials.

The corporate aviation community has special needs.

With world conditions changing at an unprecedented pace, there is an increasing demand for security specialists to help organizations respond to the escalation of incidents, threats to assets, and costs due to terrorism, kidnapping and information misuse.

Before you and your company become a target, learn to take whatever precautions are necessary to insure everyone's safety.

It is now more obvious why business travelers are routinely at risk. You won't be able to put all of these strategies in place overnight; work at it in "bite-size" pieces. Start today! Always act in ways that are most likely to reduce your risks. Remember....Risks vary according to circumstances.

You say that you know this by now? Good! Learning is finding out what you already know...doing is demonstrating that you, indeed, know it!

MR. SECURITY SAYS........

Remember......

➤ With many new overseas markets opening up, the number of robberies, kidnappings and other crimes against US business people continue to rise.

➤ Be inconspicuous; do not advertise your business status.

➤ Travel information must be on a "need-to-know" basis.

➤ Corporations need to conduct a risk analysis of areas that are traveled to frequently or infrequently.

➤ If you believe you may be a high-risk target, hire protection to travel with you, or take in-depth security training classes in anti-terrorist procedures.

CHAPTER 9

HOTEL SECURITY

"Where thou art — that is home."

Emily Dickenson

As a serious sports fan, I'll always remember my first Dodgers game. I had waited years. Each time I had business scheduled in Los Angeles, it was either during the off-season or when the team was out of town. Anyway, when I finally entered the ballpark, it even *smelled* like heaven!

Another reason I remember the game so well is the conversation I had that day with my friend. He had moved to the beach a year ago and was selling me on why I should move my family out there. He told me I couldn't afford **not** to move there. When I last saw him, a few years later, he told me that he had sold his home for <u>six</u> times what he had paid for it! He had followed that most famous piece of real estate advice ever uttered, the three most important considerations when buying property: LOCATION, LOCATION, LOCATION!

Today, when it comes to choosing a hotel, the only considerations which we hear people discuss are:

☞   *location and price...*

which means you would probably be shocked to learn that over 60% of all crimes committed in hotels occur in the more expensive ones in the best locations!

Of course, consideration of location and price are crucial, but there is much more to talk about than just assuming that location and price are adequate security safeguards. Let's examine:

First, you will select a hotel, ***preferably from a major chain,*** at each location which adheres to the following criteria:

🏛   Three stories high, or more...

🏛   Minimum of two entrances/exits...

🏛   Access to/from streets that vary so that it is possible to change travel routines...

🏛   Security department and personnel...

You only get what you give yourself, so give yourself the best.

But your choice is still not finalized yet... we want you to:

🏛   Stay at large, relatively busy hotels rather than out-of-the-way accommodations.

🏛   If possible, avoid hotels on "embassy row" or in known high-crime areas. Generally embassies cluster together on one street or in one area.

Now you can make your decision! But don't get complacent...your security responsibilities don't end here. **Which room are you going to accept? Do not accept a room assignment on the ground floor or the top floor unless there is no alternative.** *These locations increase the risk of breaking into the room from the street or from the roof. A corner room or suite is most desirable — close but not next to an emergency exit. Avoid rooms across from elevators.*

While you are finalizing your room assignment at check-in:

🏛 Do not provide any information beyond that required when registering.

🏛 Instruct all hotel staff to refrain from revealing any information about your activities, timetable, plans, room number, etc.

🏛 Ensure that baggage remains under observation at all times until delivered to the room.

Trust me...you'll feel better...and your family will too! You and your family's safety is too important to leave to hotel security or the police. We need to be on the lookout ourselves!

We recommend that you make prior arrangements with hotel management for deliveries...postal, flowers, packages, gifts, messages, etc... to be checked by the hotel security officer before being delivered. After a delivery is checked, a hotel employee should deliver it, not the messenger. The hotel employee making the delivery must be instructed to ask if the delivery is expected and if the sender's name is known. Are you getting all this?

After check-in, you should inspect surroundings to locate and identify emergency exits, stairwells, secondary entrances and exits, fire extinguishing equipment, fire escape routes, etc. Establish a meeting place for all concerned in the event of an emergency.

Other precautions:

🏛 Do not admit to your room unexpected visitors before they are screened. If the caller claims to be on the hotel staff, check with the concierge or front desk.

🏛   Use a travel lock to secure hotel room doors from the inside. Keep doors and windows locked.

🏛   Compile a list of contacts and telephone numbers in each hotel, including the manager, security head, closest fire and police stations, etc.

🏛   Keep valuables and classified documents in a personal safe in your room. If a safe is not available, store valuables with the company you are visiting or on your person in a concealed moneybelt. By the way, in smaller hotels, do not use a shared safe if offered.

THE POSSIBILITY OF FIRE

The possibility of fire also exists no matter how large the structure, or how much safety equipment the hotel boasts. Your security is generally based on how the fire is handled. However, many people do not know, or follow, correct procedures in coping with a fire. This is another step you, as a traveler, can take to protect yourself and your family.

When you and your family check into a hotel, do you and the children sit down together and discuss an escape plan from a fire before you start "running" to your eagerly awaited activities? Get real...I doubt it. Think "what if?"...because when a fire occurs, if you are prepared, you can all act without panic and without wasting time.

By choosing a secure hotel, especially here domestically, you're choosing a well made, fire resistant property. However, many hotels abroad are not as fire resistant as those here:

🏛   It may be difficult to contact a fire department.

🏛   There may not be reliable smoke detectors or sprinkler systems.

🏛   Escape routes may not be posted in hallways.

🏛   There may be too few exits and escape routes may not be posted.

🏛   Fire-fighting equipment and water supplies may be limited.

I want you to make certain that you and your family locate exits and stairways as soon as you check in. Count the number of doors between your room and an exit or stairwell. You may have to feel your way to an exit if the hallway is full of smoke. **Form a mental map of your escape route.** If there is a fire alarm system, find the nearest alarm. Be sure you know how to use it — you may have to activate it in the dark or in heavy smoke. The smoke detector has a test button — test it. If it does not work, we recommend you move to another room if the hotel cannot fix it. It's good security to do so.

IF A FIRE STARTS

Experts tell us that if a fire starts, try to call the fire department or police for help — do not rely on a security guard. If you speak the language, tell the fire department or police your room number. If you cannot reach the fire department, call the front desk — tell them your room number.

 Grab your key and crawl to the door on your hands and knees. Don't stand — smoke gases rise while the fresher air will be near the floor. Before you open the door, feel it with the palm of your hand. If the door or knob is hot, the fire may be right outside. Open the door slowly. If your exit path is clear, crawl into the hallway. Be sure to close the door behind you to keep smoke out in case you need to return to your room. Take your key as most hotel doors lock automatically. Stay close to the wall to avoid being trampled.

I know that this is beginning to sound and look like one of those "disaster dramas"... a made-for-TV movie of the week! I'm glad—it will grab your attention so you'll keep watching...I mean reading!

 Firefighters remind us to not use elevators during a fire. They may malfunction, or if they have heat-activated call buttons, they may take you directly to the fire floor. They recommend that as you make your way to the fire exit, stay on the same side as the exit door. **Count the doors to the exit.** Follow the plan that you organized. When you reach the exit, walk down the stairs to the first floor.

If you encounter heavy smoke in the stairwell, don't try to run through it. You may not make it. Instead, turn around and walk up to the roof fire exit. Prop the door open to ventilate the stairwell and to keep from being locked out. Find the windward side of the roof, sit down, and wait for fire fighters to find you.

If all exits are blocked, or if there is heavy smoke in the hallway, you'll be better off staying in your room, according to the Fire Department. If there is smoke in your room, open a window and turn on the bathroom vent. Don't break the window unless it can't be opened. You might want to close the window later to keep smoke out, and broken glass could injure you or people below.

Fill the bathtub with water to use for fire fighting. Bail water onto your door or any hot walls with an ice bucket or wastebasket. Stuff wet towels into cracks under and around doors where smoke can enter. Tie a wet towel over your mouth and nose to help filter out smoke. **If there is fire** outside your window, take down the drapes and move everything combustible away from the window.

Don't let me hear you say, "I can't remember all this," or "this is too much." WRONG! Our mind is a powerful instrument...use it to protect yourself!

EMERGENCY EVACUATION

Emergency evacuation is part of Hotel Security Procedures. It is especially relevant in high risk countries. Here are the general guidelines:

★   First, you must verify source and validity of a notification of danger. Is this rumor or fact? IF there is a real danger...

★   Move directly, without delay or hesitation, on the predetermined escape route (to the emergency meeting place, if appropriate).

★   Consider airport security conditions and proceed accordingly. If the airport is determined to be unsafe use alternative means of transport.

HOTELS...AND COMMUNICATION SECURITY

✯   **Hotel rooms are not safe places** for discussions of confidential business matters or classified information.

✯   Hotels in certain countries invariably put business visitors in designated rooms...presumably for ease of eavesdropping. In China, travelers should expect that their conversations will be monitored on the telephone, in hotel rooms, and in restaurants. Also, in China, travelers are cautioned to avoid bringing Chinese nationals to their hotel rooms, as authorities will assume that something illegal is taking place.

✯   Use the hotel to practice your communication skills when traveling abroad. For example: One noted expert says that when you leave for your first business meeting in a foreign city, the lobby is the best place to practice the procedures for using a public telephone. Your ease-of-use will come in handy later.

✯   Learn to break down the language barrier with hotel personnel.

Communication specialists say:

- Remember that your listener may not understand what you are saying, but that doesn't mean he's deaf. Don't insult him by shouting at him. Simply speak as clearly and slowly as possible.

- Avoid slang and jargon at all costs. Would you know what someone meant in Italian if he used his country's equivalent of "catching the red eye to L.A." or, "his sales pitch was all smoke and mirrors?"

- Even exaggeration may confuse. Your listener may understand enough literal English to wonder if you really meant to call your boss an idiot...or was lunch really a disaster just because the salad bar lacked chives.

- Over punctuate by your tone of voice.

HOW TO GET DIRECTIONS FROM THE LOCALS

Hotel security also involves effectively utilizing hotel personnel as resources for information. Inevitably this includes asking for directions. There is an effective, or right way...and an ineffective or wrong way to get directions.

Why is this important?

Ineffective directions can lead you to the wrong place at the wrong time!

The problem with asking directions of local folks, whether in Des Moines or in London, is that they know the territory and you don't. Sounds obvious, but that's exactly why getting directions sometimes confuse us more than ever. Local people tend to refer to "Old National Highway" instead of Route 279...which is how your map shows it...and they seldom know Interstate exit numbers.

The most useful tool for getting or giving directions is a map. Be sure to have one with you when you ask for help. It is much clearer to mark out a route than to describe it.

Be sure you are stating your destination clearly. Better still, write it down. Ask the person to point out the place on your map. No map? Ask them to sketch the route...and to estimate distances in blocks or miles.

Write down instructions, with notes on landmarks, and read them back. Don't be embarrassed to ask for clarification.

––––––––––––––––

Being security conscious is taking care of all the details... these details left unattended will serve to increase your vulnerability.

CHAPTER 10

BACK SEAT DRIVING: VEHICLE SECURITY

"Unless we change our direction, we are likely to end up where we are headed."

— Old Chinese Proverb

When my wife glanced at the title of this chapter, she accused me of sharing marital secrets of our driving experiences with the public! I assured her that absolutely nothing in this chapter was based on our personal relationship. I don't think she believed me.

Why are we including this chapter? Why is this chapter so important?

90% OF ALL TERRORIST ACTS TAKE PLACE WHEN THE TARGET IS IN A CAR!!

Wake up! Stop worrying about a scratch on your car and start worrying about what you need to do to protect yourself and your family!

Your rental car company can't give you the information contained in these pages. Neither can your Department of Motor Vehicles. **Who's going to warn you that you're in the wrong car, in the wrong place, at the wrong time?** I will. Count on it!

Security professionals are highly alert to the risks involved with riding and driving. Secure transportation is an integral part of minimizing risk.

Let me give you an example—and, believe me, **something like this happens every day, somewhere...**

A few weeks ago in Lima, Peru, two separate groups of American citizens were stopped by individuals they thought were police; one of the "police" vehicles even had a dome light. The first group of victims was robbed and then briefly abducted in their own vehicle before being released. The second victims were able to escape, but were chased and shot at for two miles. Both groups of victims were driving sport utility vehicles and were presumably targeted for their perceived wealth.

This chapter delivers over 50 strategies and recommendations. READ SLOWLY!

 VEHICLE SECURITY CHECKLIST

When we talk about the type of vehicle, we are referring to recommendations that are more relevant when you are out of the country ... and they are more specifically geared towards the business traveler. The recommendations, however, for *locking* and *entering* the vehicle apply anywhere, anytime.

Type of Vehicle

It is preferable to use a powerful, quick-response vehicle, one which could, in an emergency, break through barriers, make a quick getaway and ram other vehicles. Standard model vehicles which do not call attention to themselves are preferable... avoid American makes when abroad. *License plates can be a sign for the adversaries. And make sure that your rental agency does not use special license plate designations or bumper stickers. These are known to professional thieves.*

When it comes to locking the vehicle, check to see that the style of lock makes it difficult to open the doors without a key. Always lock the car, even when you are in it. Do not unlock the door to a stranger. Remember to protect your car keys at all times. Do not put your name or identifying logo on keys.

There are security rules for entering the vehicle as well. Check all around the vehicle prior to approaching the door, and look for occupied vehicles parked nearby. Check inside the car before unlocking it.

Know your license number and be able to describe your vehicle, if necessary. Keep the gas tank at least half full, and use a locking gas cap. Keep the car well-maintained. Don't get out of the vehicle if you have a breakdown and another motorist stops to help before you have called for help. Lower the window slightly and ask the motorist to call police or other assistance.

This may seem like an "endless" list…but the bottom line is safety and security. Don't let an act of terror rob you of your dream!

My niece just turned 16 and she's studying hard to pass her driving exam. I'll bet that some of you will feel like she does when you read and study our CHECKLIST FOR DRIVING AND RIDING. This checklist applies to you, wherever you live. Follow these rules especially when you are in an unfamiliar city.

 CHECKLIST FOR DRIVING AND RIDING

   💡   If your vehicle does not start, get assistance or get away. It may have been deliberately disabled.

   💡   Never leave an unattended vehicle running. Never leave the vehicle without checking for suspicious activities around you.

   💡   Select main roads over narrow side streets. Avoid known crime areas. Choose well-lit roads at night.

- Maintain distance from the vehicle in front to ensure ease of maneuverability, especially at stoplights or intersections.

- Stop in the center lane at an intersection or a traffic light, not the lane next to the side of the road, to prevent an attack by a pedestrian.

- Remember to keep doors locked when driving and when you park the vehicle. If someone appears to need assistance, don't stop. Telephone as soon as possible to send assistance. **ACCIDENTS CAN BE STAGED.** And never pick up hitchhikers.

- Park in well-lit, populous areas. If possible, park in a closed and protected garage or area. Park in reverse so that when you leave the space, you will have an unobstructed view of the area in front of and around you. Whenever possible, avoid leaving your car with an unknown attendant.

- Do not accept unsolicited offers of assistance. If a stranger remains around your locked vehicle and appears to be a menace, sound the horn continuously and put your lights on.

- If someone attempts to force you to stop, do not do so, even if it means a collision. Sound the horn continuously to get attention, and drive toward lights or wherever you may find assistance. Get the license number and vehicle description.

- If someone attempts to enter your vehicle at a stoplight or sign, drive away, sounding your horn, even if it means running a red light.

- **Vary travel routes and times,** especially those used to reach a routine destination.

- Look in the back seat before you enter your vehicle.

- Always keep your car in gear when you are stopped in traffic. Be prepared to quickly take elusive action.

- **Hire a driver** or get a limousine in high-risk areas.

PROBLEMS WHILE DRIVING

I mentioned earlier that it is not so much that we look at things as we overlook them. Sharpen your powers of observation.

OBSERVATION is your most valuable "weapon." Try this activity: next time you enter your familiar convenience store to pick up an item or two, after you pay the cashier and leave, stop and remember:

- ◆ The color hair and eyes of the clerk.

- ◆ What "impulse items" were in front of or next to the cash register.

- ◆ The most prominent display ads.

- ◆ The number of people in the store.

You can't drive straight on a twisted road.

Build some practice skills into your daily life—you can always practice observation. Hey...**every 10 minutes, two people are killed and 350 suffer disabling injuries in auto accidents** here in the US. Be alert! Observe! Remember Yogi Berra's famous words: "You can observe a lot just by watching!"

When your observation leads to a case of *suspected surveillance*, try to confirm or resolve the suspicion by taking the following measures:

- ☿ Change routes. Do not travel directly to your predetermined destination.

- ☿ Slow down, or accelerate; watch the response of the suspicious vehicle.

- ☿ When you approach a green light, slow down and observe the suspected vehicle's reaction. Alternatively, try to reach and cross an intersection just before the light changes to red; observe whether the suspected vehicle crosses on the red light or stops.

Do not reveal your suspicions. Try to avoid steps which will initiate a confrontation. Collect as much information as possible on the suspicious vehicle, including license number, description of the car and the passengers. If you are fairly certain that you are indeed being followed, go as quickly as possible to a safe place and request assistance. In no case, under no circumstances should you leave the main road for deserted side streets. If your vehicle has a cellular telephone, remember that it can be used to summon help.

If you observe an obstacle ahead on the road, stop immediately and assess the situation. If people rush toward you from the front or the sides or point a gun at you, you have an *attack is in progress*. Check the following possibilities of escape:

★   Quick reversing.

★   U-turn.

★   Driving on sidewalk or shoulder to go around the obstacle.

If none of the above will work, remember that you still have the option of breaking through the barrier by ramming through the obstacle. By ramming at the correct point, the average-sized European car can push a heavy American car off the road, burst through the barrier, and leave the scene. **For those of you who have never seen a Bruce Willis or Arnold Schwarzenegger action movie, here's what you do:**

✓   Stop the vehicle.

✓   Select the ramming point.

✓   Shift in the power gear.

✓   Grasp steering wheel firmly with both hands.

✓   Sit as far as possible from the wheel, leaning against the seat back.

✓   Warn passengers of your intent to ram.

✓ Press the gas pedal to the floor. ***Ram decisively and as fast as possible, in the power gear. Boom!*** (Stay in the power gear until you have broken through the barrier.)

✓ Continue driving rapidly to the nearest safe place. Phone for help.

REMEMBER: ***Do not worry about the damage done to the car by ramming. You may be fighting for your life.***

USING A TAXI

If you see this sign in a taxi — in Boston or in Paris — switch cabs!

> ◆ **Driver Speaks No English**
>
> ◆ **Driver Hates Job**
>
> ◆ **Driver Hates You**

Many business travelers routinely use taxis without using any security considerations. This is an important area of concern to me, especially in strange cities. One of my business partners travels quite frequently to Wall Street on business. He mentioned a recent incident to me. He routinely hailed a cab from La Guardia Airport to get into the city. He began to read his papers in preparation for his meeting. About 15 minutes into the ride, he looked up and was shocked. He was riding through some of the toughest-looking neighborhoods in Queens he had ever seen, and he's seen quite a bit. There were as many as six police cars on some corner! He actually feared for his life.

MORAL OF THE STORY: **KNOW YOUR ROUTES!**

TOP 10 TAXI SECURITY RULES

1. Enter the taxi at a well-lit, populous location.

2. Do not use the same taxi stand twice. Do not permit others to direct you to a particular taxi.

3. Examine the taxi driver license displayed in the cab and compare it with the driver's face.

4. Be familiar with the area, tell the driver the desired route, and insist on compliance with your directions.

5. If suspicion arises, do not hesitate to tell the driver to stop the taxi. Get out immediately and summon help.

6. Avoid getting into a taxi when there is someone else inside.

7. Know your fares. Ask airline personnel, for example, how much it should cost. Agree on a fare before taking off. You can always have hotel personnel or airport personnel negotiate on your behalf.

8. A trusted cab driver is an asset...you can always hire one for various services.

9. Order from a well-known company.

10. Do not use the first taxi.

ADDITIONAL RECOMMENDATIONS...

♦ Avoid minibuses wherever possible.

♦ Bus terminals are hazardous, frequented by robbers and criminals. Avoid long waits in these places.

♦ Always stay alert in all kinds of waiting areas.

♦ There is safety in numbers.

♦ Never lose control over your baggage and other personal items.

♦ Choose arrival times in daylight hours.

♦ Hire a driver or limousine service in high risk areas or where you may have serious problems if you get into an accident.

♦ There are several defensive driving schools that can train you to protect yourself when it comes to vehicle security. One noted authority has suggested interviewing:

BSR, Inc.
P.O. box 190
Summit Point, WV 25446
(304) 725-6512

The Scotti Defensive Driving School
11 Riverside Avenue
Medford, MA 02115
(800) 343-0046

Bob Bondurant School of High Performance Driving
P.O. Box 51980
Phoenix, AZ 85076
(602) 796-1111

◆ **Do your homework** before choosing train routes. Are thieves known to ride as passengers?

◆ **When traveling by subway,** don't sit right next to the door. Thieves have become experts at the timing needed to dash aboard, grab a purse or package, and be gone just as the doors close you in and them out.

Take an aisle seat whenever possible so you can get up easily and get away if the person next to you bothers you. Stay awake! If you must carry a handbag or briefcase, hold it on your lap or wedge it between your feet.

Vehicle security awareness applies to all of us...all the time.

> **STOP BEING PREOCCUPIED!**
> **STAY ALERT!**
> **DRIVE SAFELY!**

CHAPTER 11

CHOOSE THE SAFEST FLIGHT

"I like terra firma—the more firma, the less terra."

— George S. Kaufman

There is a scene from the movie, "The Rainman," with Tom Cruise and Dustin Hoffman that security professionals all over the world still chuckle over.

THE SCENE: Charlie, played by Tom Cruise, has just "kidnapped" from an institution his autistic brother Raymond, played by Dustin Hoffman. Charlie and Raymond are at the Cincinnati airport, about to fly to Los Angeles. Raymond suddenly announces that he will fly only to L.A. if they fly on Qantas Airlines because the airline has never had a crash!

The pair end up driving across country!

Most of us have our own ideas about how safe we believe flying is. Times change: what consumers now want is not information about whether air travel is safe, but about which airlines are the safest.

HOW DO YOU CHOOSE THE SAFEST AND MOST SECURE FLIGHT?

This is a question I've been asked time and time again by the media, by my clients, by my friends ...even by my mother-in law!

Unfortunately, it's easier for the corporate executive to choose a secure flight than it is for the leisure traveler or frequent flyer.

Why? Corporations subscribe to specialty services that extensively examine the safety records of aircraft, as well as security and safety features. These reports are customized for the corporation's international travel routes and they come with recommendations.

This kind of information has never been readily available to the general public. However, years of pressure from consumer and safety advocates intensified after the ValueJet and TWA crashes.

The public clamor is paying off...

Starting this February, airline safety records went on-line!

The FAA is now declaring it will take more and more steps to provide safety information to the public. You see, up to now, the only way that you or I, as members of the traveling public, could obtain safety information was to file a formal request under the Freedom of Information Act.

Senator Ron Wyden (D-Ore.) has said that if the FAA, under pressure from the airlines, shies away from requests to rank the airlines in terms of safety and accident records, outside groups and the news media would compile their own rankings based on the information made public.

Here's what I want you to do:

✈ Keep current on the FAA's timetables in delivering this safety information. Call them. Use the Internet. Utilize whatever they provide. File a formal request with the FAA for the information you want.

Follow these recommendations:

1. **Whenever possible, fly with major carriers.**

2. Avoid the the airlines of countries that are involved in international or domestic disputes.

3. *Choose alternatives to EASTERN BLOC, AFRICAN, LATIN, or CENTRAL AMERICAN airlines.*

The rate of fatal accidents in Africa is 15 times greater than in North America. Fatal accidents are four times as likely in Asia, Eastern Europe, Latin America and the Middle East as they are in the United States and Canada.

What brings planes down in Africa? Terrorism. In the Middle East, terrorism is second to weather and terrain. In Eastern Europe, engine failure is the problem. Generally, more planes crash in Third-World countries because of poor aircraft, maintenance and pilot training. The poorer countries also are lacking sophisticated landing and weather-radar systems

Even worse: If you do crash in a Third-World country, you're twice as likely to die than if you crash in the United States.

4. **Approach on a selective basis:**

   ✈ Charter aircraft

   ✈ Commuter aircraft

   ✈ Small but not regularly scheduled aircraft

5.   Book airlines that are in good financial condition (those companies that buy new planes and are generous with their maintenance budgets).

6.   Avoid flying on start-up airlines.

7.   Book those airlines that are unlikely to be a terrorist target in your destination country.

8.   On international flights book nonstop, non-change flights where possible. Instruct your travel agent to book the most direct routes, avoiding unnecessary stop-overs and transfers. You may spend more money, but you'll be at less risk!

Keep in mind that North America is the safest place to fly. The Massachusetts Institute of Technology calculates that the odds of being killed in a crash flying coast-to-coast on a U.S. carrier is about one in 11,000,000. *Flying on a commuter airline (30 seats or less) increases your odds by four.*

The odds increase against you when you fly on a plane with 30 seats or less because:

✈   Pilots are less experienced.

✈   Planes fly lower.

✈   Planes take off and land more often.

✈   Planes are not subject to the same safety standards as larger airlines.

---

9.   **Choosing a safe flight involves choosing a safe airport.** Spend as little time as possible in foreign airports. Avoid executive lounges so as not to be marked as a target for terrorists, thieves, or corporate spies. As we've said over and over again, maintain a low profile and try to blend in. Avoid the use of luggage tags, or anything else that would advertise a corporate affiliation when you are traveling abroad.

EVALUATING SAFETY INFORMATION

When we assess the safety and security of a particular foreign airline, there are many factors to consider. Before actually analyzing the different facts involved concerning a particular airline's security and safety, we need to consider the particular geographic region to which the airline belongs. For example, if we were to analyze AEROFLOT, THE RUSSIAN AIRLINE, we would first take a brief look at the aviation industry in Russia and ask the following questions:

THE STATE OF CIVIL AVIATION

1. How has the U.S. Federal Aviation Administration rated Russia?

2. Is there a civil aviation authority in place? What are the requirements, as set by the country's civil aviation authority, that must be met when granting an airline a license to fly in Russia?

3. What is the English proficiency of air traffic controllers?

4. What kind of aviation problems are peculiar to Russia?

5. What is the state of airports in the country? What is the state of security at these airports?

Once all of these questions are answered, we can get a good picture of the environment in which the airline operates.

Is this too time consuming for you to read and research? Regardless of who you are or what you might do, remember, nothing is more important than "getting there and back!" If you only have a need *once* in your life to use this safety information, it's worth it! What price is too much to pay for personal safety?

Your safety information will also consider:

AIRLINE FLEET

What kind of aircraft comprise the airline's fleet? How old are the aircraft?

FINANCIAL STATUS

What is the financial status of the airline? This information is crucial as we need to know whether the airline has enough hard currency to purchase spare parts for planes, run routine maintenance checks, provide routine pilot training, etc.

MAINTENANCE

Who provides the maintenance for the airline's aircraft? How frequently and where? If the airline provides for its own maintenance, are its repair centers FAA-certified?

PILOT TRAINING

What kind of pilot training programs are in place for airline pilots? Do they receive training abroad or in-house, and how frequently?

SAFETY RECORD

What is the safety record of an airline? How many crashes has it experienced in the recent past? What are the reasons for the crashes; in other words, is there a discernible pattern behind these crashes?

SECURITY RECORD

What is the security record of the airline? How many and what type of security breaches have occurred, such as bomb threats and explosions, weapons and drug smuggling, hijackings, air space violations, or sabotage?

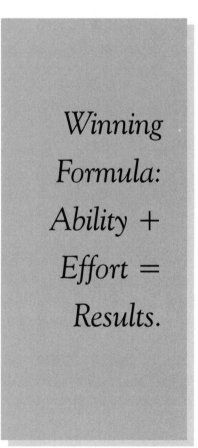

Winning Formula: Ability + Effort = Results.

The answers to all of the above questions allow us to have a comprehensive analysis of the safety and security of an airline.

I want you to read over this criteria so you can be aware of the kind of assessment you can request from the FAA.

Look–there are no shortcuts to personal safety and security. Locating and reading this information takes a commitment.

Is it worth it? Does it really make a difference?

Listen to this...and then tell me:

Of the seven new airlines that began operation during 1990-94, ValuJet had an incident rate 40% higher than the average, but it was inspected only about one-third as frequently as all new large airlines through calendar year 1994!! (AN&ST May 20, 1996 . . . pp. 26-28)

. . . and this:

"We have to halve the accident rate by the year 2000 just to stay where we are. Otherwise, we could face a major commercial jetliner accident somewhere in the world every couple of weeks."

Paul D. Russell, Chief of Product
Safety, Boeing Commercial Airline
Group, April 26 1993

...NOW YOU KNOW WHY I WANT TO KEEP YOU UP TO DATE!

NEED MORE CONVINCING?

Why do you suppose start-up airlines experienced higher incident and accident rates than established air carriers? I believe:

✓ They find it difficult to absorb this growth.

✓ They find it difficult to maintain more aircraft.

✓ They find it difficult to control and oversee multiple contract maintenance functions outside of their core organization.

THE TRICK TO SAFETY IS OVERCOMING OUR INSIDIOUS TENDENCY TO IGNORE IT! Ask yourself, "What's really important?" Ask

yourself this every morning before you embark on your day's journey!
EMBARK ON YOUR DAY'S JOURNEY!

You have choices! Where do you put your energy? Where it matters the most! Stay focused!

If you're really serious about wanting to research safety—just do it! Get involved in your own safety! If you choose not to…Then don't complain about your fears and concerns. Choosing to ignore safety awareness is what I call *"ostrich behavior."*

An ostrich is a creature who buries his head in the sand and becomes oblivious to all around him. When you ignore possible problems, you become vulnerable to all kinds of trouble. "Ostrich behavior" is shown through our sense of complacency.

COMPLACENCY CAN COME FROM:

a) **Laziness** —"it's not worth the effort."

b) **Vanity**—"I've read the statistics. I'll be okay. Nothing every happens to me."

c) **Ignorance**—"It's not important."

d) **Misplaced priorities**—"I'd rather squeeze in another movie before we travel rather than spend time and money in order to read those safety reports."

Keeping up-to-date with safety and security information is essential in today's changing world as new security threats regularly emerge. Those who pretend that these threats do not pertain to them or their families may be denying reality. "Let's be careful out there!"

TODAY'S AIRPORT SECURITY SYSTEMS

While you are learning to evaluate safety information, you need also to become familiar with today's airport security systems. *"As terrorist tactics change, it will become increasingly important to be proactive rather than reactive in developing technologies to protect the public"*...according to a U.S. Congress report. Airport and aviation safety go hand-in-hand.

In effect today, airport security systems have many of the following elements:

❏ **X-ray luggage screening**. The latest equipments "view" the item from all angles and can detect fine copper wire behind steel plate. Plastic explosives and bombs can also be detected by other equipment that uses two curtains of collimated X-rays operating at different frequencies and levels of intensity. The weaker scan shows plastics as solid shapes while the stronger one shows metal black.

❏ **Metal detector gateways.**

❏ **Explosive detectors.** New electronic devices with computer controlled logic promise to detect explosives that are tightly wrapped in metal foil or cling film. They detect minute quantities of emitted gases and by use of a computer memory identify and indicate the substance. Even plastic explosives can be detected.

❏ **Body searches.** This simple but effective technique slows the "processing" of passengers and is, therefore, used only when metal detectors indicate a case for suspicion.

❏ **Separation**. – air/ground sides. In order to reduce the problem of providing security at airports, security screening may be applied only to those members of the public who are to travel; it is therefore essential to keep the two categories of the public separate after the security screening process has been carried out.

❏ **Security patrols**. Major airports occupy many square miles of land and it is impossible to provide perfect security.

❏ **Identification** – airline/airport employees. These persons should be subject to special security measures, particularly those who perform duties that require them to pass from the "ground" to the "air" side. They are normally require to wear identity badges that include a recent photograph...but the system is only as good as the checks made on the identities of the employees.

MR. SECURITY SAYS........

Remember......

➤   Keep current on FAA timetables in providing safety information.

➤   Fly with major carriers whenever possible.

➤   Avoid Eastern Bloc, African, Latin and Central American airlines.

➤   Approach selectively: charter aircraft, commuter aircraft, and small but not regularly scheduled aircraft.

➤   Avoid flying on start-up airlines.

➤   Book non-stop, non-change flights on international flights when possible.

CHAPTER 12

HOW TO HANDLE IN-FLIGHT EMERGENCIES

"God helps those who help themselves."

Folk Wisdom

I remember walking through London's Heathrow Airport with my wife over 20 years ago and seeing for the first time these new machines. When you inserted a credit card or currency, you received an additional insurance policy for your flight!

"What is the world coming to?", I asked my wife, in my amazement of this marketing gimmick. I knew, though, that people were fearful and were looking for any means to protect themselves and their loved ones.

People are still fearful about traveling today!

Do you carry life insurance? That's the real subject of this chapter. This kind of life insurance is called: **"Think safety and security!"** The present moment is where you are! Pay attention to what is happening now...alertness pays off in an emergency.

This chapter deals specifically with emergencies in progress. Unlike other parts of the book which focus specifically on preventing disasters, we now confront disasters as they are happening.

Though emergencies are rare occurrences, you must know how to be prepared for them. ***The Federal Aviation Administration says that an alert, knowledgeable person has a much better chance of surviving a life-threatening or injury-threatening situation.*** If you think about it, it makes sense that education can directly affect the number of injuries, deaths, and even hijackings that occur. Remember the saying, "Forewarned is forearmed." This is what *The Security Connection* is all about.

What action would you take, or not take, if a plane you were traveling in were to suffer a mechanical failure, or was hijacked by terrorists? ***Most of you do not know.*** We are going to help change that.

We bring you the following encouraging facts:

✈   Sizable numbers of passengers do survive hijackings!

✈   Most crashes have survivors!

✈   *"Airplanes may kill you, but they ain't likely to hurt you!"*
                                          — Satchel Paige

The role of passengers has been extensively studied, and passenger training has resulted in increased odds for survival.

PART I: IN THE EVENT OF A HIJACKING . . .

Every hijack attempt is a serious flirtation with death. Obviously, it is a time when emotions are in a heightened state. A hijacking usually lasts for a considerable period of time. The hijacker must face obstacles to the plans he has prepared and also to his state of mind. The passengers will be unpredictable in their behavior. This produces a number of unforeseen variables and unpredictable outcomes.

Some hijacks have ended in a few hours; some have lasted for days. One even lasted on and off for forty days. Regardless of the length of the hijacking, there are critical moments when interpersonal relationships can affect the outcome of the entire event. This is why it is important for you, as a passenger, to understand the patterns that are created during this type of crisis.

The initial fifteen to seventy-five minutes of a hostage situation is the most volatile and dangerous. Hijackers are ready, from the time they stand up to take control of the aircraft, to fight to the death and kill anyone who challenges their authority or tries to thwart their purpose. For the most part, the passengers will demonstrate acute fear and helplessness.

A certain amount of tension subsides once the flight attendants resume their "normal activities." Many passengers begin to feel numb. This is the stage when a person is most open to hypnotic suggestions. Fear tells them that they will be executed as long as they explicitly obey their hijackers. At this point, passengers may regress into a submissive internal state. Psychologists call this state "Traumatic Psychological Infantilism," which, to you and me, means childlike behavior. This is why passengers are in need of training and education about the mental states and behaviors that can occur in the event of a hijacking.

Trouble is only opportunity in work clothes.

Any unexpected incident can set off a terrorist's rage and he can appear even more dangerous than at the outset. Fear within the passengers escalates. When the plane finally does land, negotiations will take place. Passenger emotions can range from quiet hysteria to desperation, depending on the conflict between the authorities and the hijackers.

I'm writing this so you can observe the emotional "curve," rising and falling. By being able to intellectualize what is happening, it can enable you to remain alert land in conscious control of your feelings...strength is a matter of the made-up mind.

Training is something that all of us are given throughout our lives. Most of us have been through some sort of driver's education. Kids in school and office workers in high-rise buildings must participate in fire drills. Passengers aboard ships and boats are put through drills so that they'll know how to handle emergencies.

Yet millions of passengers, of all ages and incomes, regularly board airplanes bound for domestic as well as international destinations without the slightest idea of how to behave should their plane run into trouble or be hijacked by terrorists. Be truthful—how much training do *you* have?

They know enough who know how to learn.

After thirty years of hijackings, this is one form of terrorism that shows no signs of abating. It's time now to learn how to handle the situation, to possibly help save your own life and the lives of your family members.

During a hijacking, the emotional roller coaster is far greater for passengers than for flight attendants and pilots. The crew, at least, are able to remain busy doing things, whether it's in the line of safety, direction, or passenger comfort.

Passengers are anonymous and, to terrorists, expendable. Therefore, it is the passenger who is the target for threats and intimidation. Passengers are psychologically and subconsciously manipulated and often turn out to be the most damaged.

Because such a small percentage of those of you reading this book have actually received training on what to do and how to cope with the trauma of a hijacking, it's important to provide a few words about the roles of the crew, the pilot and the flight attendants.

THE PEOPLE IN CHARGE

The pilot is obviously the prime "supporting player" in this drama because he controls the aircraft and the crew even though the hijacker has assumed authority of the flight. Assuming the hijacker(s) cannot operate the controls, **the pilot must be granted a certain amount of trust.** What you should be aware of is that, because of this trust, the pilot has an opportunity to thwart the hijackers and bring about an end to the hijacking.

The pilot has a number of secret ways to notify ground authorities that the plane has been hijacked. There are special frequency "codes" that the pilot can implement as part of the airline's radar system. There are also special codes for emergency situations. Specific code words are another way for the pilot to transmit this message. There is, of course, also a time when the hijacker instructs the pilot to make the hijacking known to those on the ground.

Necessity does the work of Courage.

Once the ground system is advised of the hijacking, the goal is to talk the hijacker into agreeing to land at a more favorable or advantageous site for the crew. The crew will try to convince the hijacker, for example, that an immediate landing is necessary because of bad weather or low fuel. By this time, ground controllers will already be in the process of obtaining any necessary clearances for the aircraft to penetrate unfriendly airspace or to land at a given airport. They will also notify the police or military. In order to direct the plane where ground controllers want it to land, fake weather reports have been used to foil the hijackers' plans.

There was a case where a hijacked plane left Los Angeles and the hijackers intended to stop the plane in Miami for refueling before attempting to cross the Atlantic Ocean. El Paso ground control sent a fake weather warning to the plane that caused the terrorists to divert it. In New Orleans, the same strategy was repeated. When the Miami controller firmly told the hijacker that the plane could not go on due to weather conditions, the hijacker accepted and the skyjacking ended.

Although the pilot is most often the focus of a hijacking, flight attendants nearly always play a major role. They become, in effect, the pilot's eyes and ears. They may have to coordinate passengers' actions, as in the case with evacuation. They are responsible for generating as calm an atmosphere as possible to reduce stress and anxiety for both the passengers and the hijackers. Their composure, confidence, and positive attitude increases the odds for a successful outcome. A flight attendant's training includes being alert to self-defeating moves by the hijackers.

A HERO'S STORY

There are many accounts of flight attendant bravery, mental alertness, and preparation that have contributed to "happy endings." This is one of them:

This particular flight attendant had trained herself to be psychologically prepared for a hijacking. She had also received professional training and had worked hard to assimilate the knowledge. When the hijacking did occur, she was able to make decisions wisely and without hesitation. She prevented the situation from escalating into total destruction. She calmed the hijackers and demonstrated cooperation and understanding without necessarily doing everything they told her to do.

She could see their vulnerabilities, and this gave her confidence on how to act. The time came when the terrorists demanded passports. Because she was prepared, she managed to get rid of all passports that might have placed certain passengers' lives in jeopardy because of their religious affiliation. Then she actually persuaded the terrorists to cancel their request.

She intervened on more than one occasion when her own life was at risk.

She reboarded the plane after she was freed to negotiate the freedom of female passengers and the rest of the flight crew.

She even put $12,500 of gasoline charges on her Shell credit card in Algiers.

Our hero, Uli Derickson, saved people's lives because she took responsibility. She was prepared for a crisis because she was trained.

WHAT CAN YOU DO TO REDUCE THE RISKS OF BEING HIJACKED?

First, recognize which international flights may pose the greatest risks. When possible, avoid traveling to countries that are being affected by the following events:

✈ Recent political acts which may touch off retaliatory actions...

✈ The recent capture of a well-known terrorist, or the capture of a group of terrorists, which can cause the group to attack an airliner affiliated with the country responsible for the capture...

✈ A major political or national holiday...

✈ The anniversary of an important event to a terrorist group...

✈ Recent widespread media statements made by terrorists against a country or a group of people...

✈ Keep abreast of high-risk travel areas. Be alert to current events.

Additionally:

✈ Avoid first-class seating if you are flying on high-risk routes.

✈ Maintain a low profile keep from looking like a wealthy American.

IN THE EVENT THAT YOUR FLIGHT IS HIJACKED

Listen carefully and follow the hijackers' instructions. Security experts tell us....

✈ Never speak unless spoken to. Appear neither hostile nor overly friendly. This means offer no suggestions, ask no questions, and do not become a spokesperson. Do not argue. Reactions will only serve to agitate the terrorists and your fellow passengers.

✈ Do not offer political opinions or make comments, either for or against the hijackers' cause. If you are asked for an opinion, say that you are not knowledgeable enough to comment. If the hijackers wish to talk about their cause, listen attentively, but without voluntary agreement or disagreement.

✈ Do not display authority appear neutral.

✈ Be prepared to wait. Most hijackings are over in 72 hours. The first hour is the most dangerous. The hijackers are in their most intense and nervous condition. Avoid making eye contact, especially during that first hour.

"Whether you think you can or think you can't, you're right," said Henry Ford. You *can* do something to be prepared for a potential disaster and reduce the odds of harm to you and your family. Remember: Courage is resistance to fear, not absence of fear.

PART II: SURVIVING AN AIRPLANE EMERGENCY

"Many people are still dying in survivable crashes."

— Association of Flight Attendants

Once you are aboard an airplane, you naturally expect to arrive safely at your destination. But the fact is that recently, **the United States has experienced its most deadly year for commercial aviation. Commuter airlines alone nearly doubled their number of accidents.**

✈ **Approximately 80% of all aviation accidents occur during landing or take-off.** Today, passengers take off and land more often, changes brought about by the factors of airline industry deregulation.

Historically, airlines previously would fly what is referred to as linear routes, meaning the plane would fly directly from Phoenix to Cleveland. These days, however, the industry utilizes what is known as the "hub and spoke" method. A hub is a major airport where a large airline concentrates its operation. What has happened is that the smaller commuter aircraft now carry passengers from smaller cities to one hub airport where the major airlines will then fly the "gathered" passengers to the final destination another hub.

✈ Start-up airlines experience higher incident and accident rates than established air carriers.

✈ 2500 FAA aviation inspectors must oversee 200,000 aircraft, 5000 repair stations, and 655,000 active pilots. Whew!

A review of major aviation accidents over the past few years reveals that most crashes have survivors. ***In fact, of the seven major plane accidents in the United States since 1988, four times more people survived than were found dead.*** In the tragic 1989 United Airlines crash in Sioux City, Iowa, an engine explosion took the lives of 111 passengers, but 187 people survived. This shows you that being in a plane crash does not inevitably lead to the grave.

> *If you make the decision, your thought process will make the provision.*

WHAT'S YOUR ATTITUDE REGARDING AIRLINE EMERGENCIES:

Denial   "It will never happen to me!"

Fantasy   "If it does, I'll just wait for the flight attendant to tell me what to do!"

Naivete   "If it does occur, I can't do anything about it anyway!"

HELP WANTED: ATTITUDE ADJUSTMENT!!

We all need to eat well. Yeah! Be assertive...take charge...IT'S YOUR TRIP! Act like it! Hey – you can even order a special meal if you don't like what the airline serves...some of their food is a state of emergency! No, you don't have to have a note from your doctor to order a special meal from an airline. All you have to do is ask. Low-sodium meals...seafood...kosher meals... plates for the vegetarian and fruit platters with a slice of cheese...all can all be yours at no extra cost. Airlines claim that there is no difference in quality between their regular meals and their special meals. But the special meals are often healthier and more freshly prepared. Airlines try to keep a low profile on their special-meal service because they create extra work for the flight crew. Most airlines require a day's notice to prepare a special meal, so call early. Be in charge of <u>all</u> your flight responsibilities!

When we refer to other emergencies, **EMERGENCIES** range from minor to major situations that can occur at any moment during a flight.

Like the time when...

...turbulence caused passengers to hit the ceiling, resulting in severe head injuries.

...an overhead bin popped open causing a briefcase to hit a man's head, which resulted in the loss of his eyesight.

...an aborted take-off crashed a child's face into the back of the tray table, resulting in a broken nose.

...a man scorched his lungs because he didn't have a smoke mask available when the cabin filled with smoke.

...a woman's nylons melted, causing third degree burns after impact.

...a man's polyester shirt melted on his body from heat intensity following an aborted take-off.

...a woman tried to crawl down the aisle during an evacuation but got trampled instead.

...an elderly women stepped incorrectly out of a window exit, tripped and fell forward, breaking her arms.

...a man incorrectly jumped down an evacuation slide and broke his collarbone.

BUT ISN'T IT THE FLIGHT ATTENDANT'S DUTY TO RESCUE EVERYONE?

While they may be trained to evacuate the airplane, a lot of things can happen in an emergency, and the flight attendants may not be able to respond to your needs.

Why? Because they may not have survived all the free-floating, flying suitcases that have been thrust out of the overhead bins into their faces;

OR, they could be shouting commands, but the sound of scraping metal has drowned out their directions;

OR, you could simply be too far from their jump seats to hear them;

OR, smoke and fire could be preventing their vocal cords from shouting at all!

Realistically, you could be left on your own!

THE GREATEST DANGER OF ALL

Remember your basic science?

You need fuel, oxygen, and heat to create fire.

If any one of these elements is removed, the fire will go out or will not catch. Heat is the temperature to which a material must be heated before it will burn. Oxygen sustains the burning process. Fuel sustains the material being burned.

As many as 85% of passengers are alive after impact on a survivable aircraft accident, but it is the smoke and fire that takes the lives of the majority of people.

Create your own emergency evacuation plan decide where you will go, what exit you will use, and how many rows there are to reach it. Too many people head for the door in which they boarded the plane, which is usually in front of the first class cabin. This wastes time and blocks the aisles.

Put down your USA Today and listen to the safety announcements! Read over that safety card in the pocket of the seat. **Know the procedures!**

Remain seated with your seat belt fastened, and you'll greatly reduce the risk of danger.

Put on your oxygen mask if there is rapid decompression. (Read the safety card instructions.) You can only live 4 to 5 minutes without oxygen. Oxygen masks aren't the same on all planes. Sometimes they drop in front of you. Sometimes you have to pull them out of a compartment in front of your seat. In either case, you must tug the plastic tube slightly to active the flow of oxygen. If you don't understand the instructions on how to use the mask, ask a flight attendant to explain it to you.

There are a few **"security basics"** that safety experts unanimously agree on as being common-sense precautions:

- Know that fire will probably be your most deadly killer in the event of an accident. Therefore, the kind of clothes you wear can favorably or unfavorably impact the risk to your safety. Synthetic blends melt into skin in severe heat. Go natural wear real fabrics. Bare arms and legs are particularly vulnerable, so cover them up.

- Not only will the heat from fire kill you, but so will the particles and often gases from burning products. The threat of an in-flight cabin fire is always present. Although they are rare, they are usually catastrophic. We agree with Ralph Nader and other safety specialists who recommend "B.Y.O.S.H." Bring Your Own Smoke Hoods.

As I write this chapter, the FAA is considering mandating smoke hoods for passengers. The purpose of smoke hoods, as mandatory equipment, would be to provide passengers with several minutes of protection from smoke, toxic fumes, and the gases that can cause asphyxiation during a post-crash fire.

The debate over smoke hoods began as a result of a tragic accident in 1985 at Manchester Airport in Great Britain an event commonly referred to as "Manchester." The plane's take-off was aborted. A fire had broken out in the No. 1 engine and the wind blew the engine's fire to the back of the fuselage—the central structure of the airplane that contains passengers and cargo. Fire broke through the windows in the rear and heavy black smoke filled the plane. Eight-two people survived, but fifty-five people died; and of those fifty-five, forty-six were overcome by toxic smoke and fumes. No one was killed by fire.

At Air Security in Houston, we offer what we believe to be the finest, most comfortable device available: **QuickMask** – which weighs only five ounces.

If you are ever in an air accident:

✈   Stay calm.

✈   Listen to what the crew members have to say.

✈   Leave your carry-on luggage behind. There are too many crash survivor horror stories of fellow passengers who blocked aisles and risked lives by trying to save their carry-on luggage.

✈   Assuming you have one, put on your smoke hood. If you don't, place a cloth over your nose and mouth.

✈   Do not crawl through the plane, but stay low, since smoke rises.

✈   Remember to re-count the number of seats to the exit.

✈   Exit quickly, but before you try to open an emergency exit, look outside the window. If you see a fire, do not open the door, because flames may spread into the cabin.

✈   In case of a water landing, take your flotation device with you (seat cushion, life vest, etc.).

✈   If you must slide out in order to evacuate, jump into the center of the slide with your feet together and your arms folded.

Have the courage to act—not react!

Your survival instincts need to be sharpened, not lulled to sleep by the sound of airplane engines.

Fire extiguisher

CHAPTER 13

CIVIL UNREST

"Beam me up, Scottie!"

Captain Kirk

Where I grew up, soccer was the king of sports. In talking soccer with a group of business executives, I discovered that one of them was actually in the stands at a game in South America when a melee erupted between the fans of the opposing teams. Spectators were trampled and crushed; luckily, he escaped injury. We then started talking about getting caught in the wrong place at the wrong time. He told me about an incident involving one of his employees and a US diplomat.

It seems that Jakarta (Indonesia), a city that attracts numerous Western businessmen, recently witnessed its worst rioting in 20 years. During the weekend rioting, two Americans, the employee and a US diplomat, were two of the more than 100 people injured when they were accidentally caught in the melee. They were fortunate to have escaped injury.

The odds against being involved in serious local uprisings are in your favor…but violence directed toward Americans and foreigners as part of civil unrest is common in some areas of the world. More and more "dangerous places waiting to happen" pop up without warning.

> **Six years ago UNICEF spent 4% of its budget on emergencies; now it is over 30%.**

If you're not traveling on business, my best advice to you is:

- **Stay away from countries that are politically unstable and have inadequate security!**

And, if you must visit an "unstable" country...

- Stay away from American installations and American Fortune 500 business sites in those countries.

There are obviously few Americans who become victims of war. However, civil disturbances can "find you" when you least expect it.

Are you aware that America is seen as an "international bully" by many smaller countries? Just because you know very little about foreign policy matters not to adversaries of American foreign policy. If terrorists or political factions need a scapegoat or a hostage to negotiate, **US citizens are high on the list as desirable candidates.**

The mob has many hands, but no brains.

You should also be aware that in some areas of the world like Southeast Asia and the Middle East, where US citizens rarely frequent, a visit there will be assumed to be one in connection with American intelligence—and with a purpose of gathering information.

Expect harassment at the very least.

Remember how you got in trouble as a kid when you went where you weren't supposed to? ...or you got hurt by being where you shouldn't be? What has changed? Only the "price of the toys!" *If you choose it, trouble will find you.*

In the world today we find

- regions in crises. . .

- nations in social disintegration. . .

- urban areas seized by gang warfare. . .

- random violence almost anywhere. . .

Violence directed toward civilians on a worldwide basis in unconscionable. CNN regularly brings us an horrible and numbing diet of atrocities.

The United Nations reports that the vast majority of armed conflicts in the world today are **not** between nations, but are civil wars and insurgencies.

Religious dogma and fanaticism, wealth...minerals, resources, waterways, etc...food and famine and exploding population all create tensions worldwide. It is no wonder we see so much political and civil unrest.

The world has obviously a long way to go to actualize universal brotherhood. Too many people and too many places focus on conquering rather than uniting. Political self-interest dominates the interests over group cooperation in too many places.

What this means for you as a traveler is:

1. There are certain regions and certain areas of the world where civil unrest can be commonplace. War zones are a travel reality.

2. Civil unrest can occur even where we don't expect it. Remember Tienneman Square?

When you travel abroad, you need to be alert to indicators of civil unrest. Obviously, if unrest looks likely before you leave, cancel!

❖   Keep up-to-date on political events in the area in which you travel. Your knowledge may help save your life.

❖   Find out who's fighting who. Realize there will be two sides to every story, and those forces have a history of conflict long before you arrived on the scene.

❖   Travel tough and travel smart. Read. Listen. Plan. Understand your risks. Carry as little luggage as possible. Make sure both hands are free when you are carrying bags, etc., etc.

What happens if civil unrest breaks out during your travels?

1.   If in your hotel, stay there. Contact the US embassy, consulate, or another friendly embassy. Hire someone to take a note to them if the phones are out of order.

2.   If you're not in your hotel, get to a safe place. Your own hotel is obviously most preferable. If the street scene turns violent, find a nearby hotel. Take a bus—a cab—whatever you must do to get to your hotel or a safe place. By the way, the American Embassy is not necessarily a safe place. This can be an instant target if the mob has anti-US feelings.

3.   Maintain a low profile. By now you know that your Rolex watch and $500 briefcase have no business being along on your trip.

4.   Review your pre-trip homework: know if there is a "friendly side" for Americans. There may not be, and there may be no one to trust. However, one side may be less likely to harm you than another. Do not attempt to take sides. Play the tourist who just wants to get home to your family.

5.   Be wary of "truces." **Get out of town.**

Travel history is full of stories of travelers who got caught in the middle of mobs.

Horrible actions can take place amidst the frenzy of mass hysteria.

Never, never get involved as a bystander intrigued by the situation.

Do not even watch activity from your window. Sleep in an inside room which proved greater protection from gunfire, rocks, grenades, etc.

You can't rely on "Scottie" to beam you up—the transporter has a malfunction!

MR. SECURITY SAYS........

Remember......

➣   Civil unrest pops us more and more without warning. In some areas it is common place.

➣   If you're not traveling on business, stay away from countries that are politically unstable and have inadequate security.

➣   Keep up-to-date on political events in the areas in which you travel. Understand your risks.

➣   If you must visit an unstable country, stay away from American installations.

CHAPTER 14

KIDNAPPING

"Life is what happens when you are making other plans."

John Lennon

Because of my hectic travel schedule, my wife Miri and I hadn't been to a movie for some time. Miri reminded me that it was her turn to choose. She tells me that her favorite movie star, Mel Gibson, has a new movie out which she just has to see.

"What's it called?" I innocently inquired. *"Ransom"* she proclaimed.

Great, I thought—here it is...a chance to relax...and now I've got to go see a movie about my job!

Well, Mr. Gibson not withstanding, the subject of kidnapping is really a foreign or misunderstood subject for 99% of families today.

What you probably do not also know is that kidnapping is big business in many areas of the world. And Americans make excellent commodities.

You may have seen headlines like:

AMERICAN TEACHER KIDNAPPED BRIEFLY AND RELEASED

or

AMERICAN LANDOWNER RELEASED AFTER RANSOM PAID

And, most likely you have never made a connection with your own travels. Behind the scenes of those headlines, here's what happened.

It was in Guatemala City recently where an American teacher was abducted in the parking lot of her apartment building in a poor residential area by four gunmen wearing ski masks. She was released unharmed after the kidnappers reportedly realized they had seized the wrong person. Also in Guatemala City recently, American landowner Howard Turner and his chauffeur were released after their captors reportedly received an undisclosed ransom. Turner and his driver were kidnapped as they left their car to open the gate of Turner's farm near Pueblo Nuevo Vinas, some 40 miles southeast of Guatemala City. Legislators say that 150 people were kidnapped in 1996— but reports indicate as many as four to six abductions *a day* take place.

As you've learned, threats to security vary, depending on the location.

Did you know that:

Statistically, 90% of all kidnappings are reported from the following countries:

Brazil	Lebanon	Philippines
Columbia	Mexico	Spain
India	Pakistan	United States
Italy	Peru	Venezuela

Because kidnapping is big business and Americans make excellent commodities, some reports indicate that mid-level executives can yield $500,000 or more. Some ransoms for US executive have yielded over $2,000,000.

What this says is that victims are certainly worth more alive than dead. Remember this. The real motivation is cash. Security statistics reveal:

- Close to one-half of our hostages are released safely after the ransom is paid

- Another third are rescued before the ransom of the hostages is paid

- The remaining victims are either killed, released without payment, or escape. Only 5% escape—and the odds are not great if you try.

What can you do to be aware of the possibilities of this threat?

First

In doing your pre-trip planning, you'll want to consider:

➤ Do you work for an American company?

➤ Has there been a history of kidnappings where you are traveling?

➤ Is the host country in conflict with our foreign policy?

➤ How much anti-US sentiment exists there?

➤ Is your business oil, investment mining, or fuel?

➤ Could you be an individual target because of your personal wealth?

If you believe you are at risk:

1.   Avoid routines...

2.   Check in regularly...

3.   Follow our "Business Travel Rules" —no jewelry, no American flag accessories, no company logos, etc...

4.   Minimize communication about your schedule on a need-to-know basis...

5.   Have your financial affairs in order back home...

6   Have a plan of communication if you are kidnapped...

7.   Follow "safe driving and riding rules"...

8.   Reduce your profile...

Most kidnappings occur as the victims are traveling between places in relatively close proximity to each other.

Be aware also that there is such a thing as kidnapping, rescue, and extortion insurance, which obviously facilitates "cash flow" for the kidnappers. Major insurance firms who provide such coverage report a jump in policies written over the past several years.

There are two facts about terrorism and kidnapping that you should keep in mind:

1.   **The overwhelming majority of victims have been kidnapped from their vehicle on the way to or from work.**

2.   **A large number of people taken hostage ignored the most basic security precautions.**

Your real challenge is to see your struggle with apathy and indifference towards acts of terror...to invest your time to learn how to become security conscious. Get to the point where you feel OK and comfortable with personal security.

If you go to work for a company and your travels take you to high risk areas, your company most likely has a crisis management team and plan available if a situation occurs. If not, they need to develop a plan—with outside specialists. Your company must have a communications infrastructure in place.

IF YOU ARE TAKEN HOSTAGE

The U.S. State Department provides guidelines and bulletins about security awareness every year, including suggestions if you are taken hostage. They recommend the following:

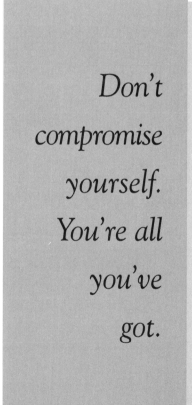

Don't compromise yourself. You're all you've got.

1. In the event you are taken hostage, you can expect your response to be various degrees of fear, denial and withdrawal. You may be blindfolded, drugged, handled roughly, or even stuffed in the trunk of a car.

2. You need to be aware that a hostage-taking situation is at its worst at the onset. The terrorists are nervous and unsure, easily irritated, often irrational. It is a psychologically traumatic moment for the hostage. Violence may be used even if the hostage remains passive, but resistance could result in death.

3. If taken hostage, your best defense is passive cooperation. You may be terrified, but try to regain your composure as soon as possible and to organize your thoughts. Being able to behave rationally increases your chances for survival. The more time that passes, the better your chances of being released alive. ***Maintain your dignity and self respect at all times.***

ESCAPE

The U.S. State Department writes that efforts to avoid capture or to attempt escape have in most cases been futile. The decision, however, is a personal one, although it could affect fellow hostage by placing them in jeopardy. Several other considerations should be weighed.

They go on to say that, to have any chance of success, you should be in excellent physical condition and mentally prepared to react before the terrorists have consolidated their position. This, also is the riskiest psychological time. You would need to have a plan in mind, and possibly have been trained in special driving tactics or other survival skills.

If you are held in a country in which you would stand out because of race or other physical characteristics, if you know nothing of the language or your location, or if you are held in a country where anti-American or anti-Western attitudes prevail, you should consider the consequences of your escape before attempting it.

> If you conclude that an escape attempt is worthwhile, take terrorists by surprise and you may make it. If their organization has a poor track record of hostage safety, it may be worth the risk.

We are told by the State Department that even in a voluntary release or surrender by the terrorists, tensions are charged and tempers volatile. Very precise instructions will be given to the hostages, either by the captors or the police. Follow instructions precisely. You may be asked to exit with hands on the air, and you may be searched by the rescue team. You may experience rough treatment until you are identified and the situation has stabilized.

🌐 ***Build relations with fellow captives and with the terrorists.*** If hostages are held apart, devise ways to communicate with one another. Where hostages are moved back and forth, to bathrooms for example, messages can be written and left behind. However, do not jeopardize your safety or the safety or treatment of others if attempting to communicate with fellow captives seems too risky.

🌐 ***Maintain your physical and mental health***; it is critical to exercise body and mind. Eat food provided without complaint; keep up your strength. Request medical treatment or special medicines if required. Establish exercise and relaxation programs. Exercise produces a healthy tiredness and gives you a sense of accomplishment. If space is confined, do isometrics. Relaxation reduces stress.

🌐 ***Keep your mind active;*** read anything available. Write, even if you are not allowed to retain your writings. If materials are not available, mentally compose poetry or fiction, try to recall Scripture, design a house, even "play tennis" (as one hostage did). You can expect to be accused of working for the government's intelligence service, to be interrogated extensively, and to lose weight. You may be put in isolation; your captives may try to disorient you. It is important that you mentally maintain control.

🌐 ***Take note of the characteristics of your captors and surroundings:*** their habits, speech, contacts; exterior noises (typical of the city or country); and other distinctive sounds. This information could prove very valuable later, especially if you are selected for early release, consider it an opportunity to help remaining hostages. Details you have observed on the terrorists and the general situation can assist authorities with a rescue.

We cannot guarantee that you will never be taken hostage. But if you avoid those high-risk areas, you've certainly enhanced the odds in your favor.

Preventing kidnapping from occurring involves the same commitment you make to reduce the risks of a security breach in your daily life.

Victims ignore precautions. If you're always on the run...to the grocery store...to the mall...to the restaurant...you must ask yourself, "Am I taking enough precaution and thinking security?"

Program yourself to be alert.

CHAPTER 15

WHAT IF YOU GET ARRESTED ABROAD?

"Good judgment comes from experience…and experience comes from bad judgment."

Barry LePatner

A friend of mine called me about 10:30 the other night saying she had just received a call from the police; they were about to arrest her teenage son because he failed to make his court dates for several traffic violations. My friend's husband was out of town, and she didn't know any attorney whom she could call at this hour of the night.

So she called me. I guess when you're in the security business, you're the next best thing to law enforcement authorities! After all, I *am* exposed to very stressful situations on a regular basis.

Can you imagine what the stress for my friend would be like if something like this happened in a foreign country where she had no friends?

In my work, one stressful situation that I see over and over again, one that could easily be avoided, is where a traveler gets into serious trouble precisely because he/she did not appreciate the uniqueness of a particular culture.

Here's what happened a few months ago:

At a birthday celebration for an employee working for a Fortune 500 in Saudi Arabia, the Mutawa (religious police) raided a private party where liquor was being served by a number of multinationals working in the country. During the arrests, a number of foreigners, including the "birthday girl", were roughed up. The women were traumatized. They had never experienced anything like this before, and could not believe that such abusive actions were caused by people drinking white wine.

What they failed to realize is that in Muslim countries, the religious police have not hesitated to harass or arrest foreigners who fail to comply with the Sharia, or Islamic laws. In some instances, Western women have been harassed by the religious police for their "provocative" clothing, and Americans and other Westerners have been consistently arrested for consuming alcoholic beverages.

There has been an increase in the number of Americans arrested, detained, or in trouble while traveling abroad. Approximately 3,000 Americans are arrested abroad each year. Over half of these arrests are drug-related, with Jamaica and Mexico accounting for over half of these drug-related arrests. The other "top 5" countries where Americans are incarcerated are Canada, Great Britain, and Germany.

If you are arrested in a foreign country, or taken into custody by the police...***ask to call your embassy. Do not expect the US Embassy to get you out of jail—they will not; you are in a foreign country and subject to its laws.***

Injustice

never

rules

forever.

The American Consulate will provide you with a list of English-speaking lawyers. The Consulate will notify your relatives and track your situation. Consular officers can work to protect your legitimate interests. They can transfer money, food, and clothing to the prison authorities from your family. They can try to get you relief if you are held under inhumane or unhealthful conditions. Your local attorney will have to explore your options for release, including contacting your friends and having them call local and national media, if required.

YOU MUST UNDERSTAND THAT THIS IS A SERIOUS SITUATION TO YOUR SECURITY. Jury trials may be uncommon, bail impossible, and solitary pre-trial detention may last months. Physical abuse may be commonplace — and guards and officials may not speak English. In some places, you may be required to pay your room and board while incarcerated.

You must be prepared for the worst...to avoid this situation:

➤   Know the rules and customs of the culture.

➤   Know the laws and how local law enforcement works (you may be expected to pay).

➤   Stay away from drugs.

➤   Driving laws must be thoroughly understood; it may be more prudent to avoid driving altogether.

❖   You may be able to pay your fine on the spot...

❖   You may need road permits...

❖   Car accidents may mean automatic jail time...

➤   Do not enter restricted areas.

➤   Do not sell your personal items, i.e., jewelry.

Also.......

➤   Do not deliver packages.

➤   Avoid arguments with law enforcement officers.

➤   Do not take anything illegal through customs.

➤   Pay attention to how your medicine is marked and how it may appear to the local law.

➤   Find out about currency regulations before you attempt to remove currency.

➤   If the US Embassy, local friends, or your outside contact cannot get you released from jail, have your local attorney call the International Legal Defense Counsel who specializes in gaining release of jailed Americans. The phone number is (215) 977-9982.

Of course my loudest travel warning very simply is: NO DRUGS!!

You don't need a lecture on drugs from me. You already know the consequences of using drugs. If you don't know the consequences, you need help to be better educated.

I want to inform you, though, about the consequences of buying drugs when you travel abroad.

And while I'm on the subject of drugs, there's something else I want to remind you about — in the context of fighting terrorism:

Many of the world's terrorist organizations finance their operations through drug sales. In countries like Thailand, Mexico, Peru, Pakistan, Afghanistan, and Columbia, the profits from illicit drugs and drug lords are used to intimidate local officials. And some countries like Panama, Cuba, and Cambodia have made huge profits by being a conduit for drug smuggling by these terrorist groups. You know, of course, the old saying: "You're either part of the problem or part of the solution," right? Think about this saying when people you may know decry terrorism, and yet purchase recreational drugs.

Negative thinking is mental malpractice.

Of the nearly 3,000 Americans arrested abroad each year, over 30% ended up in jails because they assumed they couldn't get arrested for drug possession.

Each country is sovereign and its laws apply to everyone who enters regardless of nationality. From Asia to Africa, Europe to South America, Americans are finding out the hard way that drug possession or trafficking equals jail in foreign countries.

There is very little that anyone can do to help you if your are caught with drugs. It is your responsibility to know what the drug laws are in a foreign country before you go, because "I didn't know it was illegal" will not get you out of jail.

Of all Americans arrested abroad on drug charges, marijuana was involved in 30% of the cases. Many of these possessed one ounce or less of the substance. The risk of being put in jail for just one marijuana cigarette is not worth it.

I'll say it again: Once you're arrested, the American consular officer CANNOT get you out! You may say "it couldn't happen to me" but the fact is that it could happen to you if you find yourself saying any of the following:

❖ *"My family has enough money and influence to get me out of trouble."*

❖ *"If I only buy or carry a small amount, it won't be a problem."*

❖ *"As long as I'm an American citizen, no foreign government will put ME in THEIR jail."*

FOR THE THIRD TIME: Foreign countries take drug possession and selling very seriously. The law in some countries does not differentiate between being arrested for one ounce of marijuana and selling one pound of cocaine.

In fact, your arrest can mean:

♦   **Death in some countries!**

♦   **Years in prison!**

♦   **Heavy fines!**

♦   **Trials that drag on for 2 years!**

♦   **Physical abuse and interrogation for as long as one year!**

Be aware that once you leave the US, you are not covered by US laws and constitutional rights. Bail is not granted in many countries when drugs are involved and the burden of proof in many countries is on the accused to prove his/her innocence.

In some countries, evidence obtained illegally by local authorities may be admissible in court. Few countries offer drug offenders jury trials or even require the prisoner's presence at his/her trial. Many countries have mandatory prison sentences of seven years or more without parole for drug violations.

IT IS NOT WORTH IT ON ANY LEVEL!

Another security note about drug warnings :

Ralph T., a business consultant from Southern California, had hurriedly scheduled an important meeting with his Mexican partners in Mexico City. Because of a serious health problem, Ralph was carrying prescribed medication containing a narcotic.

In his dash to the airport, he overlooked taking the necessary security precaution about which he had familiarized himself:

☞ Label prescribed medication very clearly.

☞ Know the generic name of any medication.

☞ Obtain a letter from your doctor attesting to the need for your medication.

Ralph was fortunate. He was detained at customs for 4 hours, and through the aid of his partners, "escaped" with just a warning. Some American travelers are not as lucky, spending time in jail for the same oversight.

> *Remember that a kick in the ass is a step forward.*

You have now been warned: **"He that blows in the fire must expect sparks in his eyes!"**

PLAY IT SAFE - AVOID CUSTOMS PENALTIES

While you may not suffer in jail...you certainly can suffer financially by failing to understand and consequently obey the laws of the U.S. Customs Service.

Custom officials tell us the following:

Your Declaration

You must declare all articles acquired abroad and in your possession at the time of your return. This includes:
- Articles that you purchased
- Gifts presented to you while abroad, such as wedding or birthday presents
- Articles purchased in duty-free shops.
- Repairs or alterations made to any articles taken abroad and returned, whether or not repairs or alterations were free of charge.
- Items you have been requested to bring home for another person.
- Any articles you intend to sell or use in your business. In addition, you must declare any articles acquired in the U.S. Virgin Islands, American Samoa, or Guam and not accompanying you at the time of your return.

The price actually paid for each article must be stated on your declaration in U.S. currency or its equivalent in country of acquisition. If the article was not purchased, obtain an estimate of its fair retail value in the country in which it was acquired.

The wearing or use of any article acquired abroad does not exempt it from duty. It must be declared at the price you paid for it. The Customs officer will make an appropriate reduction in its value for significant wear and use.

MR. SECURITY SAYS...

Remember...

➤ Being arrested abroad is a serious situation to your security. You must be prepared for the worst.

➤ Know the rules, laws, and customs of the culture; know how local law enforcement works.

➤ Driving laws must be thoroughly understood.

➤ Find out currency and customs regulations.

➤ Register with the US Embassy; know their role in finding you a local attorney. The International Legal Defense Counsel (215) 977-9982 can be called for help by your local attorney.

➤ NO DRUGS!

➤ Every country's system of justice is different.

CHAPTER 16

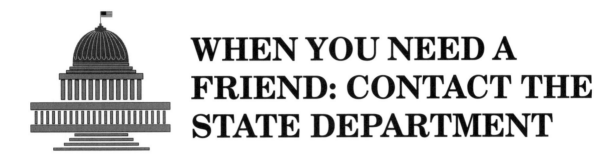

WHEN YOU NEED A FRIEND: CONTACT THE STATE DEPARTMENT

"We all need someone to lean on..."

— The Rolling Stones

I have a friend who built a company that currently generates over $1 billion annually in sales. He has told me on more than one occasion that one of the keys to his success is a philosophy of doing business that says: ***Plan for the 'down-side' of your projects because the upside will take care of itself.*** In other words, what are your alternative solutions if something doesn't go the way you expect? How many of us build a variety of contingency solutions into our plans in anticipation of the unexpected?

That's the reason for this chapter.

We want you to be prepared 'for the down-side' of your international travels. You see, the State Department can become your only friend and lifeline to the United States when things go wrong. And yet many travelers are unaware of what services the U.S. State Department can handle. There are numerous publications available from the State Department for American traveling internationally. This chapter covers some of their basic guidelines and recommendations.

For your information, there are U.S. embassies in 144 capital cities of the world. Each embassy has a consular section; consular officers in these sections of our embassies have the main function of helping U.S. citizens abroad.

Consular officers perform a range of services some emergency, some nonemergency. U.S. consuls are most often assisted by local employees, citizens of the host country. Their expertise and knowledge is invaluable to U.S. travelers.

For those of us here at home when our loved one is abroad, the **State Department's** *Citizens Emergency Center* is the point of contact in the U.S. for the family members and others who are concerned about an American abroad. The *Citizens Emergency Center*, working through our embassies and Consulate abroad, is the link, then, between the citizen in distress and the family here.

When you get to the end of your rope, tie a knot and hang on.

In addition to individual emergencies, the *Citizens Emergency Center* is also the State Department's focal point for major disasters involving Americans abroad: plane crashes, hijackings, natural disasters, terrorist incidents, etc.

The *Citizens Emergency Center*'s telephone number is (202) 647-5225. It is staffed by 25 officers and clerical personnel and is open 8:15 a.m. to 10:00 p.m., Monday through Friday, and 9:00 a.m. to 3:00 p.m. Saturday. At other times, during holidays, a duty officer can be reached through the State Department's main number (202) 634-3600.

Emergency assistance generally pertains to four categories: death, arrests, financial/medical problems, and welfare/whereabout queries. The *Citizens Emergency Center* is responsible also for administering the State Department's travel advisory program.

WHEN YOU NEED HELP ...ABOUT DEATH

Americans traveling abroad on business, pleasure, or on a study program rarely think about death. Nevertheless, approximately 6,000 Americans do die outside of the U.S. each year. The *Citizens Emergency Center* assists with the return of remains of approximately 2,000.

When an American dies abroad, a consular officer notifies the American's family and informs them about options and costs for disposition of remains. Costs for preparing and returning a body to the U.S. are high and are the responsibility of the family. Often local laws and procedures make returning a body to the U.S. for burial a lengthy process.

WHEN YOU NEED HELP...ABOUT WHEREABOUTS

The *Citizens Emergency Center* receives approximately 12,000 inquiries a year concerning the welfare or whereabouts of an American abroad. Many inquiries are from worried relatives who have not heard from the traveler. Others are attempts to notify the traveler about a family crisis at home.

Most whereabouts and welfare inquiries are successfully resolved. However, occasionally, a person truly is missing. It is the responsibility of local authorities to investigate. The State Department and U.S. consuls abroad do not conduct investigations.

WHEN YOU NEED HELP...ABOUT MEDICAL ASSISTANCE

The *Citizens Emergency Center* works with U.S. Consuls abroad to assist Americans who have become physically or mentally ill while traveling. The *Citizens Emergency Center* locates family members, guardians, and friends in the U.S., assists in transmitting private funds, and, when necessary, assists in the return of ill or injured Americans to the U.S. by commercial carrier.

WHEN YOU NEED HELP...FINANCIAL ASSISTANCE

If destitute, Americans can turn to a U.S. consular officer abroad for help. The *Citizens Emergency Center* will help by contacting the destitute person's family, friends, or business associates to raise private funds. It will help transmit these funds to destitute Americans.

The *Citizens Emergency Center* transfers approximately $3 million a year in private emergency funds. It can approve small government loan to destitute Americans abroad to tide them over until private funds arrive.

Also, the *Citizens Emergency Center* can approve repatriation loans to pay for destitute Americans' direct return to the U.S. Each year, over $500,000 are loaned to destitute Americans.

WHEN YOU NEED HELP ...ABOUT BEING ARRESTED

THE RIGHTS AN AMERICAN ENJOYS IN THIS COUNTRY DO NOT APPLY ABROAD. Each country is sovereign and its laws apply to everyone who enters regardless of nationality. The U.S. Government cannot "spring" Americans from foreign jails. However, a consul will assist on prompt access to the arrested American, provide a list of reputable attorneys, provide information on the host country's legal system, offer to contact the arrested American's family or friends, visit on a regular basis, protest mistreatment, monitor jail conditions, provide dietary supplements if needed, and keep the State Department informed.

The *Citizens Emergency Center* is the point of contact in the U.S. for family members and others who are concerned about an American arrested abroad.

Yes...these are emergency situations. Maybe they seem remote because you're not planning a foreign vacation in the near future. But what about all the possible emergencies that can exist in your daily environment? ***Think emergency*** is the message here.

BEHIND THE SCENES

Let's go behind the scenes and see how the State Department helps us in a disaster or crisis . . . . an earthquake, hurricane, political upheaval, or act of terrorism.

When a crisis occurs, the State Department sets up a task force
or working group to bring together in one set of rooms all the people necessary to work on that event. Usually this Washington task force will be in touch by telephone 24 hours a day with our Ambassador and Foreign Service officers at the embassy in the country affected.

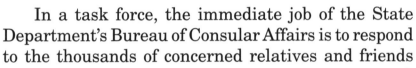

In a task force, the immediate job of the State Department's Bureau of Consular Affairs is to respond to the thousands of concerned relatives and friends who begin to telephone the State Department immediately after the news of a disaster is broadcast.

Relatives want information on the welfare of their family members and on the disaster. The State Department relies for hard information on its embassies and consulates abroad. Often these installations are also affected by the disaster and lack electricity, phone lines, gasoline, etc. Nevertheless, foreign service officers work hard to get information back to Washington as quickly as possible. This is rarely as quickly as the press is able to relay information. Foreign Service officers cannot speculate; their information must be accurate.

As concerned relatives call in, officers of the Bureau of Consular Affairs collect the names of the Americans possibly involved in the disaster and pass them to the embassy and consulates. Officers at post attempt to locate these Americans in order to report on their welfare. The officers work with local authorities and, depending on the circumstances, may personally search hotels, airports, hospitals, or even prisons. As they try to get information, their first priority is Americans dead or injured.

Sometimes commercial transportation entering and leaving a country is disrupted during a political upheaval or natural disaster. If this happens, and **it appears unsafe for Americans to remain,** the embassy or consulates will work with the task force in Washington to charter special air flights and ground transportation to help Americans to depart. The U.S. Government cannot order Americans to leave a foreign country. It can only advise and try to assist those who wish to leave.

MARRIAGE AND BIRTH ABROAD

If your travel abroad unexpectedly or expectedly involves a marriage or birth, the *Bureau of Consular Affairs* provides clarification to assist U.S. citizens. Please be advised of their information:

Marriage Abroad
Consular officers abroad cannot perform a marriage for you. Marriages abroad are generally performed by local civil or religious officials. Once your marriage is performed overseas, U.S. consular officers can authenticate your foreign marriage. A marriage which is valid under the laws of the country where the marriage was performed is generally recognized by most states in the United States. If you are married abroad and need confirmation that your marriage will be recognized in the United States, consult the Attorney General of your state of residence in the United States. Marriages abroad are subject to the residency requirements of the country where the marriage is performed. There is almost always a lengthy waiting period.

Birth Abroad of a U.S. Citizen
Most children born abroad to a U.S. citizen parent or parents acquire U.S. citizenship at birth. As soon as possible after the birth, the U.S. citizen parent should contact the nearest American embassy or consulate. When it is determined that the child has acquired U.S. citizenship, a consular officer prepares a *Report of Birth Abroad of a Citizen of the United States of America.*

Finally, it is important to recognize **what the State Department cannot do.** Don't ask the State Department to:

- Give or lend money or guarantee or cash personal checks.

- Provide direct legal representation or advice.

- Serve as a travel agency, information bureau, or bank; search for missing luggage; settle disputes with hotels; help get work permits or jobs.

- Act as couriers or interpreters.

- Provide bail or get you out of jail.

- Arrange for free medical or legal services.

- Receive or hold mail for you as a private citizen.

Remember, in asking for help, the State Department is paid to promote and establish good relations with the host government. Discriminate on asking for help...be a good friend!

MR. SECURITY SAYS...

Remember...

➤   The State Department can become your only friend and lifeline to the US when things go wrong. Know their services.

➤   The Citizens Emergency Center's telephone number is (202) 647-5725; off hours and holidays (202) 634-3600. The Center is the point of contact in the US for family members who are concerned about an American abroad.

➤   Understand the Center's policies when you need help about: whereabouts, death, medical assistance, financial assistance, and being arrested.

CHAPTER 17

THE FUTURE OF AIRPORT SECURITY

"What are we here for, if not to walk with each other along life's journey?"

— Charles Dickens

I wrote this book because it bothered me that people treat their most valuable asset...themselves... so carelessly...without thought of personal safety and security. People leave the important task of safety and security to the government, the airlines, the police, and security experts.

We must think for ourselves. **Security is a battle of wits: use yours!** There are countless examples in your own life where you learned something new and solved a problem because you decided to think for yourself, to "just do it."

Personally, I like to solve problems. Take airport security for example.

When we improve airport security, we improve our future!

You see, I get many questions put to me about the future of airport security - by the media, by my clients — and by every guest that comes into my home!

I want to share my views with you. As an advisor to The White House Commission of Aviation Safety and Security, I take an active interest in bringing the private and public sector together to deepen our joint commitment in this area.

I believe that my conclusions can lead to resolving many of the specific security problems now facing the aviation industry.

You see, today, people take either one of two schools of thought — or approaches — to apply security to commercial aviation.

❖ **One approach** emphasizes the importance of employing sophisticated machines aimed at virtually eliminating the risks inherent in air travel in the current global security environment.

❖ **The Second approach** also recognizes the value of technology. However, this second approach stresses the importance of performing a risk assessment, to evaluate the nature and level of the threats facing the industry, so that an appropriate response can be developed.

I doubt if implementing option one would be possible, and even if it were, I wonder how expensive it would be.

One must care about a world one will not see.

> You see, the philosophy which seeks a security program that will ensure absolute security overlooks the fact that the measures which would be required would be so stringent that air carriers would be unable to conduct business. Clearly, even technologically advanced security devices/systems cannot ensure anything approaching absolute security.

In fact, such systems may end up having the opposite effect. Suppose we are determined to scan and match all baggage prior to loading it onto the aircraft. When the system detects something unusual, we are obliged to locate the passenger, and then open the suspect piece of luggage in his presence. Obviously, this takes a great deal of time, and to leave unresolved baggage behind will increase carriers' expenses dramatically. And even expensive, high-tech machines occasionally give false alarms.

Security has been breached even at airports which employ the most advanced security technology, not because the machines failed to operate correctly, but because security personnel failed to interpret their findings appropriately.

We will be mistaken if we believe that technology alone can reduce our vulnerability.

As far as I am concerned, it is because we have not made a conscientious study of the nature and severity of the threats facing the aviation industry today that we still expose ourselves to unnecessary risks.

Unmatched baggage is still loaded onto aircraft.

The background of airline and airport staff are still not adequately scrutinized.

IN SHORT, WE ARE STILL HIGHLY VULNERABLE.

THE THREATS TODAY

Commercial aviation is under constant threat from a number of sources. The first step in addressing this threat is to create an environment which will prevent explosives or lethal weapons from infiltrating the aircraft. However, the first step in developing an overall security concept is to identify the threat and then to determine what is the magnitude of the threat the aviation community is facing.

The three primary threats to the American aviation community today are:

> **Terrorists from fundamentalist religious groups**
>
> **American extremist groups**
>
> **Unstable individuals**

One of the most dangerous tactics employed by terrorist groups is to infiltrate the aircraft with explosives and then to detonate those explosives while the plane is in the air, in order to maximize damage. Of all the groups which pose a threat to the aviation community, terrorists are both the most  dangerous and the most sophisticated. While extremist groups and unstable individuals will usually deliver a lethal device themselves, terrorist groups will often select a "naive passenger" to bring an explosive device aboard an aircraft for them. The aircraft ultimately targeted for such an act is almost always selected because the airline's security practices are reasonably easy to circumvent, making the aircraft a "soft" target.

Once we are familiar with our adversary and the way he behaves, we can begin to evaluate our *Vulnerability* to him. **Our vulnerability can be defined as how exposed we are to the threats facing us.** Once we have identified the *Threat* and our *Vulnerability* to it, we can assess our **Risk**, according to the formula $TxV=R$. The level of risk to which we are exposed is inversely proportional to the effectiveness of the security measures we have implemented in response to this threat. Obviously, these security measures are designed to reduce our vulnerability to a particular threat. The entire process is known as making a RISK ASSESSMENT.

However, because of the logistical and scheduling pressures in the aviation community, **it would be impractical to respond to all threats with the same intensity.** Each carrier must determine the level of response appropriate to each threat, based on the nature and severity of the existing threat and the company's vulnerability to it. This process will enable the airlines to identify the calculated risks it is willing to take. Identifying calculated risks is not the same as ignoring risks; the calculated risk is the risk we have carefully considered and yet decided to take anyway, because we believe our exposure to danger is small enough to be acceptable.

For instance, every time we get behind the wheel of a car we are taking a calculated risk. By making a comprehensive risk assessment, we strike a balance between the threats we face, our vulnerability to those threats, and our capabilities to meet them.

CALCULATED RISK

The calculated risk we are willing to accept will determine our security concept. Obviously, our security concept must respond to the specific threats facing our airline. It is crucial to remember that there is nothing we can do to eliminate threats against us! The airline industry will always be under threat by fanatics, extremists, and unstable individuals. OUR POWER LIES IN THE FACT THAT WE CAN DECIDE HOW TO RESPOND TO SUCH THREATS.

To improve aviation security, we must alter the existing conception of what constitutes security. To do so, we should establish a program which integrates the five elements of security:

> Intelligence

> Procedures

> Technical Means

> Motivated Personnel

> Control and Supervision

INTELLIGENCE

In order to counter the threats facing the industry, we must first have the right information both about the nature of those threats and our vulnerability to them. Such intelligence should be distributed to all relevant members of the aviation community worldwide.

PROCEDURES

The Profiling System

In order to reduce our vulnerability yet still remain in business, we must begin examining the profiles of our air travelers. Based on events that have historically affected the aviation world, **I suggest that over 99% of airline passengers could be classified as non-threat passengers; based on an analysis of their profiles, we believe it is likely that these passengers will pose no security risks.** Remember that this assumption is still a calculated risk. This means that less than 1% of the passengers must be viewed as a potential threat.

The Profiling System I propose is unique in that it takes a positive approach to security. It does not attempt to single out the "bad" or "dangerous" passengers. Rather, the profiling system attempts to identify the passengers who are least likely to pose a direct threat to the security of the aircraft.

Most families with young children traveling together, older passengers, and especially "frequent flyers" who fly regularly for business can be quickly identified as non-threat passengers. We can reasonably assume that the frequent business traveler is unlikely to smuggle a bomb onto an aircraft and that a father would not deliberately place a device on a plane his young children were about to board. But these assumptions are not certainties; here again we are taking a calculated risk.

Because we know that terrorists sometimes use a "naive passenger" or a "supporter" to unwittingly bring a bomb onto an aircraft, we must look at more than 1% of our air travelers. **From my experience, it is conservative to focus on about 10% of airline passengers, to take into account individuals who pose both a deliberate and an inadvertent threat to the aircraft's security. This 10% will be termed "selected passengers." These individuals will undergo a special security screening before being cleared to join the flight. Such a security screening will drastically reduce the risk posed to the flight and its passengers. The "Passive Profiling System," which I suggest, evaluates the threats posed to an airline, and to a particular flight, and seeks to minimize those threats in a manner that will still allow the plane to take off on time. This system accomplishes both these goals by taking only calculated risks.**

The Profiling System has received a great deal of negative media attention, especially because it is believed to be discriminatory. The System does discriminate, but not on the basis of ethnic background. The Profiling System deals only in probabilities.

For example, if you have been a first class business traveler for the last five years, you are most probably a non-threat passenger, regardless of your ethnic background. However, if you have flown very infrequently, and consequently we know very little about you, and you meet several other criteria, you are likely to be scrutinized very closely. I have not tried to provide an exhaustive explanation here of exactly how the Passive Profiling System operates; the above examples are intended only to demonstrate how the Passive Profiling System attempts to classify passengers based on a set of positive criteria. I believe that this system would reduce the vulnerability of the aviation community to the various threats it now faces, by integrating the concept of calculated risk into our security concept.

TECHNICAL MEANS

The term **technical** means refers to the means necessary to implement a security program.

Step one is to construct a computerized database which will compile all the data carriers regularly collect on their passengers. For obvious security reasons, the details of such a database should not be discussed publicly. Such means will also include training the airlines' agents on how to use such a database in order to effectively and accurately use the Profiling System without disrupting the airlines' operations or alarming or offending its passengers.

The future is not a gift, it is an achievement.

Equally important, technical means also refer to the deterrent measures the airline employs; for added security these measures (such as check-points, screenings, and questioning) should be applied to every passenger without exception.

MOTIVATED PERSONNEL

> Security personnel are the most important element in the system. But, ironically, personnel generally constitute the weakest link in the security equation.

Although many crucial aspects of the security system will be automated, these measures will be ineffective without motivated personnel to operate such machines. Staff performance as a whole is affected by each individual's personality, motivation, temperament, and health. The employee's performance is also very much affected by the quantity and quality of the training, supervision, and testing he receives, as well as the financial incentives his employer offers for outstanding performance.

CONTROL AND SUPERVISION

The success of any security program is measured by its ability to identify and respond to threats, so that security breaches are prevented. If a system is not sufficiently controlled, supervised and tested, it is not possible to know if it is adequate or how it will perform in an emergency. It is necessary to constantly analyze and reevaluate the system to identify its weak points, faults, and gaps in coverage on a timely basis.

Once a security system is in place, the job is far from over; to ensure adequate security one must remain vigilant.

SUMMARY

There is no doubt in my mind that the aviation security system as a whole must be improved before we can hope to respond effectively to the many threats and hazards facing the aviation industry.

To date...we have been simply ignoring many of these dangers.

However, it is clear that any revision to our conception of air security must take into account the massive number of air travelers served each year and the tremendous logistical demands placed on carriers to keep those passengers moving on schedule.

I feel confident that the security system I have outlined here will provide the aviation community with the tools it needs to meet not only today's security challenges, but also some of the as-yet unforeseen challenges which surely lurk in our collective future.

I believe that identifying the threats we face and performing a risk assessment to reduce our vulnerability to these threats can make air travel considerably safer for all passengers.

We cannot assure absolute security for every passenger.

And technology alone is not the answer.

If we implement the Passive Profiling System I have described here, along with high-tech machines operated by motivated and capable personnel, we will have the capability to focus on the potential threat presented by the "selected passengers" and thus reduce our vulnerability. The threats remain. How we decide to deal with them will determine how safe or how dangerous it is to board an airplane in this country. In my view, we must agree to accept a series of calculated risks, as I described, in order to resolve the specific security problems now facing the industry.

WHITE HOUSE COMMISSION ON AVIATION SAFETY AND SECURITY

On July 25, 1996, President Clinton directed Vice President Gore to establish the White House Commission on Aviation Safety and Security. The Commission recommended how to deploy the latest technology to detect the most sophisticated explosives...as well as non-technology improvements... primarily the shift away from an adversarial relationship between government and industry to one of partnership.

The future agenda of the Commission will include the long-term financing of security equipment and operations, as well as a thorough investigation of issues involving safety and air traffic control. Among the future issues that will be considered are:

- The development of advanced voice and data recorders.
- The impact of new technologies such as global positioning systems on air traffic control
- Synthetic vision and advanced sensors.
- Accelerating the development of terrain avoidance warning systems based on digital mapping.
- The use of new composite materials in making aircraft both stronger and cheaper.
- New ways to detect and defend against exotic new threats terrorists may employ, like chemical agents.
- Human factors.
- Changing economic pressures and influences in the airline industry.

In all these endeavors, the commission will seek non-intrusive ways to assure Americans that air travel is safe and secure so that the traditional regard for individual liberty and privacy is also assured.

CHAPTER 18

WORLD WIDE INTELLIGENCE REPORTS

"Knowledge is of two kinds: we know a subject, ourselves, or we know where we can find information upon it."

— Samuel Johnson

With world conditions changing at an uprecented pace, access to current, reliable and comprehensive information is a vital tool for today's domestic or international traveler. Good planning and preparation means to be aware of security conditions in your destination city.

The following CITY WATCH® reports provide you with security intelligence for major U.S. and international cities. We believe that the review of these reports is part of today's precautions necessary to take in order to reduce your chances of becoming a victim.

ATLANTA

CITY

The city of Atlanta (pop. 3 million) is a major center for business, entertainment and education in the southeast. Host to the 1996 Olympic games, this growing cosmopolitan and international city is proud of its history. Home to the Martin Luther King, Jr. Center, CNN and the Carter Presidential Center, "Hotlanta" offers endless tourist sites which attest to its richness and diversity. The main entertainment center is glitzy Buckhead, where clubs and restaurants abound. Midtown offers such sites as the upscale Virginia Highlands restaurant district, Georgia Tech University, the funky Fox Theater, the center of Atlanta's alternative community - Little Five Points, and cafes galore. Stone Mountain Park offers summer laser shows at night and plentiful opportunities to skate, hike or boat. This bustling city is also home to several international corporate headquarters from CARE to Delta Airlines to Coca-Cola. **Areas to avoid include the downtown section of the city, especially at night, and the housing project areas (Summerhill and Techwood) that lie very close to the city's new $209 million Olympic Stadium complex. These are areas where a great deal of crime, drug dealing and gang violence occur.**

SECURITY CONCERNS

Crime is the number one concern for travelers in Atlanta. Although statistics vary, the main message is clear: Atlanta's crime rate is high. In 1996, Money magazine ranked the city as the nation's second most dangerous. In 1995, a report published by the Atlanta Journal-Constitution indicated the city had the second highest crime rate among cities of at least 250,000 residents in the U.S. In 1995, the city recorded 184 murders, 441 rapes, 8,859 assaults and 34,221 thefts. Per 10,000 residents, the city had 1,741 crimes - 372 violent crimes and 1,369 non-violent crimes.

Nearly 60% of the city's business district's violent crime occurs after 6 p.m. In 1996, the homicide rate increased in Atlanta. In an effort to reduce the homicide rate, youth under 18 are under curfew and banned from Atlanta's streets at night.

AIRPORT

Atlanta is serviced by the Hartsfield International Airport, located 12 miles from downtown (about a half hour drive). The airport is easily accessible from Interstate I-85 which runs along the West/Northwest side of the airport. Hartsfield International Airport is one of the busiest airports in the world; the facility sprawls over 3,700 acres.

Facilities/Services at Hartsfield
The airport completed 90 different projects aimed at renovating and modernizing the facility for the 1996 summer Olympics. These include an increased number of signs and international symbols, several restaurants designed to give the visitor a "taste" of Atlanta, retail shops, a new security communications center, eight new smoking lounges (centrally located on Concourses A, B, C and T), and a huge four-story Atrium designed to be a center of relaxation for the passenger in transit.

The airport has two terminals: North (the international E Concourse is located on the East end of this terminal), and South. Both lead to the airport's six concourses: A, B, C, D, T and the new E international concourse. A and B Concourses are occupied by Delta Airlines. Concourse T is for domestic flights. Travelers may walk, use the moving sidewalk or ride the internal transit system to get between the terminals and concourses.

Ninety percent (90%) of all crime at Hartsfield involves auto theft and pickpocketing.

TRANSPORTATION

To/From Hartsfield Airport
Trains, taxis, hotel shuttle buses and rental cars are available for transport to the city center. A taxi trip from Hartsfield to downtown will cost about $18 flat rate. The Atlanta Airport Shuttle leaves from the ground transportation area every 15-20 minutes. MARTA (rail transit system) is efficient and relatively safe; it departs from the airport terminal's ground transportation area from 5 a.m. to 1 a.m. Monday through Friday, and from 6 a.m. to 12:30 a.m. weekends and holidays. One-way fare is $1.50. The airport station (phone number 404-848-3325) is the final stop on the southbound line. There is no direct MARTA public bus service from the airport into downtown.

Transportation Within Atlanta
Taxis, buses, trains and rental cars are available in the city. Public transportation is generally safe and reliable during the day. MARTA (Metropolitan Atlanta Rapid Transit Authority) operates 33 rail stations and 150 bus routes in DeKalb and Fulton counties. Fare is $1.50. MARTA has won the American Public Transit Association's "Safest Transit System in America" award 17 times in the past 20 years; the MARTA has won the award for the safest transit system in all of North America six times. Public buses are clean and reliable and require exact change or tokens. Atlanta has many roads named "Peachtree" which has often caused visitors some confusion. Be alert as to whether an address has "Boulevard," "Street," "Road," etc. attached to "Peachtree."

C AREA CODE: 404 (Central Atlanta) or 770 (outer parts of the city).

ATLANTA TIPS

☞ Areas of the city best avoided due to high crime are: the downtown to Midtown section, running from the Atlanta-Fulton County Stadium to north of 14th Street. This commercial district ranks very high in crime during the evening and night hours. Also, it is best to avoid the Fairlie-Poplar district, and the housing projects area situated close to the Olympic Stadium.

☞ High crime rate areas also include the area around the Atlanta University Center (on the streets around Clark Atlanta University and Spelman College); the bar zone in Buckhead (along Peachtree, Roswell and Piedmont Roads) between 8 p.m. and 4 a.m.; and the University-Lakewood area (south of Ponce de Leon Avenue). Also, nearly 28% of property crimes reported in Atlanta occur at Lenox Square.

☞ Pickpockets work the areas of Underground Atlanta (a network of underground shops and restaurants), Five Points and downtown shopping centers. Thieves also operate along Cobb Parkway from Cumberland Mall to Barrett Parkway, Roswell Road and Buford Highway.

☞ It is best not to take MARTA after dark if you are alone.

☞ It is best not to walk in Piedmont Park at night.

BALTIMORE

CITY

Baltimore (pop. 2.4 million) is a historical city with a seafaring heritage that dates back to the nation's beginning. Baltimore, like Boston and New York, is one of the country's oldest metropolises. Baltimore was named in honor of the first British "proprietor" of the Colony, Cecilius Calvert, 2nd Baron Baltimore. The city is the point of origin of the first railroad line in the United States in 1827, the legendary Baltimore & Ohio. The city also boasts a rich cultural history. The oldest Catholic Cathedral in the country is Basilica of the Assumption. Fort McHenry, held against the British during the War of 1812, attracts almost one million visitors each year. Baltimore's museums are rich and varied, including such diversity as the Babe Ruth Birthplace and Baseball Center, the B&O Railroad Museum, and the H.L. Mencken House. Baltimore is also home to the renown John Hopkins University. It's ethnic neighborhoods like Little Italy, Little Lithuania, or Highland Town, "Corned Beef" Row, and Greek Town provide culinary delight!

The sights and attractions of Baltimore make it a truly unique destination for visitors. There's also the Edgar Allen Poe House, the Star-Spangled Banner House and the US Frigate Constellation (the oldest US warship still afloat). Cultural events abound throughout the year. The Preakness Stakes, a famous horse race since 1873, and one of the three events that makes up thoroughbred racing's Triple Crown, takes place mid-May. "I Am An American Day" in early September is the biggest patriotic parade in the country. The city offers history and entertainment for every cultural taste. The majority of the city's attractions are located in the Inner Harbor area, filled with hotels, shops, restaurants and tourist sites. This area has been called one of the finest examples of urban renewal in the United States; in fact, some say that this area alone is worth the trip to Baltimore.

SECURITY CONCERNS

Baltimore has seen a significant rise in crime in recent years. The tourist areas have remained generally safe, aside from the occasional incidents of petty theft in crowded areas of the Inner Harbor. In 1995, Baltimore had more than 21,500 violent crimes, 325 murders, 9,100 aggravated assaults, and 25,600 motor vehicle thefts. Normal security precautions should be taken: avoid flashy watches and jewelry, guard against pickpockets, stay alert in unfamiliar territory, keep your car locked at all times, etc. Stay at relatively busy hotels rather than out-of-the-way accommodations. avoid hotels on "Embassy Row" or in known high crime areas. Upon hotel check-in, do not provide any information beyond that required when registering. Ensure that baggage remains under observation at all times until delivered to the room.

AIRPORTS

Baltimore/Washington International Airport (BWI) is located 10 miles from downtown off Route 295.

Facilities/Services
Baltimore/Washington International Airport handles more than 300 commercial flights each day. The Currency Exchange is open from 6:30 a.m. to 9 p.m.. ATMs, shops, and restaurants are located throughout the airport for travelers' convenience. Also, a Business Service Center includes conference rooms, copiers and fax machines.

TRANSPORTATION

To/From BWI

Several means of transportation are available at the airport. A taxi ride to downtown takes 20 minutes and the fare is around $20. Limousine service is available at the Ground Transportation Desk, lower level of central terminal, for $25. An airport shuttle bus to Inner Harbor hotels leaves every 30 minutes, 6:00 a.m. to 12:30 a.m. with a fare of $8 per person. Public buses depart from the lower level to Charles and Lombard Streets. The trip takes 55 minutes, but using the bus is not recommended for travelers with luggage.

Transportation Within Baltimore

Baltimore has a variety of transportation options for travelers. Taxis are generally the best option for persons unsure of their surroundings. The MTA light rail operates daily from Pratt Street/Camden Yards north to Timonium and south to Glen Burnie. The minimum fare is $1.25 and departure times vary. Metrorail trains operating from the Charles Center run Monday-Saturday 5 a.m. to 12 am to Ownings Mill in the northwest suburbs and east to Johns Hopkins Hospital. A water taxi is also available around Inner Harbor from Little Italy to Fells Point. City buses run 24 hours but are not recommended as they are probably the least secure method of public transport in the city. Rental cars are recommended only if traveling outside the downtown area. Amtrak trains and Greyhound buses offer extensive routes from Baltimore to various cities. The Greyhound bus station is located at 210 W. Fayette Street, and Amtrak service is available at Penn Station located at Charles Street at Mt. Royal Avenue. A two hour guided tour of Baltimore's principal attractions in a replica of an old time trolley is available. Cruises along Chesapeake Bay and water shuttle with landings around the Harbor take place on a daily basis.

C AREA CODE: 410

BALTIMORE TIPS

☞ Areas of the city best avoided due to high crime are areas east of Little Italy and west of Camden Yards.

☞ Avoid using public transportation at night if traveling alone.

☞ Travelers are advised against traveling around Lombard Street east of Cornbeef Row at night.

BOSTON

CITY

Boston (pop. 4 million) is New England's most important city as well as a center of high finance and high technology. The city's Irish heritage is evidenced in everything from its many cozy pubs to its basketball team, the Celtics. Boston boasts a glorious history. The arrival of the Colonists; the Boston Massacre and Tea Party; the battles of Lexington, Concord and Bunker Hill all have made Boston a leading player in US history. With the possible exception of New York, Boston has produced more noteworthy intellectuals, politicians and writers than any other US city, including Benjamin Franklin, Paul Revere, John Adams and Ralph Waldo Emerson. Boston also produced the first American newspaper. Today, Boston hosts two of the world's finest universities: Harvard and Massachusetts Institute of Technology (MIT). One Bostonian in six is a student. This deep cultural heritage makes Boston the most European of American cities. Everywhere you go you encounter landmarks of Boston's 350 year-old history. With world renowned culture, museums, libraries and more, Boston is affectionately referred to as the Athens of North America. This historic city is meant for walking as a majority of its attractions are found in a compact area. Strolls throughout Beacon Hill reveal Boston's aristocratic neighborhood, with old gas lamps and cobblestone streets. A must see is Louisburg Square. The North End is a picturesque area of Boston's old harbor, made up of small, narrow streets with red brick houses, surrounded by war houses and docks. A stroll through freedom trail offers 16 colonial and revolutionary sites.

SECURITY CONCERNS

Boston has its share of seedy neighborhoods which should be avoided, similar to that in any large US city. In particular, the Combat Zone, the seediest district in town, should be avoided due to high crime rates. The area extends about a block in each direction from the Chinatown subway station (Orange Line) along Washington and Essex streets. Public transport in Boston is safe well into the evening.

AIRPORT

Logan International Airport (BOS) is located 4 miles from downtown. In 1996, the airport added extra security measures, including bomb-sniffing dogs and extra police officers, in response to the US government's directive to beef up security at US airports. Of note, Boston becomes foggy during mid-winter, especially in the early morning and late evening; this often delays air traffic. Logan ranks worst in on-time arrival among major U.S. airports.

Facilities/Services
Logan International Airport is a major international gateway to Europe and points around the US and Canada. Shuttle flights to New York City are frequent. The airport has five terminals, each of which is connected by a frequent shuttle bus (No.11). The currency exchange is open from 8:00 am to 10:00 pm. ATMs, restaurants and shops are located throughout the airport. A Traveler's Aide desk is located in Terminal E, where international flights arrive and depart.

To/From Logan
Travel time to downtown from the airport ranges from 15-30 minutes depending on traffic. Taxis are readily available outside the terminal and cost around $17 for downtown trips. The MBTA operates a subway (BlueLine) from the airport to downtown. The fare is $0.85. The Airways red-white van costs about $6.50 and operates hourly from 8:00 am to 10:00 pm. A 10-minute boat trip across the harbor via the free van (departs every 15 minutes) arrives at Rowe's Wharf next to Boston Harbor Hotel. The $5 boat ride operates from 6:00 am to 8:00 am weekdays, and noon to 7:45 pm every 30 minutes on weekends.

Transportation Within Boston
Boston has a variety of transportation options for travelers. The MBTA, known locally as the "T," operates subways, elevated trains, and trolleys along four connecting lines (Red, Blue, Green, Orange). Trains run from 5:30 am to 12:30 am with fares $0.85 per person. The MBTA also operates bus routes, but they are not recommended for travelers unsure of the city. Taxis are available throughout the city and are recommended for night travel.

Taxis, however, may be hard to find - and expensive. Priority response goes to waiting lines at the major hotels and phone orders rather than to those hailing on the street. The guided tours are highly recommended - from seasonal catamaran services, bus tours, and a turn-of-the-century streetcar replica. Check with the Greater Boston Convention and Visitors Bureau.

✆ AREA CODE: 617

BOSTON TIPS

☛ Travelers should be aware that pickpockets work the crowded downtown shopping areas such as Fanueil Hall and Washington Street.

☛ One area of Boston that should be avoided due to high crime is the Combat Zone area, a seedy area where many of the city's sex shops are located.

☛ Travelers should always monitor their bags and valuables as pickpockets do work the terminals.

CHICAGO

CITY

Chicago (pop. 6.2 million), the "Windy City" runs in a long north-south ribbon along Lake Michigan. The main business and tourist sectors of the city are in areas known as the "Loop," the "Magnificent Mile" and the university and museum area between Jackson and Washington Parks, although many sites are outside of these places. The Loop gets its name from an elevated train that runs in a loop along Lake, Wabash, Van Buren and Wells streets, roughly marking the area's boundaries. Wacker Drive, on which the Sears Tower and the Chicago Mercantile Exchange lie, is two blocks west of Wells, between Jackson and Randolph streets. The Magnificent Mile is really a stretch of Michigan Avenue running from the Chicago River to Lincoln Park. Chicago refers to itself as "The City of Big Shoulders". It claims not only one of the busiest airports in the world (O'Hare International), it claims the largest railroad station, the tallest sky scraper (Sears Tower, 110 stories), the tallest church (The Chicago Temple), the largest inland port, the largest convention center, and the world's most important grain exchange. Chicago is a sprawling city full of contrasts, home to one of the most extraordinary ethnic mixtures on the planet.

SECURITY CONCERNS

Even the tourist areas in the Loop and other areas suffer from sporadic robberies, murders, assaults and rapes. Two recent shooting incidents in the area highlight the sort of crime that takes place there. The first incident occurred when two men were shot and wounded outside the Western Grant Park Hotel on South Michigan Avenue when they got into their car parked outside. No motive was given for the shooting. The second incident occurred when an armed man fired his gun during a snack shop robbery on E. Adams, but was followed out by the cashier and captured by police. The Loop, Downtown-South Loop and Near North areas are generally quite safe when compared to the rest of the city. For example, the district recorded two shootings in the month of January, 1996 while the other 24 districts reported 884 shootings in total during the same month.

AIRPORT

Chicago is serviced by two airports: O'Hare International Airport and Midway Airport. O'Hare is 25 miles west of the central business district, and the trip into town will take about 40-60 minutes. O'Hare is one of the busiest airports in the world, with more than 62 million passengers per year. Midway is about 11 miles south of the Loop, 10-20 minutes away.

Facilities/Services at O'Hare
At O'Hare, all terminals have traveler information booths. The Airport Transit System is available between terminals 1, 2, 3, 5 and remote parking.

CHICAGO TIPS

☞ When on a bus, subway or elevated train, try to sit as close to the driver and exit as possible, rather than in the back. Avoid using subways at night; taxis are a better choice.

☞ Areas of the city best avoided due to high crime are: Cabrini Green, the Southside (south of 35th Street with the exception of Hyde Park and the immediate University of Chicago area and non-suburban areas west of the Chicago River.

☞ While one should not avoid these areas, caution is advised in the immediate University of Chicago area, the Pullman historical district, Chinatown and Little Saigon.

Facilities/Services at Midway
Midway is a far less congested domestic airport, and has three concourses and only one level. Passenger pick-up and drop-off, taxis, buses, car rental and a CTA Orange Line train station are outside the main door. Free shuttles going to the long-term economy parking lot arrive every 15 minutes.

To/From O'Hare Airport
Trains, taxis, hotel shuttle buses and rental cars are available for transport to the city center. A taxi trip from O'Hare into the city will cost approximately $30. The Continental Air Transport shuttle service can be found at the baggage claim areas of the airport, the shuttle goes to many major hotels for $15. The Blue Line train to the downtown Dearborn subway station takes 40 minutes and costs $1.50. The O'Hare Station is located under the elevated parking structure and may be reached through pedestrian corridors leading from baggage claim areas.

To/From Midway Airport
A variety of modes of transportation are available. Cab fares to downtown run about $20. The Continental Air Transport shuttle service goes to downtown for $11 one-way. The Orange Line train fare is about $1.25.

Transportation Within Chicago
Taxis, buses, trains and rental cars are available in the city. Rental cars are not recommended for use downtown due to a shortage of parking and traffic congestion. Public transportation is generally safe and reliable during the day. The fare for buses and subways is $1.25 and includes a two-hour transfer. The suburbs are most easily reached by taxi or train. Trains leaving from the Northwestern Station head to the north and northwest areas; trains from Union Station travel to the west and southwest suburbs; southern suburbs can be reached from Randolph Street and LaSalle Street stations.

✆ AREA CODE: 312 or 708 (downtown, O'HARE airport, and suburbs).

DALLAS

CITY

Dallas/Ft. Worth (pop. 4 million), otherwise known as the "Metroplex" is a vast suburban web of small cities built on former corn fields and cattle ranches. Dallas is the largest and most commercially visible city in the Metroplex and is bisected northwest-southeast by the Trinity River, east-west by the highways I-35 and US75 and north-south by I-30. Known as the "New York of the South," Texas' largest city is also one of the country's three great fashion capitals. Dallas also has more retail shopping space per capita than any other U.S. city. (It also is proud of the fact there are more Cadillacs per capita than any other city!) The culture is renowned: The famous Dallas Symphony Orchestra, Dallas Opera, Museum of Art, and Southern Methodist University, one of the most prestigious schools in the South. The main business areas are the central business district (just north of the river), Las Colinas (near DFW Airport) and North Dallas/Richardson/Plano (North Dallas and two northern suburbs). Most of the shopping malls are in North Dallas and most of the tourist attractions, such as Six Flags Over Texas and the sports stadiums are in the western suburbs of Arlington and Irving. A car is essential for navigating the city as public transportation is not well developed. **Areas generally best avoided due to crime are all in the south, southwest and southeast sectors of the city.**

SECURITY CONCERNS

Dallas has one of the highest per-capita crime rates in the US, but like many cities, the violent crime rate has fallen during the past year. There were 219 people murdered in the city during 1996, down from 276 in 1995 and the lowest level since 1991. Violent crimes occur mostly in the poorer areas of Dallas, generally south of the Trinity River. Each suburb also has a poorer area, but these are usually small and easily identifiable. However, street crime is not unknown even in the "better" parts of the city. For example, recently a man was killed while walking on a sidewalk in Oak Lawn, a trendy entertainment area just north of downtown, when he refused to give his wallet to an armed robber. The robber made off with $20. The victim was the third person to be shot and the second to die under similar circumstances in three months. Normal security precautions should be taken: avoid flashy jewelry, guard against pickpockets, stay alert in unfamiliar territory, keep your car locked at all times, etc.

AIRPORTS

Dallas has two airports; the very large Dallas-Ft. Worth International Airport (DFW) and the smaller Love Field. DFW is 40 minutes northwest of the central business district, 30 minutes west of North Dallas and 10 minutes from Las Colinas. DFW is ultra modern in conception and the world's second largest airport in surface area (16,800 acres) – as big as Manhattan! It is the fourth busiest airport in the world with 42 million passengers a year. Love Field is located 10 minutes from the central business district, 30 minutes from Las Colinas and 30 minutes from North Dallas.

DALLAS TIPS

☞ Areas of the city best avoided due to high crime are: East Oak Cliff, Pleasant Grove, Fair Park and East Dallas south of I -30.

☞ While one should not avoid these areas, caution is advised in the immediate area around the Galleria and Valley View shopping malls, Oak Lawn, neighborhoods around Love Field (especially a strip of bars and topless clubs on Northwest Highway), and the West End and Deep Ellum (both popular nightclub areas in the central business district.)

☞ Suburban cities such as Plano, Garland, Duncanville, Richardson, Mesquite, Irving, Arlington and Carrolton are generally safe bedroom communities.

Facilities/Services at DFW Airport

Terminals 4E, 3E and 2W handle most international flights and currency exchange is located there. ATM machines are located throughout all terminals. The airport is very large and there is a tram system that should be used for fast transit between terminals. A 24-hour post office, conference facilities and computer facilities are also available.

Facilities/Services at Love Field

Love field is only serviced by Southwest Airlines, Dallas Express and private aircraft; the facility is much less busy than DFW. The airport has only one main terminal, and all flights are domestic. ATMs are available, but currency exchange and tourist facilities are not. Conference facilities, fax and copy machines are available on the first floor.

TRANSPORTATION

Transportation Within Dallas

Taxis, buses, trains (very limited service) and rental cars are available in the city. A rental car is recommended due to a lack of easily accessible public transportation and because parking is generally inexpensive and plentiful. Seat belts are mandatory.

Buses are not recommended due to the great inconvenience involved in using them. A new light rail service was initiated in the fall of 1996, but the lines are designed more for commuting rather than getting around town.

To/From DFW Airport

Taxis, hotel shuttle buses and rental cars are available for transport to the city. A taxi trip from DFW to the central business district will cost approximately $28. A taxi to downtown Ft. Worth costs $32. A shared van to Dallas costs $10.

Train: Amtrak (toll free 800-872-7245) has stations in Dallas (Union Station) at 400 S. Houston St. and in Ft. Worth at 1501 Jones St.

To/From Love Field

Taxis, hotel shuttles and buses are available. Cab fares to the central business district run about $15. A door-to-door shuttle costs about $10.

✆ AREA CODE: (Dallas) 214 or 972; (Ft. Worth & Arlington) 817

DENVER

CITY

Denver (pop. 1.7 million) is the focal point of Colorado commerce, government and transportation and an economic center of the Great Plains and Rocky Mountain regions. This intriguing city, a combination of a modern American city mixed into an Old West town, extends from the Rocky Mountain foothills on the west far into the plains to the south and east. Denver often is referred to as the "Mile High City," because when you climb the State Capitol steps, you're precisely 5,280 feet above sea level. Lying at the foot of the Rockies against the magnificent natural backdrop of the mountains, the mountains have made Denver one of the great capitals of American tourism. The city also has regional federal offices and rapidly growing other industries like rubber and food processing associated with the rapidly growing stockyards. A branch of the U.S. Mint (1906) is located there, as well as a number of military installations. Denver is home of the University of Colorado Medical Center and the University of Denver. Other cultural institutions includes the Colorado State historical museum and the Buffalo Bill Cody Memorial Museum (Lookout Mountain). With dozens of winter sports resorts, the Rockies are a skier's paradise. Like many of its sister cities of the West, Denver has experienced an economic boom since World War II. Denver is one of the energy capitals of the country with its oil, gas, coal, uranium, solar energy and synthetic fuels.

The one drawback is that automobile emissions and industrial fumes are caught in the atmosphere. Whenever the winds blow westward, a thick cloud of pollution occurs Most of Denver's attractions are concentrated downtown, a compact area that can be toured on foot. A popular place for most visitors is the Lower Downtown District, referred to as "LoDo" by the locals. The area has been rebuilt and many popular restaurants, bars, shops and art galleries are now located there.

SECURITY CONCERNS

Denver is not unlike many of the other large metropolitan areas in the US in that it suffers from the same problems like crime and violence. The city has certain places where caution is warranted, although such neighborhoods are off the typical beaten path of most travelers. Persons should use normal precautions in Denver as they would in any large city. In 1995, Denver reported 4,300 violent crimes, including 81 murders, 320 rapes, 1,400 robberies, and 2,500 aggravated assaults. Higher rates of criminal activity are reported in the northern and eastern parts of the city.

AIRPORT

Denver International Airport (DIA) is located 23 miles northeast of the city. The airport, which opened in 1995, replacing Stapleton Airport, is the nation's largest, encompassing 53 square miles. The airport's stunning architecture has gained much notoriety, while the cost of building the facility has generated a great deal of criticism.

The airport opened eight months late (1994) and $1 billion over initial cost estimates. DIA is the first airport to be built from scratch since Dallas-Fort Worth 20 years ago. DIA is projected to become the second busiest airport in the U.S., after Chicago's O'Hare transporting 32 million people annually. DIA has the ability to handle three simultaneous landings or 99 arrivals an hour.

Facilities/Services

Denver International Airport is comprised of a main terminal and three concourses, all connected by underground train. Persons changing concourses should allow extra time. The airport has five runways and can land up to three planes simultaneously. The visitor information telephone number is 303-892-1112

TRANSPORTATION

To/From Denver International Airport

Bus, taxi and limousine service are available at the airport. A ride on the City Bus to downtown cost $6 each way. Also the Airporter shuttle service provides door-to-door pick up; fares range from $20 to $40 each way, while the Denver Airport Shuttle provides transportation to most major hotels with fares varying. A taxi trip to downtown ranges from $30 to $50. Drive time from the airport to downtown Denver is 35-45 minutes by car.

Transportation Within Denver

Public buses, light rail and taxis are the easiest means of transiting downtown Denver. Fares range from $.50 to $1. Rental cars are not advised unless travel to suburban parts of the city is required. The downtown district has limited parking. During weekday rush hours, traffic becomes very congested on highways leading to mountain suburbs. Amtrak trains and Greyhound buses provide service between cities and mountain resorts. Guided tours of the surrounding Rocky Mountains are available through hotel contacts. Taxis are few and may not be hailen on the street. Winter sport resorts: Aspen Mountain and Aspen Highlands is the luxury resort of the Rockies. Vail is the poshest of the Colorado resorts. Copper Mountain, Keystone Ski Areas, Snowmass, Telluride, and Winter Park are also very popular.

✆ AREA CODE: 303

DENVER TIPS

☛ Women walking alone at night are particularly vulnerable on Colfax Avenue between Colorado Boulevard and Broadway.

☛ Due to criminal activity caution is warranted at night around City Park, Curtis Park, Sun Valley, North Capitol Hill, and Five Points.

DETROIT

CITY

Detroit, the "Motor City," is a major port and industrial center, the ninth largest city in the US, and the 5th largest metropolitan area in the US (pop. 4,590,500). The word détroit is French and means "on the strait." The city was so named because it is on the west bank of the Detroit River, a strait connecting Lake St. Clair and Lake Erie. It is known as the Motor City because it accounts for approximately 70% of domestic automobile production. Led by such magnates as Henry Ford, Walter P. Chrysler, William C. Durant, and Ransom E Olds, the automotive industry in the beginning of the 20th century converted Detroit into its world-wide capital. Detroit is also a steel-producing center that furnishes both raw metal and finished products for the automobile industry. The city is located as a gateway to Canada on the Detroit River in southeastern Michigan, and it is the oldest city in the Midwest. While downtown is largely quiet, Greektown is a popular tourist destination, full of traditional Greek restaurants, night clubs and cafes. Within Greektown, Monroe Avenue is the main hub of street action. Every weekend during the summer, Detroit's cultural and ethnic diversity is celebrated in festivals held at Hart Plaza on the river front. Detroit is also home to Motown sound and every September holds the Montreax-Detroit Jazz Festival. Also, Detroit hosts the world headquarters for both Ford Motor Company and General Motors Corporation. **The main area to avoid due to crime is downtown, which is largely deserted day and night.**

SECURITY CONCERNS

Street crime is a concern in Detroit. Visitors should employ normal security precautions to protect against petty theft. In 1996, there was a 15% decline in the city's murder rate. The actual number of homicides in Detroit has declined from 234 in the period January to June 1995, to 210 for the same period in 1996. In all of 1995, the number of murders stood at 475, while in 1994, it stood at 541. The situation has improved in part due to the city's youth violence prevention programs and the implementation of community "safety zones." However, in a survey published by Money magazine, Detroit was still ranked as the fifth most dangerous US city (of 100,000 residents or more) for overall violent crime and burglary in 1996.

DETROIT TIPS

- ☛ In general, the northern sections of Detroit are safer and more picturesque.

- ☛ It is best not to travel on public transportation after dark if you are alone.

- ☛ Areas of the city best avoided due to crime are: the are north of the theater district and the Red Light District (Second Avenue, Woodward Avenue between 6 and 8 Mile Roads, 8 Mile Road and Southfield Road intersection area).

- ☛ The downtown area, because of its lack of tourist sites, is generally empty during the day and night hours. Caution is advised.

- ☛ Pickpockets work the areas surrounding the Amtrak train and Greyhound bus stations, especially at night. Some incidents of crime have also been reported around Wayne State University campus.

AIRPORTS

There are two airports that service Detroit; Detroit City Airport (located 10 miles from downtown), which provides mostly private access, and the Detroit Metropolitan International Airport (located 19 miles southwest of downtown).

Facilities/Services at Detroit Metropolitan International Airport
The Detroit Metropolitan International Airport is the 15th most busiest in the world, with about half a million flights arriving or departing every year. A tremendous increase in air passenger traffic has led to a massive expansion and modernization program at the airport worth nearly $1 billion, including the building of a modern Northwest Airlines terminal by year 2000. This also includes the new Airport Movement Area Safety System (AMASS), the first of its kind in the US, which detects and alerts operators to potential runway dangers, especially in fog.

TRANSPORTATION

To/From Detroit Airport
Taxis, buses, hotel shuttles and rental cars are available for transport to the city center. A free shuttle service exists between the airport's terminal facilities and the SMART (Suburban Mobility Authority for Regional Transportation) bus stop; the pick-up/drop-off areas are located on the upper departure level curb front of each terminal. Commuter vans to most major downtown hotels takes 30 minutes and costs approximately $13; they depart every 30 minutes until midnight.

Transportation Within Detroit
Taxis buses, the People Mover and rental cars are available in the city. Public bus transportation is coordinated by DDOT (Detroit Department of Transportation) and SMART (the Suburban Mobility Authority for Regional Transportation). DOT buses run inner-city services for $1 per ride, while SMART services suburbia and fares are $1.50 per ride. The bus services do not provide a large network of routes, nor do the buses run very frequently. Driving your own car around town is the best way to see the city. Also, during the day, the Attractions Shuttle minibuses run between major points.

 AREA CODE: 313

HOUSTON

CITY

Houston (pop. 3.5 million) is situated on former swampland about 20 miles northwest of the Gulf of Mexico coast. Where 150 years ago there was nothing but a mosquito-infested tent town, today stands the world's energy industry capital and a skyline dominated by the corporate headquarters of energy industry giants. The city owes its name to the first elected president of the Republic of Texas, Sam Houston. Houston today is sometimes call "the Bayou City" (on the shore of Buffalo Bayou), and is the country's third-largest port. As a world center of Energy, Houston is also a city of culture. The Lyndon B Johnson Space Center, headquarters for the country's space program, has guided every space flight launched from the Kennedy Space Center. The Astrodome is the second largest covered stadium in the world and is one of the most vivid examples of the contemporary American architecture. The Texas Medical Center is the world's largest hospital complex, considered the most up-to-date in the world. The city is divided by several highways: I-10 runs east-west, I-45 runs north-south, and US59 runs southwest-northwest. Additionally, there are several loops around the city: I-610, Beltway 8 and Highway 6. Businesses and major hotels are concentrated in the central business district and Galleria area. Many people in the city refer to places being either inside or outside the "Loop," which is I-610. One thing that many visitors notice about Houston is that there is no formal zoning, which often means that the distinctions between "bad" and "good" neighborhoods are less clearly defined than in other cities.

SECURITY CONCERNS

The main concern for a traveler to Houston is crime, specifically armed robbery and theft. The city has a reputation for being a bit rough around the edges, a reputation substantiated by its crime rate. Houston ranks number 12 among the most visited US cities in violent crime (murder, rape, aggravated assault) with a rate roughly one-third that of Miami or Atlanta. The most worrisome crimes that a traveler might encounter are carjacking and armed robbery, which can occur even in "safe" areas. A recent example: a group of four youths, age 16 to 20, participated in a swift crime spree in an upscale area of southwest Houston, during which they either robbed at gunpoint or carjacked six people in two hours. The robberies took place in parking garages, convenience store parking lots, an intersection and a woman's own driveway. No one was injured and the youths were later apprehended.

HOUSTON TIPS

☛ In general, areas to avoid are the sectors north, east, northeast and southeast of the central business district that are within Beltway 8.

☛ Areas best avoided because of high crime are: the area east of US288 inside Loop I-610, either side of I-45 north of downtown to F.M. 1960, either side of I-45 south of downtown until NASA Road and downtown after 8 p.m. as it is largely deserted.

☛ Other areas that should not be avoided but where caution is advised are: the Texas Medical Center area, Hermann Park, Memorial Park, Sharpstown, Vietnam Town, Little India, Chinatown, Pasadena and the immediate Ship Channel Turning Basin area.

☛ There have been a number of shootings recently on US288 south of downtown following minor traffic altercations and at random. Avoid antagonizing fellow motorists and drive defensively on this road and everywhere in Houston.

AIRPORTS

Houston is served by two airports; Houston Intercontinental Airport and Hobby Airport. Intercontinental is by far the larger of the two; all international flights to Houston arrive through Intercontinental. Intercontinental is located 20 miles north of downtown; Hobby is 10 miles southeast of the city.

Facilities/Services at Intercontinental

The airport has several terminals, but all are contiguous. ATM machines, a post office and meeting rooms are available 24 hours per day. Currency exchange is open daily from 7:30 a.m. to 9:30 p.m.

Facilities/Services at Hobby

The airport has only one main terminal, and all flights are domestic. ATMs are available, currency exchange and tourist facilities are available. Conference facilities, tax and copy machines are also available.

TRANSPORTATION

To/From Intercontinental Airport

Taxis, hotel shuttle buses and rental cars are available for transport to the city. A taxi trip from Intercontinental to the central business district will cost approximately $35 and takes 40 minutes. Special airport shuttles are available to the Galleria, Medical Center and downtown for $9.75. A helicopter is available for flights to Hobby Airport.

To/From Hobby Airport

Taxis, hotel shuttles and buses are available. Cab fares to the central business district run about $22 and take 30 minutes. Shuttle vans to major business centers, Greenway Plaza and South Post Oak cost $10.

Transportation Within Houston

Buses, taxis and rental cars are the only method of travel in the city. A rental car is the easiest way to get around the city as the bus system covers too large an area to be time-efficient and taxis generally have to be phoned for in advance, rather than hailed, except during the day downtown. There is an abundance of inexpensive or free parking around the city, but traffic at rush hour can be horrendous. Road construction on the major highways is seemingly endless so checking with the Texas Department of Transportation at (800) 452-9292 for the latest information can save a lot of time.

 AREA CODE: 713 or 281

LAS VEGAS

CITY

Las Vegas (pop. 500,000) is currently one of the fastest growing cities in the U.S in terms of population growth. The city also continues to attract around 30 million visitors each year, most of whom come to this desert city seeking riches in Las Vegas' countless casinos. The city was founded by Mormons on the colonial trail from Santa Fe to California; it fell on hard economic times until the construction of the Union Pacific's first track in 1905. The adoption of new gambling laws by the State of nevada in 1931 made the fortune of Las Vegas. The city in recent years has transformed itself from a gamblers-only destination, as new hotels/resorts have become more family oriented, with theme parks and attractions geared towards persons of all ages. Still, most first-time visitors are overwhelmed by the thousands of lights, people and the ringing of slot machines that can be heard throughout the night along the famous Las Vegas Strip — a 3.5 mile long row of hotel/casinos along S. Las Vegas Boulevard. Such night life has won Las Vegas a reputation as a city that never sleeps. With annual gambling revenues approaching $4 billion, there are even slot machines in rest rooms! Las Vegas has more churches, chapels, and other places of worship per thousand residents than any other city in the U.S! Dozens of "wedding chapels" are open until midnight on weekdays and around the clock on weekends..."armed" by ministers called "Marying Sams". Food at restaurants, cafeterias and snack bars cost about half of what it would cost anywhre else in the country...as an incentive for tourists to get back to the tables! Travelers should be aware that Las Vegas is located in the desert and that extreme hot temperatures are common during summer months. **Areas of Las Vegas best avoided at night due to high crime are the city's Upper West side and North Las Vegas.**

SECURITY CONCERNS

The Strip and downtown areas are relatively safe at all times of the day and night. The hotels/resorts put security and safety as a top priority to protect their patrons and casino operations. However, some pickpockets do work these areas looking for easy targets among unsuspecting or inattentive tourists. Public buses are fairly safe, but they are best avoided at night. Overall, the influx of new residents and increased tourism has hampered the Las Vegas police department's ability to fight crime effectively. In 1995, Las Vegas reported 118 murders, 571 rapes, 3,700 robberies, 5,100 aggravated assaults. The city also racked up over 30,000 thefts in 1995.

AIRPORT

McCarran International Airport (LAS) is located 10 miles from downtown Las Vegas and 1 mile from the Strip. The airport, an extremely modern facility, is the 10th busiest in the U.S. Currently, the airport has several construction projects underway, among them an east-west runway expansion and D concourse expansion. Also, a $10 million expansion of the north ticketing area of the airport will add 25 counters by spring 1997. The airport recently opened a new $84 million, nine-level 6,000-space parking garage.

Facilities/Services

McCarren International Airport has all the modern conveniences, like moving walkways and trains, to allow travelers to arrive at their gate with east. Currency exchange, ATMs, restaurants and shops are located throughout the airport. Tourist information desks are located on the second floor and in baggage claim areas. Gamblers can play at the many slot machines located throughout the airport almost the moment they get off the plane.

Transportation Within Las Vegas

Taxis are the best means to transit Las Vegas but they can be hard to find during rush hour. Frequent traffic jams along the Strip have made some taxi rides expensive. The meter starts at $2.20 and each two blocks or so costs 30 cents. The Citizens Area Transit (CAT) bus service operates along the Strip and in downtown, stopping at all major hotels along the way. The cost is $1.50 per person. The buses are generally safe during the day but it is preferable to use a cab after dark. The Las Vegas Trolley also operates 8 vehicles which run every 30 minutes up and down the Strip from 9:30 a.m. to 2:00 a.m. The fare is $1.30. Rental cars are not recommended unless venturing out of the city. Free parking areas are available at most hotels, but drivers are generally required to make a long walk from such remote parking lots. Valet parking is quite expensive. The Greyhound bus station is located at 200 S. Main Street. The Amtrak station also is located downtown. Because of low car rental rates, Las Vegas is also a good base for exursions to near by Lake Mead, Hoover Dam, Red Rock Canyon...or further to the Grand Canyon and Utah's national parks.

✆ AREA CODE: 702

LAS VEGAS TIPS

☛ If venturing between downtown and hotels along the Strip, use city buses or taxis. Walking between these areas is unwise.

☛ At night, it is best to stick to the beaten path around hotels and casinos. Use caution and common sense when venturing down dark side streets.

☛ When looking up to watch the Street Experience light show, remain aware of your surroundings and possessions as pickpockets look for attractive and inattentive targets.

LOS ANGELES

CITY

Los Angeles (population 10 million) is one of America's most exciting and sprawling cities. A broad corridor running 25 miles west from downtown Los Angeles to the Pacific Coast offers a multitude of sites, including glamorous Hollywood, Beverly Hills, Disneyland, and the sandy beaches and palm-tree resorts of Santa Monica and Malibu. The heart of LA is downtown, a microcosm of everything the city has to offer, including its ethnic, social and cultural diversity. West LA ("Westside") is the avant-garde part of town, encompassing all that is new and happening in the city. It includes Sunset Strip, a multitude of restaurants, hotels and nightclubs which represent the best of LA night life, and Beverly Hills, one of the world's wealthiest residential neighborhoods. **Areas to avoid include South Central LA, which is the heartland of LA's infamous gang warfare. There are reportedly over 70,000 gang members in the area. Fueled with drug money and automatic weapons, these gangs fight violently for "territory" and occasionally engage in drive-by shootings. Do not drive through South Central LA after dark; it is inadvisable to drive through this area even during the day. Also, Venice Beach (south of Santa Monica) should be avoided at night, which it is overrun by gang members and drug dealers. In fact, walking on the beach after dark is illegal.**

SECURITY CONCERNS

Crime is the number one concern for travelers in Los Angeles. According to FBI statistics, in 1995 the city ranked as the seventh most dangerous city in the U.S. However, crime has decreased in recent years: in 1995, violent crime (murder, forcible rape, robbery and aggravated assault) declined by 8% in Los Angeles. In 1996, the murder rate fell 17% from 1995 (in 1996, the murder count was 688 as compared to 829 in 1995). Gang killings and drug-related murders account for almost half the homicides in Los Angeles. Some murders and armed assaults have occurred at ATM machines at night. However, ATM crime in Los Angeles in 1995 was one-third of its 1992 level. The actual number of reported incidents in 1995 was 261, just over half the 499 ATM-related crimes reported in 1992.

AIRPORT

Los Angeles is served by three airports: Los Angeles Airport, Burbank Airport and Long Beach Airport. The main international airport in the city is Los Angeles International Airport (LAX), located 17 miles southwest of downtown. It is one of the largest and most congested airports in the U.S.

Facilities/Services
The huge LA airport contains seven domestic terminals and the Tom Bradley International Terminal. Terminal One houses Gates 1-14, Terminal Two has Gates 21-28, Terminal Three has Gates 30-39, Terminal Four has Gates 41-49, Terminal Five has Gates 51-59, Terminal Six has Gates 61-69, Terminal Seven has Gates 71-77 and Gates 80-84. The International Terminal houses Gates 101-123. Travelers' Aide provides tourist information in every terminal on the arrivals level from 7:00 a.m. to 10:00 p.m. (Monday to Friday) and from 9:00 a.m. to 8:00 p.m. (Saturday and Sunday). The international terminal contains Skytel, small individual cabins where travelers can take naps, showers and make telephone calls. Blue, White and Green Airline connections provide free shuttle buses between the terminals.

To/From Los Angeles Airport (LAX)
Trains, taxis, hotel shuttle buses and rental cars are available for transport to the city center. A taxi to downtown or Hollywood costs approximately $30. The trip can take up to an hour. A taxi to Disneyland can cost as much as $85. Taxis are available outside the baggage claim at each terminal building. Free 24-hour shuttle buses take passengers from the terminals to the MTA Transit Center, where they can catch public city buses. A bus ride from the airport to downtown takes up to an hour with a fare of about $2. The Metro public rail service has a free shuttle service between the Aviation Station at Imperial Highway and all terminals at the airport. Shared-ride minivans go to any location in Los Angeles, Orange, San Bernardino and Riverside counties. Fares are generally around $18.

Transportation Within Los Angeles
Taxis, buses, trains and rental cars are available in the city. Many visitors find that renting a car is the best way to see LA. The next best alternative is to use express buses. However, the best way to see downtown or Hollywood is on foot. Public transportation is generally safe and reliable during the day. It runs until midnight. The Metrorail system, still incomplete, is currently made up of three lines: the Red Line, Green Line and Blue Line. Tickets cost $1.35, and trains run every 5 to 15 minutes. Public buses run by the LA County Metropolitan Transit Authority (MTA or Metro) run ever 15 minutes between 5:00 a.m. and 2:00 a.m. on the major roads between downtown and the coast. The standard single fare is $1.35; transfers cost 25 cents more. Express buses are $1.85. DASH mini-buses travel between five downtown routes and run a Hollywood service weekdays and Saturdays, for 25 cents each. Bus and commuter rail fares from LA to Long Beach are $1.35. Amtrak provides frequent connections to San Diego, Oakland and Seattle from its station at 800 N. Alameda, on the north side of downtown. Greyhound terminals are located throughout LA, although the main one is located at 1716 E. Seventh Street (a seedier part of downtown).

© AREA CODE: 213 or 818 in the San Fernando Valley and parts of the San Gabriel Valley.

LOS ANGELES TIPS

☞ By day, tourist areas, such as downtown, Hollywood, and the beaches are safe to visit. Avoid downtown and Venice Beach after business hours. Be aware of pickpockets throughout the city.

☞ Avoid South Central and East LA after dark, as these areas have especially high rates of general and juvenile crime.

☞ Be cautious on public transportation and try to not get stranded alone downtown while waiting for a public bus connection.

☞ Car-related theft is a major problem in LA. Never leave valuables in cars.

☞ Be cautious if using an ATM machine at night.

MIAMI

CITY

Miami (pop. 3 million) is located at the mouth of the Miami River on Biscayne Bay. Numerous foreigners come to the city's Atlantic Ocean beach resort hotels each year to enjoy the generally year-round warm climate. Besides its nice beaches and summer-like climate, Miami is a ethnic melting pot which offers glimpses into a variety of different cultures. The city is home to a huge Hispanic community, and Spanish is widely spoken. Just like large American cities, Miami also is facing problems, namely issues of economic stagnation and urban decay. Travelers should be aware that the transitions between rich and poor areas are sometimes abrupt in the city. **Areas to avoid include Liberty City, Carol City, Overtown and Cloverleaf.**

SECURITY CONCERNS

Miami has one of the highest per capita crime rates in the U.S. Travelers to Miami should be aware that street crime may affect them, as petty theft and robbery are common. Even tourist locations are targeted by criminals, who are often violent. Increasingly, criminals are young, and frequently gang members. In an effort to address this problem, a curfew is in place for those under 18.

The city in the early 1990's received considerable negative publicity over a number of tourist attacks. In several cases, foreign tourists were followed from rental car locations at the international airport and either carjacked or robbed. In several instances, foreign tourists (Germans and Britons) were murdered during the commission of these crimes. Recently, a Dutch tourist was shot during a robbery after the woman and her husband became lost while driving a rental car in the city. The crime was played out in seedy Liberty City when the husband stopped at a gas station to ask for directions. Police have made a major effort to correct the problem but caution should be exercised both at the airport and when traveling from it. Travelers who rent a car should follow roads designated by a sunburst symbol - a bright orange sun symbol. These symbols were posted to prevent travelers from inadvertently driving into bad areas of the city.

Thieves operate on the city's beaches, and frequent incidents of pickpocketing are reported in parts of South Miami Beach. The best advice for those spending time on the beaches is simple: do not leave valuables unattended.

AIRPORT

Miami is serviced by the Miami International Airport, which is 5 miles from downtown and about 10 miles from many beach locations. The airport is located off the East-West Expressway. Due to acts of crime against tourists, a special tourist security police unit, STARS, has been established at the international airport. STARS officers patrol the area in and around the facility. Some travelers coming to North Miami areas arrive at the Fort Lauderdale/Hollywood International Airport 25 miles away.

Facilities/Services

At the four-story Miami International Airport, tourist information centers and currency exchanges are available; these services are usually open around the clock. There are eight concourse areas at the airport; the eight concourses are marked A-H. The baggage claim area is located on the first floor, as are car rental agencies and other ground transportation connections, foreign exchange and information kiosks, and Customs and Immigration. International travelers may experience delays of over one hour in Customs. Also, delays should be expected in retrieving baggage, as airport security will match claim checks to baggage.

To/From Miami

Taxis, Red Top Vans, buses and the Metrorail provide transportation services into Miami. In addition, many hotels operate shuttle services, but generally these should be arranged ahead of time. Major rental car services are available. Rental car lots, about one mile from the terminal, are located in an area that can be tricky to get into and out of, so drivers should be attentive. In an effort to reduce the threat of carjacking and robbery against rental car users, rental agencies have removed corporate insignias from cars. The tourist police's (STARS) primary function is to advise new arrivals on rental car firms in the area and make sure tourists who have gone astray get back on the right road when leaving the airport.

Metered taxis generally take about 15-20 minutes to travel to downtown Miami; fares run about $17. Metered taxis traveling to Miami Beach usually take about 25-30 minutes to reach resort locations; fares run about $22. Red Top Van services take about 30 minutes to reach downtown Miami and the fare is $8 per traveler. Buses, which are difficult to travel on if carrying a number of bags, take about 30 minutes and cost $1.25 to go downtown. There is a free shuttle bus service to Metrorail; the Metrorail costs $2 to travel downtown.

Transportation Within Miami

Taxis, Metrobus service, trains and rental cars are available in the city. Taxis generally are the safest and quickest way to travel. Taxi drivers generally know the safe and unsafe driving areas. The elevated Metromover rail system loops downtown Miami. The Metromover connects to the Metrorail that runs to the suburbs. A Tri-Rail system connects Dade, Broward and Palm Beach counties.

MIAMI TIPS

☛ Travelers planning to rent a car should consider renting a vehicle from rental agencies located around resorts rather than at the international airport. If a traveler receives a rental car with a corporate insignia on it, ask the rental staff to remove it.

☛ If driving a rental car, follow only major routes or routes designated by the sunburst symbol. Always park in well-lit areas.

☛ Avoid possible theft from vehicles by keeping doors locked and windows rolled up. These precautions should be followed when driving, as window washers sometimes approach vehicles and reach in through open windows to steal.

☛ If involved in a minor accident, always proceed to a well populated, secure area before getting out of your vehicle.

☛ Be aware that traffic often is congested in Miami. In the beach area, parking is difficult in Coconut Grove and South Miami Beach because there is only street parking.

☛ At night, the banking district in the city center, and the area between the South Miami Beach/South Beach (also called the Art Deco District) and Miami Beach are dangerous.

☛ Avoid using the Metrorail at night, especially to the downtown area, because of crime.

 AREA CODE: 305

MINNEAPOLIS

CITY

The upbeat city of Minneapolis (pop. 360,000) mixes natural beauty (the city boasts dozens of lakes and parks) with towering skyscrapers. Minneapolis prides itself on being the intellectual capital of the Midwest ,with the University of Minnesota, well-known symphony and chamber orchestras, an opera, and many museums of high quality, and the famous Guthrie Theatre. It is also the heart of fabulous vacation land of deep forests, swift-running rivers teeming with fish, and numberless lakes...naming Minneapolis "Gateway to the land of 10,000 lakes". Some 30 of *Fortune Magazine's* 500 top-ranking corporations are based in the "Water City," companies such as Honeywell, Control Data, General Mills, 3M Corporation, and Pillsbury. In contrast to its sister city, the more traditional and slightly older capital of St. Paul, Minneapolis has proved itself to be livelier and more "artsy." Downtown Minneapolis is connected by a network of elevated, climate-controlled glass walkways, allowing the visitor to view the city without being affected by Minneapolis' harsh winter weather. Despite these harsh winters, Minneapolis and St. Paul rank among the greenest cities in the country, with 936 lakes and 513 parks or public gardens between them. Visitors will surely feel welcome by the city's polite, liberal Scandinavian descendants, who give the city a feel all its own.

SECURITY CONCERNS

Crime has increased in this otherwise placid city in recent years. In 1996, Minneapolis had 83 murders; in 1995 the city witnessed 97 murders. There were 27.1 murders per 100,000 people in 1995. This surge in crime makes the city the 25th most dangerous among the nation's 200 largest cities. In both 1996 and 1995, the number of murders have risen far above the city's previous average of about 60 murders per year. Drugs and gang warfare are reportedly responsible for almost half of 1995's homicides. Also, racial tensions have increasingly manifested themselves in gang-related crime.

The state of Minnesota has allocated almost $1 million to the city to put more police on the street and tackle inner-city problems, where drugs and gang warfare are common. Also, the city has instituted a youth curfew system; those under 18 must be off the streets by 8:00 pm on school nights, by 9:00 pm during summer break, and by 11:00 pm on weekends.

Residents of the city are conscious about the growing crime situation. It is no wonder that the McDonald's restaurant at Hennepin and Lagoon in the uptown part of Minneapolis features a built-in police substation. Two full-time officers are assigned to the McDonald's. The collaborative effort, the first of its kind in the country, is aimed at increasing police visibility and helping to deter crime in the area.

AIRPORT

The Minneapolis-St. Paul Airport is located 16 miles south of downtown Minneapolis (about a 20 minute drive). The airport is one of the nation's busiest, with over 1,100 daily arrivals and departures on 10 commercial airlines and nine regional carriers, as well as several international carriers.

MINNEAPOLIS TIPS

☞ The vast majority of murders in Minneapolis take place in poor, run-down neighborhoods, some of which are only a few miles away from downtown's glittering business district.

☞ Some areas around Lake Street should be ventured into with caution; the area between Cedar Avenue and Blaisdell should be avoided due to crime.

☞ Areas in which extra caution should be employed include south Minneapolis, which has been particularly hard hit by crime.

☞ The run-down neighborhood of Phillips is particularly known as a haven for drug dealers.

Facilities/Services at Minneapolis-St. Paul International Airport

The airport has two terminals, the main Lindbergh Terminal (which has four concourses) and the Humphrey International Terminal. The Lindbergh Terminal contains everything from bank ATMs to a barber shop to restaurants and shops. The Lindbergh Terminal contains the following concourses: the Blue Concourse (gates 41-54); the Gold Concourse (Gates 1-15A); the Green Concourse (62-90); and the Red Concourse (Gates 21-38). The Humphrey International Terminal contains Gates 1-3.

TRANSPORTATION

To/From Minneapolis/St. Paul International Airport

Trains, taxis, hotel shuttle buses and rental cars are available for transport to the city center. Information on limousine and bus service is available on the lower level of the main terminal's baggage area. Free hotel shuttles exist; also the Airport Express shuttle bus takes travelers between the airport and major hotels for around US$10 in about 45 minutes; these buses leave every half hour from the lower level. Taxis to Minneapolis cost about $25 and are available from the lower level of the main Lindbergh Terminal. The Metropolitan Transit commission (MTC) or suburban bus lines offer a wide selection of routes. Bus #7 goes to Minneapolis every 10 minutes from 6:00 am to midnight and costs about $1.25. The bus ride takes 50 minutes.

Transportation Within Minneapolis

Taxis, buses, trains and rental cars are available in the city. Taxis are widely available. The Metropolitan Transit Commission (MTC) buses operate throughout the city 6:00 am to midnight and are clean. Cost ranges from $1-$1.25. Old-style trolleys run through the city's downtown, costing about $2 a ride. Amtrak is located midway between Minneapolis and St. Paul at 730 Transfer Road, off University Avenue. Amtrak runs a major east-west line from Chicago and the East to Seattle and Portland. The convenient downtown Greyhound terminal is located at 29 Ninth Street in Minneapolis.

Mississippi Cruises: 3-10 day cruises aboard the Delta Queen or the Mississippi Queen, paddlewheel steamers built in the 1920s.

 AREA CODE: 612

NEW ORLEANS

CITY

New Orleans (population 500,000) home to the world-famous Mardi Gras, is a city divided into distinct districts: the tourist-ridden French Quarter; majestic Uptown, which contains the Garden District, famous for its picture-perfect parks and historic homes; the Faubourg Marigny, home to Bohemian restaurants and clubs; the Warehouse District; the Central Business District; and the popular residential area of Mid-City. The variety of cultures and races in the city gives it its polyethnic flavor; however, the divisions between rich and poor are very apparent, even just a short distance away from the commercialized French Quarter. The New Orleans atmosphere of cuisine, southern hospitality and jazz music, filled with college students and other party-goers, makes the city a perfect place to wind down. **Although the French quarter and Bourbon Street are full of tourists day and night, it is imperative that visitors do not wander away from the main tourist area, even a few blocks. Poor and rich neighborhoods are very integrated in New Orleans (and often such neighborhoods are actually adjacent to one another); thus, it is easy for travelers to wander into a particularly "bad" part of town inadvertently. Visitors should also steer clear of the many housing projects which are sprinkled throughout the city.**

SECURITY CONCERNS

Crime is a serious problem in New Orleans. In recent years, the city's homicide rate has sharply increased. On top of that, the city's police force has historically had a reputation for corruption and inefficiency. In the past three years, over 50 police officers have been arrested on felony charges, including rape and murder.

New Orleans has 76 murders per 100,000 citizens—a murder rate almost eight times the national average. And the murder rate in the city's public housing developments is twice the rate for the city as a whole. In 1995, New Orleans was the eighth most dangerous city in the US, with 2,219.59 violent crimes per 100,000 people. The staggering statistics have caused the City of New Orleans to invite experts from New York City to help reform police methods and tactics in combating crime.

Racial divisions have fueled the crime problem. In 1996, all but 15 of the city's 350 homicide victims were black and the city's sizable African-American community (70%) has complained that more attention is paid to crimes against whites or tourists. In 1996, 10 of the city's 350 murder victims were tourists.

Crime has become such a problem that some French Quarter merchants have erected signs warning tourists that they are entering a "high-crime area." Recent murders sparked a mass march on City Hall. After the murders, City Council voted to increase the police budget by $4 million, with most of the money to be used to buy new equipment and raise starting pay for the police. (Historically, New Orleans has had the lowest starting salaries for police of any major US city.)

NEW ORLEANS TIPS

- ☞ Although the heavily visited French Quarter area is relatively safe day or night, to wander beyond it (even a few blocks away) can be dangerous.

- ☞ Be careful of pickpockets who work in crowded areas, especially in the evening.

- ☞ Avoid going to public parks at night. Extra caution should be used when visiting the Louis Armstrong Park.

- ☞ At night, always take a cab, no matter how short the distance.

- ☞ The area near the Union Passenger terminal at 1001 Loyola Avenue, near the Superdome is dangerous at night. The area is ten minutes away from Canal Street. Extra caution should be employed around Union Station.

- ☞ The Algiers suburb, an industrial area located in the Warehouse District, is crime-ridden and should be avoided.

- ☞ The cemetery north of the French Quarter, where tours of the Voodoo High Priestess are conducted, should be avoided at night.

One thing that has helped reduce juvenile crime in particular in New Orleans is the curfew system. The New Orleans version bars youth under 18 from being out after 8:00 P.M. on school nights, 9:00 P.M. on summer weekdays and 11:00 P.M. on weekends. Police take violators to a special detention center; if a child is picked up three times, his/her parents may wind up in court. According to the city's mayor, youth crime has been reduced by nearly 25% during curfew hours.

AIRPORT

New Orleans International Airport is located 12 miles northwest of the city on I-10. It is within half an hour of the New Orleans Central Business District. The trip from the airport to the city/French Quarter takes roughly 45 minutes. Another facility in the city, the New Orleans Lakefront Airport, serves private, corporate and charter air travelers.

Facilities/Services at New Orleans International Airport

The airport has two terminals: the West Terminal and the East Terminal. The East Terminal houses Concourse A and B and the West Terminal houses Concourse C and D. Both domestic and international flights arrive and depart from the two terminals.

The New Orleans International Airport has a 3,000-space covered parking garage on site for long and short-term parking. All major credit cards are accepted. The facility is guarded 24 hours a day by security guards.

TRANSPORTATION

To/From New Orleans International Airport

Trains, taxis, hotel shuttle buses and rental cars are available for transport to the city center. Flat rate taxi fares into town are $21 for one to three people; and $8 for each extra person (not to exceed five). Pick up is on the lower level of the airport outside baggage claim. Minibuses or airport shuttle buses can take you to your hotel in the city. The official transportation company providing shuttle services for the City of New Orleans to and from the airport is called the Airport Shuttle; airport Shuttle costs $10 each way and they run every 15 minutes 24 hours a day.

Transportation Within New Orleans

Taxis, buses, trains and rental cars are available in the city. Taxis are abundant and public transportation is good, although the French Quarter is best enjoyed on foot. The Regional Transit Authority provides transportation throughout the metro area; the city for $1-1.25. Some routes, including the Streetcar, run 24 hours, while others end at midnight.

 AREA CODE: 504

NEW YORK

CITY

New York (pop. 7.3 million) represents both the best and worst of American culture. There is the majesty of Manhattan with its gleaming towers of glass and steel, but there is also the depressing site of homeless people huddled in their shadows. The sheer size of New York is at the root of most of its problems. But the city somehow manages to bounce back...restoring its title as the world's financial and cultural torch bearer. It is the country's literary and artistic capital, its greatest port, its biggest stock market and convention city, the center for communication and media, as well as the country's biggest industrial city. The revenues of New York businesses exceed the GNP of countries like Canada and Brazil! New York is actually made up of several boroughs: Manhattan, Staten Island, the Bronx, Brooklyn and Queens. Most tourists spend most of their time in Manhattan where most of the hotels and tourist attractions are located. Manhattan itself is divided into several distinct areas. Some of the more recognizable are: the financial district, the Lower East Side, Upper East Side, Greenwich Village, SoHo, Midtown, Upper West Side, the Garment District, and Harlem. **In general, areas to avoid due to high crime are the South Bronx, most of Harlem, Chelsea, Hell's Kitchen, and much of the Lower East Side.**

SECURITY CONCERNS

New York has a worldwide reputation for having a high crime rate, but in some respects it is no longer justified. The city now ranks 15th in violent crimes among U.S. cities, lower than cities like St. Louis and Minneapolis that many people consider safe. The rate is 1,577.44 violent crimes per 100,000 people. The problem with these statistics, however, is that New York feels dangerous and intimidating to many visitors. Muggings are still relatively common, especially in certain high-risk areas. And there is a general callousness among street criminals that can make a simple theft dangerous. A case in point occurred recently when an elderly woman, visiting from Finland, collapsed with a heart attack on a sidewalk in Greenwich Village. One of the passers-by, a woman who had stopped to "help" the ailing tourist, actually proceeded to yank the diamond ring off the tourist's finger instead. The thief then left the elderly visitor writhing on the sidewalk and walked away.

NEW YORK TIPS

☞ A "fake" wallet with about US$20 in it is useful to carry. If robbed, give the mugger the "fake" wallet as criminals are much less likely to become violent if given something. In general, doing whatever the mugger says is the best idea.

☞ Caution is advised in the Broadway area, Upper West Side, Central Park (during the day), the Lower East Side outside of Chinatown, Union Square, Harlem, Times Square, Washington Square and the East Village.

☞ In Manhattan, the following areas are best avoided altogether: Spanish Harlem (El Barrio), Central Park (after dark), Chelsea and areas west of Broadway in Midtown.

☞ If walking after dark, try to walk in the street or as close to the street as possible to allow you to quickly get attention if mugged.

☞ If mugged, immediately hail a cab and go to the nearest police precinct. The cab should not charge. The police probably will not do much more than file a police report, but this is needed for insurance claims.

☞ Pickpockets and purse snatchers are active around in tourist areas and target tourists. Purses should be worn across the body, wallets in the front pocket and expensive jewelry should be left at home.

AIRPORT

New York is served by three major airports. La Guardia and Newark are mostly domestic airports. John F. Kennedy is the major international airport in the region and is one of the busiest in the world. JFK and La Guardia are both located in Queens and Newark is across the Hudson River from Manhattan in New Jersey. These airports collectively handle the world's heaviest passenger traffic; nearly 80 million travelers a year.

Facilities/Services - JFK Airport
Tourist facilities, currency exchange, the post office and business conference facilities are all open from 8 a.m. to 9 p.m.

Facilities/Services - La Guardia
Currency exchange is open 6:30 a.m. to 8:45 p.m. Tourist information and a post office are available.

Facilities/Services - Newark
Currency exchange is open 7 a.m. to 8 p.m. Tourist information and a post office are also available.

To/From JFK
Licensed yellow taxis are often difficult to find, but avoid the so-called gypsy or discount taxis that are plentiful but can be dangerous. A taxi ride to Midtown Manhattan takes about an hour and costs $30. A shuttle bus to Manhattan costs $16.

To/From La Guardia
Only official, metered taxis should be used. A taxi takes about 45 minutes to Manhattan and costs $20. A shuttle to Wall Street takes 40 minutes and costs $20.

To/From Newark
New York is about 45 minutes away by taxi, which costs $40. Shuttle buses to the World Trade Center and Penn Station are $7.

Transportation Within New York
The New York subway has a bad reputation, but in most areas it is safe during the day. Taxis are best used after dark rather than public transportation or walking; be aware that many taxi drivers really do not speak English and may have a hard time finding addresses off the beaten track. There are two kinds of taxis, both licensed and regulated: metered and "gypsy" cabs! Tourists unfamiliar with New York should stick to metered Cabs. They are painted yellow and can be easily hailed on the street or taken from the waiting lines outside the major hotels. Arrange and agree to the fare before hand with unmetered cab companies. Renting a car is not advised due to horrendous traffic, inadequate parking meters and very expensive parking lots.

✆ AREA CODE: 212 (Manhattan)
718 (The Bronx, Queens, Brooklyn, Staten Island); 516 (Long Island); 917 (City-wide for beepers and cellular phones)

ORLANDO

CITY

Orlando (pop. 1.4 million) has long been known as a major tourist location for both American and international travelers. However, the city's economy is on the upswing due to the emergence of many new businesses, over 100 per year. The presence of Disney World—the Magic Kingdom, EPCOT Center and the Disney-MGM Studios—and the Sea World complex draws millions of visitors each year. Disney World draws 100,000 visitors daily; the busiest periods are mid-February to August and from Christmas Day to New Year's Day. Consequently, at these times freeways can be congested and hotel rooms hard to find. The City of Orlando generally is a quiet metropolis with its compact downtown housing a number of commercial enterprises.

SECURITY CONCERNS

In a survey published in December 1996, *Money Magazine* ranked Orlando as the 37th most violent city in the U.S. Even the tourist areas are affected by crime, especially theft. Occasional incidents of theft have even been reported in the Magic Kingdom. Muggings often occur in the parking lots of hotels; usually muggers focus on individuals walking alone to their cars in the evenings. Recently a four-year-old child was abducted by unknown persons from the hotel where her family was staying. The girl, a visitor from Northern Ireland, surfaced 20 hours later unharmed.

Travelers should keep in mind that robbers sometimes stage vehicular "accidents" or breakdown to gain attention/assistance of victims; these good Samaritans are typically robbed when they stop to render assistance. Also, because vehicular break-ins are also a problem, it is inadvisable to leave valuable items in cars, especially if they are in view. There also have been incidents in which window washers have approached cars at stoplights and stolen items through the vehicle's open windows.

AIRPORT

Orlando is serviced by the ultra-modern Orlando International Airport, which is located 12 miles from downtown Orlando, 22 miles from Walt Disney World and 18 miles from Sea World. The airport is located at the junction of State Road 436 (Semoran Boulevard) and 528 (Beeline Expressway). The local police maintain a presence at the facility. An enclosed elevated passenger shuttle system links arrival/departure gates to the tri-level main terminal. There is a 443-room Hyatt Regency Hotel atop the main terminal.

Facilities/Services at Orlando International Airport

A number of restaurants, stores and services are available at this unique-looking airport. Level one of the main terminal contains ground transportation services, including buses and car rentals. Level Two contains the foreign currency exchange, hotel phones and other ground transportation services. Level Three of the terminal contains further foreign currency exchanges, duty free shops and a number of restaurants and shopping facilities, as well as traveler information services. Banking, including ATM machines, a postal area and a business center are available on this level. Customs and Immigration are located at the airside terminals containing gates 1-29 and 60-99. Baggage claim is located on Level 2 of the main terminal. Due to the large volume of travelers handled by this airport, delays clearing Customs and claiming baggage are sometimes a problem.

TRANSPORTATION

To/From the Orlando International Airport

Rental cars, taxis, and private and hotel shuttle buses are available for transport to the city center and hotel locations near Walt Disney World and Sea World. Rental car agencies, Avis, Budget, Dollar and National are located on Level 1 of the main terminal, others are located at off-airport sites. Courtesy shuttles to off-site airport car rental agencies are located on Level 1 also. Taxis are available outside the baggage claim areas on Level 2. The average taxi rates downtown are $27; $40 to Disney World and $26 to International Drive where many hotels are located. Taxi fares to motels along Highway 192 between Walt Disney World and Kissimmee cost $25. By taxi it takes about 25 minutes to reach downtown and 35 minutes to reach Disney World. One-way fares on private shuttle buses are: $12 to International Drive. Local bus #11 run by LYNX (the metro), serves downtown Orlando; the 45-minute journey costs $.75. The bus arrives downtown at the Pine Street terminal.

Transportation Within Orlando

Rental cars, taxis and buses are available in the city. Public transportation is generally safe, but routes are limited and, in general, public transportation does not operate at night. The base fare is $.75. Besides rental cars, taxis are generally the only way to travel at night. It is recommended that taxis be prearranged via the hotel or by phone. Disney shuttle buses connect with official hotels. A private shuttle bus service also can be used on International Drive, connecting the Disney complex and other attractions. To use this service run by Mears Transportation Service call a day ahead. The service costs $7-9 round trip to attractions.

𝒞 AREA CODE: 407

ORLANDO TIPS

☞ It is a wise security precaution to always drive with doors locked and windows rolled up.

☞ The Orlando Airport has a Walt Disney World Gift Shop where tickets to the resort are available. Purchasing tickets may save time.

☞ Areas to avoid are downtown around Gore and Parramore Streets. In the downtown area, avoid walking at night. Also, areas west of the city around the Citrus Bowl can be unsafe, especially after dark.

PHILADELPHIA

CITY

Philadelphia (pop. 4.8 million), located near the Delaware and Schuylkill Rivers, is a bustling commercial and industrial center with one of the largest fresh water ports in the world. Major tourists sites, such as the Liberty Bell, Independence Hall and Carpenter's Hall, are located in the downtown area in the Independence National Historic Park, or the Historic Square Mile. Philadelphia is the "cradle of our nation". Here the Declaration of Independence was drawn up and adopted; the Constitution was approved; George Washington governed as our president here from 1790-97. In the 18th Century, London was the only English speaking city in the world larger than Philadelphia. The city has retained its sense of history. Many of the city's fine museums are located along the Benjamin Franklin Parkway, sometimes called America's Champs-Elysées. Visitor centers are located in the Historic Square Mile, and another fine visitor center is located at 16th and JFK Boulevard at the Penn Center subway station. "Philly" takes pride in its long-standing tradition of intellectual and artistic activity including the world renowned University of Pennsylvania and Temple University, as well as world famous Symphony Orchestra.

SECURITY CONCERNS

Philadelphia faces many of the same crime problems found in other large U.S. Cities. Increasingly, young criminals, many of whom are addicted to crack cocaine, have been a problem. While most crime is confined to seedier areas in northern Philadelphia, incidents happen everywhere. Even more closely-knit areas such as Germantown and Port Richmond have been affected by street crime.

Because it is a major tourist draw, the Historic Square Mile is targeted by criminals who conduct petty thefts and, in some cases, violent acts. This area, bordered by Walnut, Front, 6th and Race Streets and secured by national park rangers, is generally safe to walk in during the day. However, walking in this area after dark is not recommended. Though South Philadelphia, famous for its row houses, is generally safe during the day, seedy pockets exist and, as such, caution should be exercised. Travelers who enter South Philadelphia to visit the neighborhood's renowned Italian restaurants around Ninth Street in the evenings should take taxis and limit exposure on the streets.

AIRPORT

Philadelphia is serviced by the Philadelphia International Airport. The airport, located off Interstate 95, is six miles southwest of Philadelphia. Philadelphia police maintain a generally visible presence at the airport.

PHILADELPHIA TIPS

☞ Use taxis at night as public transportation is sometimes frequented by criminals in the evenings.

☞ Areas generally best avoided are north of the Center City, including areas around Temple University, and areas west of the University of Pennsylvania.

☞ Generally, people staying in the city center should opt not to rent a car due to the congestion and the scarcity of parking spaces.

☞ When visiting Philadelphia's main night life location, the South Street area, stay in well lit and populated sections.

☞ Travelers stand the greatest chance of being pickpocketed on public transportation. Travelers should exercise caution outside major train stations.

☞ Crime is high in nearby Camden, New Jersey, just across the Delaware River, and Chester, Pennsylvania, just south of Philadelphia.

Facilities/Services

The airport offers both tourist information and currency exchange centers. Language translation services are available in Terminal A. Customs and immigration services also are in the vicinity of Terminal A. Tourist centers re open from 7 a.m. to 11 p.m. and currency exchange centers are open from 6:00 a.m. to 8:30 p.m. ATM machines, accepting major credit cards, are located throughout the airport. Conference rooms and fax machines are available. A medical facility is located in Terminal C. A Free shuttle bus connects the domestic and international terminals. On the first floor, travelers will find the airport rail line connection, baggage claim areas, car rental information and other ground transportation services. The second floor contains currency exchanges and other tourist information services. Also, the post office, restaurants and shops are located on this floor.

To/From Philadelphia International Airport

Taxis, shuttle buses, rental cars, a limousine service and a surface rail system are available for transport to the city center. A taxi trip from the airport into the city takes about 30 minutes (longer in rush hour), and costs upwards of $20. A shuttle service called "Limo on Demand" costs about $8 to travel downtown. The rail system operates from the domestic terminal and travels downtown, stopping at the 30th Street Station, 16th Street and the Market Street East near the Greyhound bus terminal. The train, running from 6:10 a.m. to 12:10 a.m. leaves every 30 minutes and takes about 25 minutes to reach its destinations. The fare is $5 if purchased at the ticket booth, and $7 if purchased on the train.

Transportation Within Philadelphia

Taxis, buses, trolleys, subways and rental cars are available in the city. Public transportation, which is generally safe and reliable during the day, is referred to as SEPTA. The subway system is divided into two different zones: the east-west Broad Street zone, and the north-south Market Street zone. Subway and bus fares cost $1.60; transfers and zone changes are $.40. These are exact fares.

✆ AREA CODE: 215

PHOENIX

CITY

Phoenix (pop. 2 million) is the largest city in the southwest and 8th largest in the US. Phoenix covers an enormous area 25 miles long by 40 miles wide — called "A Los Angeles in the desert." Population growth has been over 900% in less than a third of a century. Phoenix enjoys the third fastest economic growth among major cities, behind Austin and Orlando; 25,000 hotel rooms, 80 golf courses, the finest Native American museum in the country (Heard), and dozens of grand hotels, including the famous Arizona Biltmore Hotel designed by Frank Lloyd Wright. The city owes its name to its Native American ancestors. As with the mythical bird that rises from its own ashes, the residents of this city have given new life to an arid plain that has been long left empty to the scorching sun. Phoenix is an oasis in many ways. The city is surrounded by a number of smaller cities with populations over 100,000 such as Tempe, Scottsdale, Mesa, Sun City, and Glendale. Together they comprise the region known as the "Valley of the Sun." The Valley has become a hotspot for millions of tourists.

Many tourists visiting Phoenix venture into the other parts of this wondrous state. Arizona's highest point, near Flagstaff, is 12,655 ft.; its lowest, near Yuma, is only 140 ft. above sea level. In between, Arizona's earth is composed of a diversity of ancient materials configured in astonishing contortions, including dramatic and plunging canyons. There are over 100,000 square miles of dry plains, sizzling desert and wild rivers.

SECURITY CONCERNS

Downtown Phoenix is generally safe although normal precautions should be taken as in any large city. In 1995, Phoenix reported 214 murders, 411 rapes, 3,700 robberies, 7,200 aggravated assaults and 21,000 burglaries. With 80% sunny days making it a city with one of the largest amounts of sunshine in the U.S., Phoenix inhabits are spoiled and cautious. Visitors must carry water in their cars — engine overheating and personal dehydration are commonplace. Problems arise when water is needed; illness and crime can follow.

AIRPORT

Phoenix Sky Harbor International Airport (PHX) is located 3 miles east of downtown. The airport serves as the home to America West Airlines.

PHOENIX TIPS

☛ Places to avoid in Phoenix due to high crime rates include areas west of Black Canyon Freeway and Camelback to Roosevelt Street on the west side.

☛ After dark, avoid south Phoenix and the Maryvale area on the west side.

☛ Downtown is generally safe. The downtown area at night can be busy with basketball, hockey, and cultural events. Take normal precautions against petty theft and street crime. Avoid walking alone in deserted areas.

☛ Limit outdoor exercise during summer months and (frequent) smog alerts. Always carry plenty of water.

Facilities/Services at Sky Harbor

Sky Harbor has three somewhat disjointed terminals (they are listed as Terminals 2, 3, and 4), which can create difficulty for passengers trying to make connecting flights. A bus service is available for travel between terminals. Persons changing terminals should allow for extra time. Currency exchange, ATMs, shops and restaurants are available at the airport.

TRANSPORTATION

To/From Sky Harbor Airport

Taxis, shuttle buses or rental cars are recommended for travel to and from the airport to destinations in the Valley. All major rental car companies are represented at the airport. A taxi ride into downtown Phoenix is less than $12 and takes about 15 minutes. Taxi service to Scottsdale is $25 and a few minutes longer. Shuttle buses, limousines and van services charge under $7 to most areas of Phoenix, and less than $15 to Sun City, Mesa, and other surrounding areas. Valley Metro buses operate every 20 minutes to downtown Phoenix with a fare of $1.25. Bus No. 13 runs from Terminals 3 and 4 to downtown and leaves every 30 minutes, Monday to Friday 5:30 am to 8:00 pm. Cost is $1 and the trip takes 25 minutes.

Transportation Within Phoenix

For most travelers, a taxi or rental car will be the best and easiest way of getting around the Valley. Public transportation is safe but limited outside downtown Phoenix. Fare is $1, and there is no service on Sundays or late at night. The Greyhound bus station is located at 5th and Washington streets. The Amtrak is located at 401 W. Harrison Street.

Rental cars with unlimited free mileage are required for making excursions to monuments of Native American civilizations, old trails of Cochise and Geronimo, shut down silver and copper mines, botanical gardens with more than 10,000 species of desert plants from around the world, and western villages "carved" from the 1800s. Further excursions include the Mogollon Rim (wonderful scenery of wooded mountains, stretches of desert lakes, and wild canyons); Oak Creek Canyon and the charming, former pioneer town of Sedona; the world's largest petrified forest; and of course the Grand Canyon.

✆ AREA CODE: 602

SAN DIEGO

CITY

San Diego (pop. 1.1 million), promoted as "America's Finest City," is the sixth largest city in the US in terms of population. The local climate, a coastal desert, approaches perfection year-round: never too hot, never too cold, rarely rainy. However, San Diego is not all *fun-in-the-sun*. The city has become a thriving center of telecommunications, biotechnology, and medicine. San Diego is also proud to be home to the largest military complex in the world. The city's revitalized downtown offers a mix of historic preservation in the Gaslamp Quarter and state-of-the-art architecture with Horton Plaza, a dramatic shopping and entertainment complex in the heart of downtown. Additionally, two thirds of the avocados consumed in the US are grown here. Tourism ranks third among San Diego's industries, bringing in $3 billion a year. As California's second largest city, San Diego has retained vestiges of Spanish and Mexican, as well as American influences.

San Diego offers superb beaches and parks. Balboa Park is a tropical park of woods, lawns and lakes in the heart of the city; it shelters half a dozen museums and the world famous San Diego Zoo, the richest and most famous zoo in the US, visited by almost four million people annually. Sea World is the huge marine life theme park containing over 5,000 sea creatures, including seals, sea elephants, dolphins, and three killer whales. The Wild Animal Park is one of the finest safari zoos in the US, featuring rhinoceroses, giraffes, lions, zebras, etc. The Natural History Museum arranges whale watching trips.

SECURITY CONCERNS

San Diego has its share of problems, including a heavy flow of illegal immigrants and poor neighborhoods plagued by drugs and crime. However, travelers who stick to the beaten path generally are not confronted with such problems. In 1995, San Diego reported 91 murders, 346 rapes, 3,200 robberies and 7,400 aggravated assaults. Also, almost within view of San Diego's modern skyline lies some of Mexico's worst shantytowns.

San Diego is located 20 miles north of Tijuana, Baja California, Mexico. Persons planning on crossing the border should be aware of a higher criminal threat posed by common criminals, drug users, and drug traffickers in these areas.

SAN DIEGO TIPS

☞ Areas of San Diego best avoided due to higher crime rates are downtown east of 10th avenue and the Greenbelt area of Balboa Park after dark.

☞ Travelers renting cars should be cautious about the models they choose and where they park due to car theft. Popular targets include Ford Mustangs and Thunderbirds, all Chrysler vans and sporty cars like the Dodge Intrepid. Hotel parking lots are frequent theft sites.

☞ Downtown business district can become deserted after working hours.

AIRPORT

San Diego International Airport—Lindbergh Field (SAN) is located two miles west of downtown. Charles Limbergh's immortal *The Spirit of St. Louis* was built in San Diego, which accounts for the airport's name. The airport is currently under major reconstruction to accommodate the rising number of air travelers. San Diego is served by all major airlines. Several airports throughout San Diego County also serve corporate and pleasure aircraft.

Facilities/Services

San Diego's airport has two terminals (East and West) plus an additional area for commuter flights. Persons changing airlines should check for signs advising in which terminal a particular carrier can be found. Allow extra time if changing terminals. Currency exchanges, ATMs, restaurants, and shops are located in each terminal.

TRANSPORTATION

To/From Lindbergh Field

San Diego's airport is served by city buses, various shuttle buses, and taxis. City bus No. 2 and No. 2A arrive and depart every 20 minutes for downtown. The fare per person is $1.50. Shuttle buses, such as Supershuttle and Cloud Nine operate to downtown for $4. Taxi fare to downtown runs around $8.

Transportation Within San Diego

An excellent freeway system makes road travel throughout San Diego County easy. Taxi service, rental cars and tours are readily available. Cars offer the best bet to see the area (make certain you have unlimited mileage!). Remember...not all rental car agencies allow their autos to be driven into Mexico. you'll need to check. San Diego Transit Corporation buses serve the metro area. Fares range from $1-$3. The city bus system is extensive but slow. The San Diego Trolley also provides service in the downtown area, between downtown and the Mexican border at Tijuana, as well as to San Diego's East Country. Fares range from $1 to $1.75. Amtrack passenger trains provide service to and from Los Angeles.

𝒞 AREA CODE: 619

SAN FRANCISCO

CITY

San Francisco (pop. 1.7 million in the metro area) is a world-class city with a truly diverse population. The city is one of the top US tourist spots, as well as major business and arts center. Most of the major tourist spots, Fisherman's Wharf, Chinatown and North Beach, are located in the vicinity of the downtown area. Downtown is centered around Market Street. No trip to California can be called complete without an attentive visit to this joyful, flamboyant city which has inspired so many poets, movie directors, novelists and song writers... from the frontiers of Chinatown...to the panoramic bay scene from the Golden Gate...the high rises of the financial district...to the quaint park of San Salito across the bay...to the vineyards of Napa Valley...to the roller-coaster hills...to the spectacular highway drive to Silicon Valley.

SECURITY CONCERNS

San Francisco has the sixth highest violent crime rates per 100,000 people in the US. The rate of violent crime was 884.3 per 100,000 people in 1995. Most crime is drug-related. Like other major metropolitan area, youth crime also poses a problem. Tourists should be aware that petty theft, purse snatching, muggings and in some cases armed robberies have occurred in tourist areas. In general, travelers should remain in populated, well lit areas and not leave valuables displayed conspicuously in vehicles. There are a large number of street people in San Francisco; some of these people can be menacing, as they conduct an aggressive brand of panhandling. As a general rule, stay clear of street people.

AIRPORT

San Francisco is serviced by the San Francisco International Airport, which is located 15 miles south of the city on the Bayshore Freeway/US 101. Security is high at the facility. As such, travelers should give themselves extra time when checking in. Only ticketed passengers may pass through security checkpoints and continue to boarding areas. The airport is comprised of three terminals: The International Terminal (comprising Concourse D); the South Terminal (comprising concourses A, B, and C); and the North Terminal (comprised of concourses E and F).

Facilities/Services at San Francisco International Airport

Information centers are located on the lower levels of the North and South terminals. The information centers are open from 8:00 AM to 12:00 AM. Currency exchanges, open from 7 AM to 11 PM, and the duty free shop are located in the International Terminal. A nursery and bank can be found on the second floor of the North Terminal. Ground transportation services (including car rentals). hotel information and baggage claim are located on the lower levels of the South and North terminals. ATM machines, accepting Plus, Interlink and Star system cards, are available at the airport. Fax machines are available in each terminal.

SAN FRANCISCO TIPS

☞ Caution should also be exercised day or night when in the Haight-Ashbury, as street people congregating in the area sometimes conduct acts of theft. Lower Haight Street is a particular spot of concern. At night travelers should avoid Golden Gate park and exercise caution when in the Mission District and the Castro district.

☞ Caution should be also exercised when visiting the busy nightlife spots in the SoMa area of south Market Street. Stay in well-lit areas when in this area.

☞ Areas to avoid include Hunter's Point on the southeast waterfront, the Tenderloin and seedier areas west of downtown.

TRANSPORTATION

To/From San Francisco International Airport

Taxis, buses, shuttle services and rental cars are available in the city. Major rental car agencies maintain booths in the lower level of the terminals. Taxis are found on the lower level of the North and South terminals. The taxi fare for the 30-minute ride downtown is about $25-30. In rush hour, travel time can be about 40 minutes. Airporter Shuttles are available to carry travelers to major hotels. The cost is about $8. Private minivans also are available and cost around $15 to take travelers to destinations around the city. The SamTrans (San Mateo County Transit) bus, called the #7F express, travels to downtown San Francisco. The express takes 40 minutes to reach downtown and only allows one small piece of hand luggage to be carried. The cost of the express is $1.75 and it leaves ever 30 minutes. The San Francisco Airporter bus, which costs $8, travels every 15 minutes to Union Square and the Financial District. The Supershuttle and Yellow Airport Shuttle minibuses, which cost about $12-15, pick up passengers every five minutes.

Transportation Around San Francisco

Taxis, buses, shuttle services and rental cars are available in the city. Many travelers use rental cars when in San Francisco, but be aware that traffic is congested and routes can be confusing. In the downtown area, parking is scarce, particularly around Fisherman's Wharf. A number of public transportation networks operate in San Francisco and nearby areas. Along Market Square downtown, MUNI, which operates light rail vehicles, electric buses, motor coaches, trolley and cable cars, and the Bay Area Rapid Transit system (BART), which operates trains, share station concourses that link major points in San Francisco with East Bay and the outer suburbs. The CalTran commuter railway, with a depot at Fourth and Townsend streets (south of Market), links the city with points along the Peninsula south to San Jose. Overall transportation base fares range between $1 and $2.70. Toll booths are in place at the Golden Gate and Bay bridges. The cost is $3 at the Golden Gate Bridge and $1 at the Bay Bridge. The Golden Gate ferry operates from the Ferry Building on Embarcadero, crossing the bay past Alcatraz to Marin County.

✆ AREA CODE: 415

SEATTLE

CITY

Seattle, (pop. 2.5 million), known as the "Emerald City," is a rapidly growing city in the Pacific Northwest. The city is surrounded by water on three sides, making sailboats, seaplanes, and other water craft permanent fixtures of the cityscape. Seattle is the leading fishing port in the U.S. Its deep and well protected Elliot Bay harbor requires no dredging, and it has long been a major Asia-oriented port as well as the principal gateway to Alaska. Its containerized shipping facilities are among the largest in the world. Seattle is also the capital of the aerospace industry. Almost one out of every two airlines now in service in the west first took off from King County International Airport, headquarters of Boeing Corporation. The central area of the city is crowded onto a narrow hilly isthmus between Puget Sound on the west and Lake Washington on the east. The suburbs sprawl to the north, south, and east of Lake Washington, which is spand by a floating bridge. Spectacular mountains dominate the horizons: cascades to the east with Mt Rainier on the southeast and the Olympics to the west. In downtown, most points of interest can be reached by foot, boat or the monorail. However, the landscape is very hilly, which can make even short hikes tiresome. Seattle has several distinct neighborhoods, all of which have their own character. Travelers should be aware that Seattle, and most of the northern Pacific region as well, has only 56 clear days per year. The rest are either cloudy or rainy.

SECURITY CONCERNS

Security concerns in Seattle are typical of other large US Cities. Normal precautions late at night should be taken by all persons, especially those traveling alone. Downtown Seattle is generally safe, but caution is warranted late at night when the streets become deserted. Also at night, the tourist areas of Broadway on Capitol Hill, University Avenue in the University of Washington district (known as the U District), streets under the viaduct at the waterfront and in alleys of Pike Place Market, become prone to street crimes. In 1995, Seattle reported 41 murders, 260 rapes, 2,700 robberies and 2,400 aggravated assaults.

AIRPORT

Seattle-Tacoma International Airport (SEA), the main airport serving Seattle, is located 14 miles south of the city. This large and busy airport, called "Sea-Tac" by the locals, is serviced by more than 30 carriers. Boeing Field–King County International Airport (BFI) is a smaller facility used mainly by private and corporate aircraft. The airport is located approximately 10 minutes closer to town than Sea-Tac.

Facilities/Services
Sea-Tac Airport has all the amenities of a large airport. A tourist information booth can be found in the baggage claim area, ATM machines and currency exchange facilities are located in each terminal, and restaurants and shops are numerous.

TRANSPORTATION

To/From the Sea-Tac Airport
The airport is connected to Seattle by Interstate 5 and travel time by car to downtown is 30-45 minutes depending on traffic. Taxis, shuttle buses and rental cars are available for transport to the city center. A taxi trip from the airport into the city will cost approximately $25. A Gray Line Airport Express operates buses from the major hotels to the airport from 6:00 a.m. to 11:45 pm with departures every 30 minutes. The fare is $7.50 one-way and $13 round-trip. Metro Express City buses to the downtown terminal take about 40 minutes and leave every 15 minutes. The fare is approximately $1.10 to $1.60. Private shuttle bus fare is $18 one-way.

Transportation Within Seattle
Taxis, buses, and rental cars are available in the city. Rental cars are not recommended for use in downtown Seattle due to a shortage of parking and traffic congestion. Roads also become slippery when wet and icy during winter. Public transportation is generally safe and reliable during the day. Bus service downtown is free from 6:00 am to 7:00 pm. At other times the fare is around $1. When going outside the downtown free zone, pay the fare to the driver when leaving the bus; pay as you enter the bus when going into downtown. A monorail shuttles between Westlake Mall and the Seattle Center every 15 minutes. The fare is $0.90 each way.

Amtrak trains and buses also run to surrounding cities each day. The Amtrak trail station is located at 303 S. Jackson Street. The Greyhound bus terminal is located at 8th Avenue at Stewart Street. Water ferry service to Canada, Bremerton, Bainbridge, as well as other nearby islands, also is available. The Washington State Ferry System provides passenger and vehicle service to Bremerton and Winslow daily throughout the year. It offers splendid service and low fares. Clipper Navigation offers service between Seattle and Victoria aboard the catamaran Victorian Clipper. The time is 2 1/2 hours each way and it is daily year round. Within easy reach, the tourist will find the magnificent forests of Olympic National Park, while the snowfields of Snoqualinie National Forests await the skiing enthusiast.

SEATTLE TIPS

☛ Areas of Seattle that have higher crime rates include Ranier Valley, Bell Town, and the Central district.

☛ Late at night Pioneer Square and First Avenue are particularly troublesome due to criminal elements.

☛ It is wise to pack appropriate rain gear.

ST. LOUIS

CITY

St. Louis (pop. 600,000), perched just below the confluence of the Missouri and Mississippi rivers, is the 17th largest city in the US. In the mid-19th century, St. Louis became knows as the "Gateway to the West," as this is where westward expansion began. St Louis has spread widely from its original site on the west bank of the Mississippi River, and its Metropolitan area now occupies the rolling hills and undulating plains on both sides of the Mississippi. The flood plain of the river, now constricted between artificial leaves, serves to separate the main part of the Metropolis in Missouri from its less extensive suburbs in Illinois. The stream, however, is spanned by seven bridges that connect the various parts of the city as well as the two states. It was from St. Louis that Meriwether Lewis and William Clark started out on their famous expedition to Oregon in 1804. St. Louis at one time was referred to as the City of Jazz; it has been the home of great paddlewheelers stemming the current of "Old Man River." St. Louis has also been referred to as a pioneer in the history of aviation. It was the Spirit of St. Louis in which Charles Lindbergh made the first solo flight across the Atlantic from west to east in 1927. Did you know that the first ice cream cone and hot dog were "exhibited" at the St. Louis World's Fair in 1904?

Today, the city boasts many attractions, among them the eye-catching Gateway Arch, Union Station and the Missouri Botanical Garden. Downtown, Midtown and the Central West End contain many of the top tourist attractions in St. Louis. St. Louis still possesses the world's largest brewery (Anheuser-Busch). St. Louis is "summed up" or symbolized by its Gateway Arch. Two million visitors each year are attracted to this stainless steel archway that is dedicated to the memory of the pioneers who won the West.

SECURITY CONCERNS

Security concerns in St. Louis are similar to those in many other large US cities. Downtown St. Louis has a higher crime rate than its suburbs, although the area is relatively safe during the day. At night, petty theft and street crimes are high near the riverfront area, which is also the main nightlife district. In 1994, St. Louis reported 204 murders, 275 rapes 5,100 robberies, 6,800 aggravated assaults.

ST. LOUIS TIPS

☞ Walking around downtown at night is inadvisable. It is preferable to take a cab.

☞ It is best to avoid public transportation at night, especially when traveling alone, due to risk of crime.

☞ Be careful at the bus station, which is known for a high rate of petty theft and muggings.

☞ At night it is best to avoid east St. Louis and the Central West End, particular Washington Avenue and areas north and west of it.

AIRPORT

Lambert St. Louis International Airport (STL) is located 10 miles northwest of the city. The airport serves as the home to Trans World Airlines (TWA). The tourist information desk is there daily from 10:00 a.m - 8:00 p.m.; it provides free maps and up-to-date city information. Fax machines and conference rooms are available. A post office in the main terminal is open 8:30 a.m. - 4:30 p.m. Monday thru Friday.

Facilities/Services

Lambert St. Louis International Airport has one main terminal that branches off into five concourses. The airport is generally not congested and easy to use; however, persons having to make connecting flights are often left with long walks. Currency exchange, ATMs, shops, and restaurants are all available throughout the airport.

TRANSPORTATION

To/From Lambert Field

Travelers should expect travel delays outside the airport because of road construction. Temporary boundaries and drop-off/pick-up spots have been made. Taxis are readily available outside the airport. The drive time to downtown is 30 minutes and fares run around $20. Other transportation means include a Jet Port van, which departs from the airport every 20 minutes from 6:30 am to 10:30 pm. The fare is $8. The city's MetroLink also connects the airport to downtown; the trip takes 35 minutes. The light rail is generally fast and clean, and the fare is only $1.

Transportation Within St. Louis

Taxis or rental cars are the easiest way of getting around St. Louis. City buses run throughout the city and to the suburbs, but they are not recommended because they are often slow and they operate infrequently. The MetroLink (light rail) is safe and reliable, and the fare is $1 per ride. Travelers should be aware that the city's highways become very congested during rush hours. Greyhound buses and Amtrak train service also are available in St. Louis for travel to other cities.

 AREA CODE: 314

WASHINGTON, D.C.

CITY

Washington, DC (metro area pop. 4 million) is perched on the banks of the Potomac River near the Mason-Dixon line which divides the North from the South. The city was designed in 1800 but, aside from the government buildings, not much was built before the 20th century. Some of the country's most historic and visited landmarks are along the Mall: The White House, The Capitol, Arlington Cemetery, Washington Monument, Lincoln Memorial, Jefferson Memorial...and make Washington a cosmopolitan city like no other in the world. The city's museums are unmatched—the Smithsonian Institute and the National Gallery of Art lack nothing that the visitor could ask for.

There are four quadrants in the city — northwest, northeast, southeast, southwest — and each has its own qualities. North-south streets are numbered and east-west ones are lettered; there are also several dozen broad diagonal avenues named for states. One thing to remember is that every address has the quadrant listed after the street name, such as 1200 Texas Avenue NW; 1200 Texas Avenue NW is a great distance from 1200 Texas Avenue SE, and the two neighborhoods are very different. Most all of the tourist sites are in the northwest quadrant inside the I-495 Beltway which is a heavily congested freeway running around the city. Georgetown and DuPont Circle are also popular areas. **In general, areas to avoid include all of the northeast, southeast and southwest quadrants of the city.**

SECURITY CONCERNS

Washington has a deservedly bad reputation for violent crime. The city has for years ranked at or near the top in murders per capita. The city currently ranks fourth among the largest U.S. Cities for violent crime. However, the vast majority of violent crimes are committed within the impoverished areas of town. The Mall, Capitol and other tourist attractions are safe during the day. At night they are largely deserted, so exercise caution if visiting these areas after dark. The crime rate has been declining slightly for the past three years, but the murder rate bucked a national trend and rose slightly in 1996 to 360 murders. For the traveler, armed robbery is the most pressing threat, although tourists are not usually victimized. Two recent armed robberies against tourists in the Metro (subway) prompted police to increase security there.

AIRPORTS

Washington, DC is served by two major airports: Dulles and National. Many people also fly into Baltimore/Washington International, which is approximately 1 hour north of the city. Most international flights come into Dulles, although some also arrive at National. Dulles is located 25 miles west of the city in Virginia and National is located just west of the Mall on the Potomac River.

WASHINGTON, D.C. TIPS

☞ The northeast, southeast and southwest quadrants of the city are much poorer and have higher crime than the northwest.

☞ Avoid straying off main streets in the Adams Morgan neighborhood after dark due to the threat of mugging. A modicum of caution is also advised on back streets in Georgetown at night.

Facilities/Services at Dulles Airport
Most international flights and many longer domestic flights come into Dulles. Business and medical facilities are available 24-hours a day, as is the post office. Currency exchange is open from 7 a.m. to 9 p.m. Tourist facilities are open from 10 a.m. to 9 p.m.

Facilities/Services at National Airport
National is almost exclusively a domestic airport. Postal and medical facilities are open from 8:30 a.m. to 5 p.m. weekdays. Tourist facilities are open from 9 a.m. to 9 p.m. weekdays. Business conference facilities are available.

To/From the Dulles Airport
Dulles Airport is located in Virginia and the trip to the city center takes 40 minutes by taxi. Fares run about $40. An express van to eight major hotels takes about 1 hour and costs $16.

To/From National Airport
National is located within the Washington city limits so a cab ride to the city center takes only 15 minutes; the cost is $12. A hotel van takes 20 minutes and costs $8. The Metro takes 12 minutes and costs $1.

Transportation Within Washington
When seeing the tourist sites around the Mall, many people simply walk. Taxis are plentiful and relatively inexpensive in the area also. Drivers may attempt to overcharge, so check the zone chart when they quote a fare. Public transportation on the Metro subway is safe, clean and reliable. Most places can be reached for $1. 10 a.m. to 3 p.m., although some fares nearly double during rush hour. Rental cars are not recommended due to heavy traffic, poor parking facilities and the high incidence of theft from vehicles.

Guided tours are excellent. Horse and carriage tours of the Washington Mall (Charlie Horse Tours) leave from the Museum of National History. Trips in a mule drawn barge along the C&O last 90 minutes on the Georgetown. Replicas of turn-of-the-century street cars are called the best sightseeing tours in town (Old Trolley Tours). There are shuttle systems and mini-cruises along the Potomic.

 AREA CODE: 202

ATHENS

CITY

Athens is the Greek capital and has a population of more than three million. It lies on a small plain that extends southward to the Saronic Gulf, a branch of the Aegean Sea. Athens is surrounded by mountains and is the center of the Greek government...the old palace of the kings of Greece which is now used to handle the parliament. Athens is also the primary financial and commercial center in Greece and is the focus of the road and rail systems. Light engineering, textiles, chemicals, and cement making are important businesses, as are distilling, milling, tanning, tobacco preparation, and the processing of other local agricultural products. Athens is the principal cultural and economical center of Greece and has a university, founded in 1837, as well as many professional schools. The city is note-worthy for its fine archeological collections, especially those contained in the national Archeological Museum. The city's most important cultural remains, however, are its numerous architectural monuments, dating from ancient times and later periods. Foremost among these is the Acropolis, the ancient fortified hill on which stands the Parthenon. To the south of the Acropolis is the Theatre of Dionysos, and to the west, the Council Chamber (Areopagus) in which St. Paul spoke.

The city, while scenic, suffers from congestion and pollution. Security conditions in the city are primarily affected by sporadic terrorist attacks, general crime, and frequent demonstrations and strikes.

CRIME

Crime in Athens is low compared to other European cities. Petty thefts, such as pickpocketing and purse snatching are not widespread but have increased. An influx of immigrants, mainly from poverty-stricken Albania, and increased drug use are blamed for the increase. Violent criminal acts are unusual.

Terrorism: Athens is the primary center for terrorist activity in Greece.

Strikes/Protests: Athens is plagues by frequent strikes and demonstrations. In the past two years, farmers' strikes, work slowdowns and shop closing have all been held to protest economic policies. Strikes have shut down banks, disrupted telecommunications, buses, trains and postal service and caused power outages. Periodic minor, non-violent anti-American protests have also been held in front of the US Embassy.

ATHENS TIPS

☛ Travelers should maintain vigilance around Omonia Square, an area where Asian refugees congregate. Crime rates are also higher in the port of Piraeus and in Exarchia. Such crowded Athens sites as the Plaka and the weekly flea market are magnets for pickpockets and purse snatchers.

☛ Athens is the most polluted city in Europe. During summer months, the city experiences almost unbearably high levels of air pollution, referred to as "Nefos." Persons with respiratory and heart problems should take precautions when pollution reaches critical levels.

☛ Greece has very severe penalties (including lengthy prison terms) for those convicted of smuggling antiquities. Travelers should be sure they do not take historic objects from Greece.

TRANSPORTATION

There are no specific security problems with using public transportation in Athens. In general, the safest and most popular means of public transportation in Athens is the taxi. However, it can be difficult to find taxis during rush hours, and overcharging is common. Licensed (as opposed to gypsy) cabs are yellow. City buses and a single-line subway are also fairly reliable. Travelers should note that ELA guerrillas have in the past bombed buses and bus stations in Athens. Because taxis are such a popular mode of transportation, and because they are often difficult to find, it is recommended that private ground transportation be arranged in advance with a reputable company.

EMERGENCY CONTACTS

Medical: Medical facilities in Greece are adequate. The International Association for Medical Assistance to Travelers (IAMAT) has identified the following facilities as meeting its professional standards:

IAMAT Center, 8 Marni Street; T: 822-90331681-4274.

IAMAT Center, 167 3rd September Street; T: 274-385

IAMAT Center (near Athens Airport), Afxentiot 7, Kalamaki; T: 984-1499/984-8228.

Police: The Athens police are well trained and generally responsive to the needs of foreigners.

However, emergency response is often hampered by traffic tie-ups. The police emergency telephone number is 100. The non-emergency telephone number is 171.

US Government: United States Embassy, 91 Vasilissis Sophias Blvd.

T: 30-1-2951 or 721-8401.

BEIJING

CITY

Beijing (pop. 12 million) is the capital and the country's most conservative city. Its Chaoyang district is home to most of the foreign resident community and many first-class hotels. Security in Beijing is mainly affected by general criminal activity and the consequences of foreigners inadvertently breaking Chinese laws. The Chinese government does not tolerate much in the way of political dissent. International security conditions are affected by wide spread competition and rapidly rising crime. Crime is, however, the current bogeyman on which the government is focusing most of its attention. "Operation Strike Hard" launched in April 1996, is a repressive police action targeted at known and suspected criminals and has resulted in at least 2,500 people being executed so far. The crimes punished range from murder to high-level corruption to petty theft. The focus of the operation is now moving towards pornography so any material which might possibly be construed as such should be left at home.

CRIME

The crime rate in Beijing is low when compared to other major metropolitan areas around the world. However, reforms in the economy have led to greater freedom and openness, as well as greater economic inequality. This inequality has contributed to large increases in crime. In fact, Beijing's crime rate has risen at an average of 10 percent per year for the last decade. In the past, criminals considered foreigners off-limits because of the severe penalties for attacking visitors. However, this has changed, and criminals have come to view foreigners as potentially lucrative targets. Most crimes are non-violent, e.g. pickpocketing, petty theft, and scams. Stealing mobile phones and mobile phone numbers is also a growing problem. Tourist areas and other crowded places are the most common areas for petty crimes. Gangs of pickpockets prey on unsuspecting tourists at the city's historic monuments, temples, hotel lobbies, bars, restaurants, public transportation hubs and parks. Also, because there is little or no credit in China, everyone is aware that most travelers carry large amount of cash.

BEIJING TIPS

- ☞ Surveillance is a normal activity in China and visitors should be prepared for such monitoring. Travelers should expect their conversations to be monitored on the telephone, in hotel rooms and in restaurants. Foreigners have been detained or expelled for engaging in improper political activities, including discussions with Chinese citizens and importing of political material. Documents may be seized if the government deems them inappropriate. This includes religious, pornographic and political material. Travelers should always carry either their passport or a photocopy. The police will hold foreigners for questioning if they do not have proper identification.

- ☞ Areas with higher crime rates include the central district of Chongwen and the northwest district of Iiaidian.

- ☞ Travelers are cautioned to avoid brining Chinese nationals (especially women) to their hotel rooms, as authorities will assume that something illegal is taking place. It is preferable to meet acquaintances in the lobby or in a cafe instead.

- ☞ It is recommended that you eat at hotel restaurants, as the food is generally better, communication is easier and you are less likely to be overcharged.

AIRPORT

Security at Beijing Airport (PEK) is adequate although not equivalent to Western standards. Security is provided by two units, the Beijing Capital Airport Public Security Branch and Armed Security Police Troop. Like all other Chinese airports, Beijing Airport suffers from outdated equipment, poorly trained personnel and the general substandard quality of service endemic to the Chinese aviation industry. In the past three years, 15 hijackings or attempted hijackings of domestic Chinese airliners have been reported. Hijackers generally demand the aircraft to be flown to Taiwan where they can seek political refuge. In most cases, there has been no violence. Chinease authorities have instructed flight crews to forcefully resist any hijacking attempts.

TRANSPORTATION

The airport is located 17 miles east of the center of the city and is a 40 minute drive from the city. It is served by taxis and buses but not rental cars, as foreigners are not allowed to drive. Unless you speak Chinese, lack of clear communications can lead to security problems. Therefore, the best way to get from the airport to the city is via private car arranged in advance through a reputable company. There are no specific problems with public transportation in Beijing. Travelers are advised to avoid unmarked taxis.

EMERGENCY CONTACTS

Police: A strong and growing police presence keeps Beijing's streets orderly. The total number of police is 4,500-5,000 officers. Few of them speak anything but Chinese, but most are helpful in spite of the language barrier. The telephone number for the Police Foreign Control Unit is 831-7303, or 831-7347 for an English speaker.

US Government: United States Embassy, Xiu Shui Dong Jie 3, Beijing 100600, T: (86) (1) 532-3831.

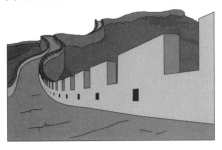

BERLIN

CITY

Berlin is a city no longer divided by a wall, but the divisions caused by the wall have not completely disappeared. There is still tension between "Ossics" (East Berliners) and "Wessics" (West Berliners), mostly over the perceived wealth of the latter and the cost of raising living standards for the former. In order to unify the city, businesses and government are rebuilding Potsdamer Platz, which was formerly divided by the Wall, and other historic areas. Berlin is currently a mass of construction sites, but its people are generally positive about all the development and hope the city will once again become a world center for politics and commerce. Security conditions in the city are primarily affected by a moderate crime rate, extremist violence, mass demonstrations against economic policies and criminal activity in the city's ethnic enclaves.

CRIME

The crime rate in Berlin has risen dramatically since the 1989 fall of the Berlin Wall. Berlin has the highest crime rate in the country, prompting many residents to stay indoors at night, something that they did not have to do when the city was divided. Genuine fear of crime and extra security precautions are now widespread in the city, and security guards accompanied by guard dogs are a regular sight in the subways

Some 580,000 crimes were reported in 1993, up 5% from 1994. Alarmingly, 78.4% of those crimes are believed to have been committed by individuals aged 12-21. There were 245 murders in 1994, which is considerably fewer murders than take place in comparably-sized U.S. cities, but still far more than the 175 killings which took place in London during the same period. Statistics are not available for 1995 or 1996, but the number of murders is believed to have increased substantially. Household robbery is up 15.9% from 1994, and street theft increased by 23.2% from 1994 to 1995. The city is home to gangs from Russia, Romania, Poland, Vietnam and the former Yugoslavia. The Russian mafia is by far the most active, with ethnic Russians in Berlin increasingly becoming the victims of blackmail, kidnappings and assassinations. Vietnamese cigarette smugglers are also gaining notoriety in Marzahn and Grossbeeren districts; 50 smugglers have been killed in power struggles between January and September 1996. Bonn is trying to deport both Russian and Vietnamese gangsters, but Moscow and Hanoi are doing little to cooperate.

BERLIN TIPS

- Visitors are most likely to be affected by petty crimes which have increased in tourist areas. Over 40 cases of pickpocketing are reported every day. Thefts from hotel rooms, even at luxury hotels, have also been reported.

- Crime Notes/Places to Avoid: The former east Berlin's large and centrally located Alexanderplatz District is especially thick with thieves. Numerous petty criminals also work the Ku 'Damm shopping district.

- In the eastern sections of the city, gangs of skinheads sometimes attack non-Caucasians without provocation. Conversely, Turkish and other foreign street gangs assault young men with short haircuts on the assumption that they belong to Germany's ultra right-wing groups.

- Organized Crime: Organized crime syndicates maintain a heavy presence in Berlin. Gangland shoot-outs and small bombings are relatively common.

- Demonstrations: There were several mass (200,000+ people) demonstrations in Berlin in 1996.

AIRPORT

Security at Tempelhof Airport (EDDI/THF) is the responsibility of the German Police, under the direction of the National Aviation Authority.

Transportation To/From Airport
The airport is located 7 miles/1 km southeast of Berlin. Taxis, buses and the subway provide service to the airport. The drive time to Berlin is approximately 10-15 minutes. All taxis are metered. There are no specific security problems with the transportation systems, although skinheads and delinquent youths sometimes harass passengers on the subway at night.

Transportation Within Berlin
There are no major security problems with the public transportation system. In an effort to increase security on the subways, the city spends US$17 million a year on private security guards accompanied by attack dogs. Taxis are a generally safe means of transportation.

Hotels
There are no reported security problems with the Berlin Hilton, Berlin Plaza or Berlin Palace Hotels.

EMERGENCY CONTACTS

Medical: The International Association for Medical Assistance to Travellers (IAMAT) has identified the following facility as meeting its professional standards and having English-speaking doctors: Institut fur Tropenmedizin, Engeldamm 61-64, Berlin; T: 274-6790, T: 431-3454.

Police: The police force is capable of ensuring basic civil order. However, the quality of police assistance varies from the eastern to western half of the city. Policemen in the east tend to be less well-trained than their western counterparts. In an effort to alleviate this problem, high ranking policemen from the west have been transferred east to help integrate the system. Police in central districts wear badges indicating which languages they speak. The police emergency telephone number is 110.

US Government: US Embassy, Neustaedtische Kirchstrasse 4-5, Berlin; T: (49-30) 238-5174. Consular Section: Clayellee 170, Berlin; T: (49-30) 832-9233.

DUBLIN

CITY

Dublin (pop. 1 million) is Ireland's capital city and the home to not only the largest university (Trinity College) but also to a great number of the nation's young people. The city, which is built on the River Liffey, has many pleasant canals, public houses, and the charming and bohemian Grafton Street area, right near Trinity College. It's name in Irish is Baile Atha Cliath (town of the Hurdle Lord); its conventional name is derived from the original Irish Dubh Linn, "black pool." Dublin was a small town until the 18th Century. It retains a rural flavor in part because of the building activity during the late 1700s, which resulted in low buildings, square, and wide streets. Few existing structures predate this period. While Dublin is a small town in comparison to many American cities, it is beginning to suffer from many of the same problems facing US cities, albeit on a much smaller scale. The main security concern in the city is crime, much of it spawned by unemployment and drugs. Several organized crime groups operate in the city.

CRIME

Ireland's image as a peaceful backwater country, isolated from European problems of crime and drugs is no longer accurate. While Ireland's crime rate is far worse than it was 10 years ago, Ireland is still a fairly safe place compared with the United States. Murder rates in Ireland are more than 500% lower than those in the United States. Dublin has more crime than elsewhere in Ireland, but violent crimes are still comparatively rare. The primary crime threat to visitors comes from pickpockets, purse-snatchers, and other petty thieves. Thieves particularly target tourists' cars for break-ins, since many tourists leave valuables inside their cars when parked. Dublin is now home to as many as 5,000 heroin addicts who surely contribute to the city's petty theft problem.

Organized Crime: Organized crime in Ireland is almost exclusively involved in the drug trade and, consequently, presents no direct threat to visitors. Be aware that Ireland's membership in the European Union has proven to be a godsend to drug profiters. Ireland's location at the western edge of Europe where its wild coastline have made it an ideal site for larding cargoes or drugs and guns. And its lack of custom barriers has made Ireland a criminal way station for smuggling illicit goods around to the rest of Europe.

Terrorism: Over the past 25 years, isolated terrorist attacks have occurred inside the Republic of Ireland, although the majority of incidents have occurred along the border with Northern Ireland. In general, both the IRA and Loyalist paramilitary groups confine their attacks to Northern Ireland. The IRA has, at times, conducted robberies of financial institutions and armored cars within Ireland to finance its operations. Attacks by loyalist paramilitary groups within the Republic of Ireland, which had been predicted in retaliation for recent IRA strikes, have failed to materialize.

AIRPORT

Security at Dublin Airport (EIDW/DUB) is adequate. While the airport has been mentioned in several bombing threats issued by Protestant paramilitary groups in the past, none have ever been carried out.

The airport is located 6 miles/10 kms north of the city. The facility is served by taxis, express buses, and local buses. Taxis are available at the front of the terminal; the ride to town takes 20-30 minutes, and costs about 9 Irish pounds, with added charges for each extra passenger and for baggage. Express bus service to bus areas, the control bus station, is available every 35 minutes, 8:10 a.m.. - 9:25 p.m.; the trip takes 20-25 minutes and costs 2.30 Irish pounds. Public bus AIA leaves every 30 minutes, 7 a.m. - 11:20 p.m., and takes about 30 minutes. For those with rental cars, the route into the city is very well-marked.

EMERGENCY CONTACTS

Medical: Medical facilities in Ireland are adequate. The International Association for Medical Assistance to Travellers (IAMAT) has recognized the following facilities in Dublin as meeting its professional standards:

IAMAT Center, 54 Woodbine Road; T: (1) 269-1581.

International Vaccination Center, 34 Grafton Street, Blackrock; T: (1) 671-9200.

Police: The Irish National Police, the Gardai, is a good police force capable of maintaining the peace and the safety of visitors. The nationwide police, fire, and medical emergency number is 999.

US Embassy: United States Embassy, 42 Elgin Road, Ballsbridge; T: 353-1-668-8777; F: 353-1-668-9946.

DUBLIN TIPS

☞ Travelers should be attentive if exploring the Ringsend/Sandymount area on foot, especially after dark. While this area is not as dangerous as inner-city areas in US cities, crime has increased 220% here in the last four years.

☞ It is believed that the IRA receives significant financial support from some Irish-Americans living in the US; consequently, the IRA would not intentionally target American citizens.

HONG KONG

COUNTRY/CITY

Hong Kong (pop. 6.3 million) is a developed and stable island/city which reverts to Chinese rule on July 1, 1997. Tensions between China and Britain regarding the hand-over continue and escalate as Beijing tries to test Hong Kong's population to democratic ideals. In fact, shipping billionaire Tung Chee-hwa has already been selected by Beijing as the new chief executive of Hong Kong after the hand-over. Hong Kong has witnessed sporadic pro-democracy and anti-Chinese protests like the one on November 3, 1996, when thousands marched on the Xinhua building, which houses China's news agency, to demand the release of democracy dissident Wang Dan. No violence was reported. Tensions continue with Japan over the Diaoyu (Senkaku in Japan) islands, which are claimed by both countries. Numerous anti-Japanese protests have taken place in the past few months, but with no serious violence. Overall, Hong Kong remains safe for visitors and residents alike. Security conditions are affected by a slowly rising crime rate. Credit card theft rings are another growing problem.

CRIME

Crime in Hong Kong is low in comparison to other major cities worldwide, with a rate of 1,484 crimes per 100,000 people. Overall crime fell 9.7% in the first half of 1996, with 1/3 of the cases involving only illegal immigration. The number of robberies, burglaries, kidnappings and murders declined while assaults, rapes and serious drug offenses increased. Theft, especially car theft, is the largest single problem in the city-state. Most thefts occur in tourist spots, shopping centers and subway stations. On December 3, 1996, a woman was robbed of $690,000 in cash in the central business district. Crimes of this sort are unusual as there is usually an armed police presence in crowded areas of the city. Police suspect that this robbery was not random, but rather the product of extensive criminal surveillance. Residential theft is also increasing in areas where Western business people and diplomats make their home. A recent spate of robberies at homes of the rich and famous has people improving their home security systems and hiring guards. There have been several recent cases in which robbers have broken into homes, tied up the residents and made off with thousands, and sometimes millions of dollars of cash and jewels. The Crown colony's reputation as a haven for pickpockets is still justified. The problem became so acute earlier this year that the Japanese Consulate began handing out warning leaflets to Japanese nationals traveling to the territory.

Credit Card Theft: Hong Kong is the center of credit card fraud in the Pacific area.

AIRPORT

Kai Tak International Airport (HKG) is the world's third busiest airport in terms of international passengers. Police have issued a warning that crime syndicates from India and South America are increasingly stealing luggage. Some instances of drug trafficking have also been reported at the airport.

HONG KONG TIPS

☞ Visitors are cautioned to guard their purses and wallets, especially in the Hang Kow Street restaurant district, Wan Chai, and in the popular Mongkok market. Pickpockets re common in crowded downtown areas and on the public transportation system.

☞ Travelers are advised to take extra measures to safeguard their credit cards, including guarding their credit card numbers, at all times. Criminals sometimes copy the cards of unwary customers waiting to pay for their purchases.

TRANSPORTATION

Transportation To/From Airport
The airport is located in Kowloon, 4 miles/6.4 kms northeast of Hong Kong. There is a regular shuttle bus that operates between the central district of Hong Kong Island, Tsimshatsui (Kowloon) and the airport. There are also metered taxis available. The most convenient mode of transportation is by private car arranged through a reputable company.

Transportation Within Hong Kong
Public transportation is widely used because of Hong Kong's notoriously congested traffic. The territory has a highly developed transportation system that is clean, efficient, safe and dependable. Metered taxis are readily available in most areas of the territory.

HOTELS

Hong Kong is home to numerous world-class hotels. There are no reported security problems with the JW Marriott Hotel, the Regal Hong Kong or the Park Lane.

EMERGENCY CONTACTS

Medical: Good medical facilities are available and there are many Western-trained physicians. The following facilities have qualified medical personnel and doctors who speak English: Admiralty Doctors' Group, 246-249 Admiralty Center, 16 Harcourt Road, T: (852) 2528 1231; CHC Group Medical Practice, 33 Queens Road, Central #901, Melbourne Plaza, T: (852) 2525 8158; Hong Kong Adventist Hospital, 40 Stubbs Road, T: (852) 2574 6211.

Police: The Royal Hong Kong Police Force (RHKPF) is comprised of 33,000 well trained policemen. Despite recent reports of corruption, the force remains well equipped and capable of providing effective assistance. The emergency number is 999.

US Government: American Consulate General, 26 Garden Road, Hong Kong, T (852) 523-9011, FAX: (852) 845-4845; American Citizen Services: (852) 2841-2323.

ISTANBUL

CITY

Home to 11 million people, historic Istanbul is situated at the mouth of the Bosphorous Straits, at the point where Europe meets Asia. This ancient city is symbolic of the confluence of East and West. Today, the city is Turkey's main commercial, industrial, and intellectual center, as well as a popular tourist destination. Security conditions in Istanbul are affected by terrorist attacks, crime, and drug trafficking. Turkey's unsettled disputes with regional neighbors Greece, Syria and Kurdish separatists pose continuing challenges for government. Economic woes including high inflation, unemployment and budget deficits plague the city and country. Turkish troops continue to act against Kurdistan Worker's Party (PKK) rebels in southeastern Turkey. Travelers should be aware that PKK reprisal strikes in Istanbul remain a possibility.

Crime: While Istanbul has less crime than many Western cities, street crimes such as pickpocketing and purse-snatching are fairly common; local pickpockets use diversion tactics which include staging a "fight," spilling something on the target, bumping into the victim, or stopping the target to request assistance in order to create a distraction while the robbery takes place. While violent crime is still fairly rare, muggings take place frequently in the city.

Terrorism: Organizations have been responsible for more than 100 terrorist bombings in Istanbul since the beginning of 1995, some directed at tourist targets. Terrorist elements also engage in sporadic gunfights with police.

Drug Trafficking: Istanbul is a primary hub of an international smuggling route that accounts for 80% of the heroin going to US and European markets. Most of the drugs arrive through the city's port. The drug trade has spawned some violence in Istanbul.

AIRPORT

Security is tight at Istanbul's Ataturk Airport (IST), located 15 miles/24 kms southwest of the downtown area. The military and police are charged with maintaining airport security.

ISTANBUL TIPS

☞ Visitors should minimize time spent in and around military and police facilities, government buildings, and political party headquarters and rallies due to increased likelihood of terrorist activity.

☞ Caution is warranted for persons visiting tourist attractions and eating in restaurants that cater to foreigners. If eating in hotel restaurants, stick to eateries lacking direct street access.

☞ Some persons, usually traveling alone, have been drugged and robbed in Istanbul, sometimes by French or English-speaking foreigners. Travelers should be careful to supervise their drinks at all times.

☞ Avoid nightclubs which invite visitors to "just take a look inside." Once inside, the traveler is not allowed to leave without paying a huge price; force is sometimes used to obtain the money. Local police have often refused to assist tourists in these instances.

☞ Foreigners are warned to avoid night clubs in the Istanbul districts of Beyoglu and Taksim.

Transportation To/From Airport

Ataturk Airport is serviced by shuttle buses, taxis and trains. Public buses, which run intermittently to the city, should be avoided as they have been targeted by both thieves and terrorists in the past. Travel time from the airport to the city center is about one hour, depending on traffic. It is advised that travelers pre-arrange ground transportation through a reputable company, in order to minimize security risks.

Transportation in Istanbul

While official taxis may be used to transit the city, a more secure alternative is pre-arranged transportation like that described above, employing a driver knowledgeable about local conditions. Due to the risk of robbery, gypsy cabs should be avoided. It is recommended that travel itineraries and transportation arrangements be kept confidential to reduce vulnerability to terrorists.

Hotels: There are no specific problems with security at first class hotels in Istanbul. Due to a recent surge in terrorist activity, many hotels have increased their security measures.

The following bars in Istanbul are known to cheat tourists:

- Karnaval, Beyoglu district
- Club 14, Beyoglu district
- Club Balim (near British Consulate)
- Carosel, Taksim district
- Beyaz Saray (The White House), Beyoglu district
- Meric Disco Bar, Beyoglu district
- 1001 GECE (1001 Nights), Beyoglu district

EMERGENCY CONTACTS

Medical: Most medical facilities in Istanbul are inadequate by Western standards. Two acceptable hospitals in the city are:

American Bristol Hospital...and
The International Hospital

Police: Police in Istanbul are adequate. Most officers do not speak English. The nationwide police emergency number is 055.

US Government: United States Consulate General: 104 Mesrutiyet Caddesi
T: (90) (212) 251-3602

JOHANNESBURG

CITY

Jo'burg, as locals call Johannesburg (pop. 1.7 million), is a modern city sitting on a vast plateau. The city is the commercial and industrial capital of South Africa. Downtown skyscrapers are fed by a large network of freeways, and the suburbs have large American-style indoor shopping malls. The vast northern suburbs, once reserved for whites but now being slowly integrated, are home to South Africa's upper-middle class. Security conditions in the city are primarily affected by a high rate of violent crime, ongoing political violence, and sporadic protests and strikes.

Demonstrations: Johannesburg is the site of sporadic protests and strikes, many of which turn violent and lead to clashes with the police. Many public gatherings, especially in the East Rand and in the downtown area, result in violent unrest among political factions. Black townships are also the site of frequent clashes.

CRIME

Crime statistics over the past year show Johannesburg as the most violent city in the world outside of a war-zone. The city's crime rate continues to spiral out of control. On average, one serious crime is committed every 17 seconds; a murder takes place every half hour; an armed robbery occurs every eight minutes. A normal weekend of crime consists of 40 murders, dozens of rapes and hundreds of burglaries and vehicle thefts. Easy access to weapons such as handguns and automatic rifles is one of the main reasons for the high rate of violent crime. Visitors to Johannesburg have a 1 in 20 chance of being affected by crime. Foreigners have increasingly been targets on the streets and in places tourists frequent, especially near hotels. Such crimes have ranged from pickpocketings to armed robberies to carjackings. In 1995 alone, 50,000 carjackings took place in Johannesburg. Several dinner-time robberies have led restauranteurs in Johannesburg to install locked gates and allow their patrons in one-by-one. Criminals in Jo'burg seem particularly ruthless. Policemen are often killed just for their firearms; average citizens are murdered for a car, a cellular phone, a camera or a fistful of money.

JOHANNESBURG TIPS

- Walking in downtown Johannesburg (central business district CBD) should be avoided due to the crime threat. It is recommended to use taxis or private transportation instead.

- The northeast suburb of Hillbrow is a no-go area, day and night. Extreme caution should be exercised in Joubert Park and the area south of the city; and the rectangle formed by Noord, Nugget, De Villiers and Eloff Streets.

- The suburb of Westbury has been declared an "unrest area" by police because of gang violence.

- If you feel your car is being targeted at an intersection, blow the horn and switch on the lights to draw attention to the criminals. Persons who are victims of carjacking incidents should offer no resistance if confronted by car thieves.

- Money should be carried in money belts and kept in separate areas on your person and in small denominations. "Muggers toll" can be handed over easier this way.

- Due to the potential for violence, travel to townships should be avoided. If you find yourself in a township, turn around and leave immediately by the route you entered.

- Always ride in cars with windows closed and doors locked. Do not stop at suspicious looking accidents.

- Plan your route before embarking on any road travel in the city. Always avoid low income areas and roads that pass close to townships. Be especially alert on the M1 motorway as the Alexandra township is next to the highway.

Carjacking: Armed carjacking occurs at a rate of one per hour in Johannesburg. More than 80% of cars are hijacked at gun point and 19% occur during daylight hours. Many hijackers will shoot to kill at the slightest provocation. Popular methods employed by hijackers are to force a driver to stop by using a car to force him off the road; bumping his car from behind or standing in his way; and attacking drivers stopped at traffic lights.

AIRPORT

Lanseria Airport (HLA) is midway between the capital, Pretoria, and the business center of Johannesburg. Lanseria is primarily used as a private corporate airport. Security at the facility is satisfactory for short stopovers.

TRANSPORTATION

Transportation arrangements in Johannesburg should be coordinated through a private and reputable company. The use of public transportation is not recommended. Hotel dispatched taxis provide adequate service, but the Rose taxi company is considered to have the most reputable drivers.

HOTELS

High crime has driven most tourists from downtown Johannesburg hotels. If a downtown hotel must be used, the Carlton Hotel, the city center's last remaining five star hotel, is adequately secured but the environs around the facility are unsafe. The northern suburbs offer better, safer choices for an overnight stay. Among the best suburban hotels is the luxury Sandton Sun.

EMERGENCY CONTACTS

Medical: Because South Africa has the worst tuberculosis problem in the world, visitors should be inoculated against the disease prior to their departure. Medical facilities in Johannesburg are well developed and comparable to those in Europe. A recommended hospital is:

IMAT Centre, 7 Third Street, Houghton; T: 728-4298

For medical emergencies dial 10111.

US Government: American Consulate General, Kline Center - 11th Floor, 141 Commissioner Street (intersection with Kruis Street); T: (27-11) 331-1681.

Police: The police telephone numbers in Johannesburg are: Flying Squad (SAPS): 10-111; Regional Headquarters (SAPS): (011) 230-239; Central Headquarters (SAPS): (011) 497-7510.

LONDON

CITY

Greater London (pop. 6.75 million) is the financial, intellectual, cultural and political center of the UK. The city consists of 32 boroughs, plus the City of London, spread out over 609 square miles. For about a century, a quarter of the world was ruled from here; London still retains an appeal that is both marvelously eclectic and yet supremely British. London is a multiracial city, with a large immigrant population from Britain's former colonies, especially from South Asia and the Est Indies. London is one of the largest ports in the UK. The city attracts millions of visitors each year, and tourism, especially in the summer, is a major industry and contributor to the economy. Because of London's long history as Britain's leading city, it abounds with major educational and cultural institutions. Historical sites are of exceptional importance...the Houses of Parliament, Big Ben, Westminster Abbey, the Tower of London, Buckingham Palace, etc.

CRIME

The crime problem in London is moderate when compared with large US cities, and, in general, the city experiences far less violent crime than its American counterparts. Opportunistic crimes such as burglary, pickpocketing, and theft are the primary concerns for visitors; many of these crimes occur in areas frequented by foreigners and tourists. Racially motivated attacks have been a problem in ethnically mixed areas of the East End.

The main security concerns in the city are crime and the threat of IRA terrorism.

IRA TERRORISM

Since the IRA ended its most recent cease-fire in February 1996 with a bombing in East London's canary wharf complex, six bombings have occurred around London. In most of the IRA bombings, the IRA called the police with a coded signal and warned of an impending attack. The City (financial district), ports and airports are on high alert, and security around Parliament and other strategic buildings, VIPs and the Royal Family have been intensified. Americans and US corporations are generally not targeted by the IRA as IRA operations are allegedly funded in part by Irish-Americans living in the US. However, travelers do stand the chance of being affected by terrorist activity by being near a targeted person or place.

AIRPORT

Due to past and present terrorist threats, the British Airport Authority (BAA) has implemented strict security measures at all London area airports.

Heathrow International Airport (LHR) is Europe's busiest, and security provided by the BAA is tight. However, criminal activity at the airport is high. More than 1,000 thefts occur each day at the airport, a large percentage of which are allegedly carried out by airport personnel and baggage handlers.

LONDON TIPS

- ☛ Travelers are advised to be cautious in the areas of Brixton, Nofting Hill, Paddington, Lewisham, King's Cross, Lambeth, Kirklees, West Yorkshire and Peckham, as these areas are subject to higher levels of criminal activity — especially at night.

- ☛ Travelers are advised to limit late-night travel on the Underground due to the increased presence of muggers and panhandlers, especially in railway stations. At night, visitors should be cautious on suburban routes operating from Victoria or London Bridge.

- ☛ A number of crimes take place when trains are pulling into stations. Be especially attentive to the presence of pickpockets at these times.

- ☛ The Piccadilly Line to Heathrow Airport, the district, Russell Square Station, the West End, particularly Leicester Square and Covent Garden are also favorite places for pickpockets.

TRANSPORTATION

To/From Heathrow

The airport is located 15 miles/24 kms west of central London. The airport is serviced by taxi, public bus, hotel shuttles, the Underground (subway) and private limousine service. Travelers should be aware of the rising incidence of robbery and pickpocketing on the Heathrow-Piccadilly line, and should try to avoid the Underground altogether if arriving late at night. Drive time into London is 45 to 60 minutes, and travel time by train is 30 to 40 minutes.

Transportation Within London

There are generally no security problems with public transportation in London. Travelers should note that pickpocketing, and occasionally even armed robbery, take place on some parts of the Underground, especially in areas of South London, parts of East London and the busy central London.

EMERGENCY CONTACTS

Medical: Medical care throughout the UK is among the best in Europe. This International Association for Medical Assistance to Travellers (IAMAT) has recognized the following facility as meeting its professional standards:

Drs. King, Clarke and Page
15 Basil Mansions
Basil Street
Knightsbridge
SW3 1AP London
T: 584-6718/6719

Police: The police are well organized and capable. The emergency telephone number is 999.

US Government: US Embassy 24/31 Grosnevor Square, W. 1A 1AE
W:1A 1AE London
T: 44-171-4999000

MEXICO CITY

CITY

Mexico City (population 22 million), more commonly known as the Distrito Federal, is one of the largest, most culturally diverse cities in the world. The city is famous for its charming Zona Rosa, excellent museums, exciting cuisine and its impoverished masses. Security conditions in the city are mainly affected by escalating criminal activity. Kidnapping for ransom, drug-related violence, and frequent demonstrations.

CRIME

The crime rate in Mexico City is high and on the rise. The rapid rise in criminal activity has been attributed to the devalued peso, record unemployment, poverty, corruption and increased drug use. While there are some especially high crime areas in Mexico City, no area can be considered absolutely safe, as crimes, especially robberies, are becoming more common in well-to-do middle class neighborhoods, which, until recently, were spared much of the violence long seen in poorer areas. The most common type of crime affecting travelers is robbery. Police estimate that about 4 murders and 150 car thefts take place each day in the city. The government has promised to spend an additional $1.6 billion over four years to prevent these sort of incidents by increasing the number of policemen and police vehicles on the streets. However, many locals do not think this will do any good as the police are often as bad as the criminals. Recently, the Mexico City police have been implicated in several armed robberies, while in uniform and on-duty. On August 9, 1996, an American and his Mexican friend were walking on Reforma at 11:45 p.m. when they were accosted by two policemen in a patrol car, one of whom was under the influence of alcohol or drugs. The two pedestrians were taken at gunpoint to an isolated location where they were told it was a crime to walk at night with another man, and that the two were required to pay a 3,500 peso "fine."

Kidnapping: Visitors to Mexico should now be especially vigilant to counter the threat of abduction, which is already fairly significant.

Demonstrations: In the past year, Mexico City has been affected by frequent public demonstrations against unemployment, the high cost of living, high taxes and sky-high interest rates and other problems. The majority of incidents take place in the downtown Central Square (Zolcalo) and The Plaza of the Three Cultures.

MEXICO CITY TIPS

☞ Mexico City's highest crime rates are reported to be in the districts of Cuauhtemoc, Gustavo A. Madero, Miguel Hidalgo, Iztapalapa, Alvaro Obregon and Venustiano Carranza.

☞ Foreign nationals should give as little advance notice of their movements as possible, to minimize the risk of abduction.

☞ When in a car, it is recommended to ride with the windows rolled up and the doors locked.

☞ If taking a taxi in the city, travelers should only use radio taxi cabs or those from authorized taxi stands (sitlos); avoid gypsy cabs and "green and white" cabs as many work with criminals and rob passengers.

☞ Visitors are advised to avoid sharing taxis with strangers as these individuals are sometimes criminals.

☞ Travelers should be alert for petty theft if using the Metro (subway) system.

☞ Female visitors are advised to avoid traveling on the Mexico City Metro during rush hours as women are frequently groped on the packed trains, when it is virtually impossible to identify or escape from the perpetrator.

AIRPORT

Security at Adolfo Lopez Mateos International Airport (MMTO/TLC) also known as Toluca, is generally inadequate. The airport is located 40 miles/64 KM west of Mexico City. Taxis and shuttle buses are available for transport to Mexico City, which takes between one and two hours. There is greater risk in taking a taxi or shuttle than in taking private transportation with a local driver, especially at night.

Transportation Within Mexico: Taxis, buses and the Metro are available in the city. The Metro is not safe at night or when it is very crowded and pickpockets are very active on it. Buses have similar problems. Taxis should only be used when arranged through a hotel or business contact. For business travelers, it is recommended to arrange for private transportation from a reputable company in advance. Armed criminals have ambushed cars at stoplights and at crowded intersections.

Hotels: Note that the vast majority of hotels in the Toluca area are located in a seedy neighborhood where many indigents walk the streets. Because of this fact, visitors are advised to avoid walking in the area around their hotels after dark; it is preferable to have the hotel contact a reputable cab company.

EMERGENCY CONTACTS

- Medical - Hospital Americano-Britanico, Calle Sur 138, just south off Avenida Observatorio in Colonias Las Americas), T: 272-8500; emergencies: 515-8359.

- The Secretaria de Turismo also provides 24-hour referrals to doctors, dentists, and hospitals; T: 250-0123/0151.

- Police - In the past year, Mexico City's chief prosecutor has cracked down on crooked cops and has fired nearly a quarter of the city's judicial police and a tenth of his department's law enforcement civil servants due to corruption and criminal activities. The police telephone number is 585-5100.

- US Government: United States Embassy, Paseo de la Reforma 305, Mexico City, T: (52) (5) 211-0042.

MOSCOW

CITY

Moscow (pop. 13 million) is the cultural, political and business capital of Russia. The Kremlin marks the center of the city, and a highway known as the outer Ring Road, 16 miles from downtown, circles Moscow and marks it boundary. The city's four airports are beyond the Outer Ring Road. While a private economy is emerging in the capital and new businesses are opening, many people are barely surviving. The security situation in Moscow is primarily affected by potential terrorist attacks by Chechen rebels or other groups, organized criminal activity, a high crime rate, and widespread corruption. In an effort to improve the city's lawless image, a police crackdown is underway.

CRIME

Organized Crime: Moscow is the center of organized criminal activity in Russia. In Moscow, 35,000 businesses are controlled by gangs — from large banks to the smallest kiosks. Gangsters sometimes conduct attacks in public areas. Many leading businessmen and politicians now surround themselves with bodyguards and travel in armored cars to deter assassination attempts. Russia mafia groups increasingly target foreigners doing business in Moscow for extortion. The situation has become so alarming that many companies now operate behind security doors with heavily armed guards. Russian bureaucrats sometimes work with mobsters or other corrupt Russians to extort Western companies.

General Crime: The crime rate in Moscow is fairly high. Street crime, like mugging, is rising. Serious crime, like premeditated murder, kidnapping, extortion and drug-related offenses, is also rising. Travelers should remember that crime in Moscow is not too much worse than crime in major US metropolitan areas like New York City.

Kidnapping: Kidnappings are on the rise in Moscow.

MOSCOW TIPS

☞ Avoid the Pyotr Razumovsky market in the northern part of the city as this is a high crime area.

☞ The Arbat shopping mall, which is popular with tourists, is frequented by groups of gypsy children who lurk in the entrances of foreign grocery stores, looking for foreigners to rob.

☞ At night, increased crime is reported in the areas around Red Square and the Kremlin.

☞ Drug dealing takes place at the following cafes: Mechta, Kabul and Gvozdika; at the following restaurants: Kashtan, Sofia and Olympia, and in the following markets: Danilovsky Market, Cheryomushkinsky Market, and the Central Market.

☞ Other high crime areas include Izmaylovskiy Park, Nevsky Prospekt, train stations, airports, markets and the "Art Park."

☞ Travelers may also be targeted for robbery near currency exchanges. In at lease one case, a currency exchange operator was in cahoots with robbers.

☞ In light of increased security checks, travelers are advised to carry proper documents and remain patient when dealing with security officials.

AIRPORT SECURITY

Security standards at Russian airports are grossly inadequate. Many terminals are dimly lit, security is disorganized and personnel are subject to corruption. The Civil Aviation Department admitted that Russian airports are short of cash to provide proper security checks on passengers and cargoes. In 1995, there were about 90,000 cases in which passengers tried to pass checks with banned objects, including arms. From 1990 - 1995, nearly one-third of attempted hijackings world-wide occurred in Russia. The mafia is involved in criminal activity at Sheremetyevo Airport. There are also reports that customs agents at Moscow airports have allowed luggage to pass unexamined for bribes of US$150 and US$250.

TRANSPORTATION

Private transportation should be arranged. Travel time from Sheremetyevo Inter-national Airport to the city is 40 to 60 minutes.

EMERGENCY CONTACTS

Medical: The International Association for Medical Assistance to Travelers (IAMAT) has recognized the following facility as meeting its professional standards and having multi-lingual staff: Mediclub Moscow, Michurinsky pr-t. 56, Moscow: T: (095) 911 5018, FAX: (095) 932-8653.

Police: Since the transition to a more market-oriented economy, many of the most competent Russian policemen have taken more lucrative positions in the now booming private security industry. The Russian police now lack the funds, equipment, training and personnel to effectively fight rising crime . In fact, there have been reports of policemen refusing to intervene even when a crime was occurring right in front of them. In Moscow the following are emergency telephone numbers: Fire: 01; Police: 02; Ambulance: 03. The city's Organized Crime Combat Division deals with cases against foreigners. Most officers do not speak English and, due to their low salaries, many officers are subject to corruption. Consequently, visitors are advised to minimize contact with the police to the extent possible. A 24-hour duty officer can be reached at T: 7-095-237-0411.

US Government: United States Embassy: Novinskiy Buivar 19/23, Moscow, T: 7-095-252-2451 through 2459.

NEW DELHI

CITY

New Delhi (pop. 8.3 million) is the capital of India as well as the cosmopolitan center of the country. The city's population is mostly Hindu, although there are also a large number of Sikhs and Muslims. Power blackouts and fuel shortages occur frequently. Security risks in New Delhi include sporadic terrorist incidents, civil unrest, demonstrations, crime, and kidnapping for ransom. Also, anti-American corporate sentiment and sectarian violence between Hindus and Muslims, issues which have not directly affected New Delhi recently, can, nonetheless, erupt any time.

CRIME

Crime in New Delhi remains moderate when compared to major US cities, although robbery and theft are increasing. In fact, the level of violent crime perpetrated against Indians has more than doubled in the past year. Rape cases have increased a whopping 30% since 1995, while kidnapping increased 6.3%. The primary crime problem for foreign visitors is petty theft, much of which is committed in and around tourist areas.

Terrorism: Since September 1993, there have been over 12 explosions in and around the Delhi area resulting in injuries and/or deaths. Targets have included public buses, restaurants, shops, movie houses and train stations, many of which are visited by Americans.

Demonstrations: New Delhi witnesses regular demonstrations, some violent, over a wide range of issues. Rowdy anti-Pakistan protests are fairly common.

Kidnapping: New Delhi continues to suffer from a high number of kidnappings for ransom. In most cases, kidnappers target the children of wealthy Indian parents and then demand large ransoms. However, persons are sometimes abducted for political reasons. While foreigners are not usually targeted, in September 1995, the U.S. Embassy put its staff on alert because of reports of impending kidnapping attempts on western officials and Indian diplomats.

NEW DELHI TIPS

- ☛ Travelers should be cautious around the Boat Club area, Parliament, Connaught Place, the Pakistani High Commission, and the President's House, as these are areas where demonstrations commonly occur.

- ☛ The US State Department has repeatedly warned that the area around Connaught Place could be a possible site of an attack by Kashmiri terrorists.

- ☛ In the crush of humanity in New Delhi's downtown areas and markets, travelers are advised to hold on tightly to their bags and wallets. In especially crowded locations, like movie houses, one may find several hands digging into one's pockets.

- ☛ The New Delhi police commissioner has advised all businessmen to maintain a low profile, keep itineraries private and to take different routes when traveling by car while in the city.

- ☛ Indian merchants will not accept dirty, tattered or torn bills. Travelers should, likewise, refuse to accept such currency as they will find damaged notes impossible to spend.

- ☛ Visitors would be wise to arrange for a contact to meet them at the airport ahead of time to expedite the check-in or customs process as airport authorities can be slow and bureaucratic.

AIRPORT

Security at Indira Gandhi International Airport (DEL) is less than adequate. Corruption is also a problem at the New Delhi Airport. Immigration officers sometimes openly solicit bribes from arriving passengers. Strikes by airport workers have resulted in travel delays.

Transportation To/From Airport:
The Airport is located 9 miles/4.4 kms south of downtown and is serviced by taxis, buses and rickshaws. The most secure and convenient method of reaching the city is by private transportation arranged in advance. Average travel time from the airport to the city is 45 minutes.

Transportation Within Delhi:
Public transportation is not recommended in the city; rather, private transportation like that described above should be utilized. If using a taxi, travelers are advised to use only marked taxis and to negotiate a price in advance.

Hotels:
There have been no reported security incidents at the Tai Palace Hotel in recent months.

EMERGENCY CONTACTS

The International Association for Medical Assistance to Travelers (IAMAT) has identified the following English-speaking clinics as meeting its professional standards in New Delhi: IAMAT Centers: 166 Jorbagh, 469-2544/461-1708, 110-A Kamia Nagar; T: 252-3107/711-5066; 62 Khan Market; T: 461-8593/469-0239.

Police: The overall quality of police assistance in New Delhi is generally good. Communication with foreigners is often a problem. Not all officers speak English very well, and even when they do, Americans may have trouble understanding them. Police corruption is a major problem. The police contact number in New Delhi (and throughout the northern part of the country) is 100.

US Government: United States Embassy, Shantipath Chanakyapuri, 110 021, New Delhi, T: 91-11-600-651.

PARIS

CITY

Paris (pop. 12 million) is one of the most beautiful and livable cities in Europe. Paris is more than 2,000 years old. Gauls of the Parisii tribe arrived there between 250 and 200 B.C., building a fishing settlement on an island in the river that is the present-day Ile de la Cité – the center around which Paris developed. Today, about 61% of the nation's bank and corporate headquarters are in the city. Much of the industry in central Paris is of the small-scale craft type. Book printing and publishing are major activities in central Paris; heavier industries are situated in the suburbs. The street plan and total urban development of Paris are divided into two parts by the Seine and connected by 31 bridges. The Rive Gauche or Left Bank (when facing downstream) contains the governmental and university sectors of the city. It is the site of the most famous landmark of Paris, the Eiffel Tower. Situated in the Seine, the Ile de la Cité is the focal point of the city and is dominated by the majestic Cathedral of Notre Dame de Paris. The Rive Droite, or Right Bank, contains the retail center, large department stores, hotels, and banks. The city's romance notwithstanding, there are a few security concerns. The biggest concern for visitors is crime, the vast majority of it non-violent petty theft. A great deal of industrial espionage also takes place in France. Travelers may also be inconvenienced by occasional strikes and other labor protests. There have been no major terrorist incidents in Paris since October 1995 when the Algerian Armed Islamic Group's bombing campaign ended. Since then security has been stepped up throughout France, especially in airports, railroad stations, and government facilities.

CRIME

Crime levels in Paris are lower than in most American cities. The most common crimes in the city are pickpocketing, baggage theft, vehicle break-ins and credit card theft. Paris is one of the world's worst cities for credit card theft. While violent crimes and murders do take place, they happen considerably less frequently than in US cities.

Espionage: Much industrial espionage is conducted in France. Consequently, it is advised that all sensitive corporate documents be kept on one's person or in a secure location. Avoid leaving such items in hotel rooms. Travelers should also be discreet in conducting business conversation on French airlines.

Strikes/Protests: Each year there are around 1,500 demonstrations (an average of four a day), many of which block the city's main arteries and cause traffic jams. So far, train and subway service in Paris has been unaffected.

PARIS TIPS

- ☞ It is best to avoid the city's northeast zone by Place Blanche, La Chapelle, and Bellevue due to crime.

- ☞ Visitors are likewise advised to avoid the Bois de Boulogne and Bois de Vincennes parks after dark as these areas are frequented by transvestite prostitutes and other unsavory elements once the sun goes down.

- ☞ Travelers should remain vigilant for petty theft on railways, especially the Gare du Nord and Gare de L'Est stations. Be attentive to pickpockets in the busy Chatelet Nation, Les Halles, Concorde, Barbes-Rochechouart-Pigalle, Republique, Montparnasse and Porte de Clingnacourt stations.

- ☞ The sections of Paris with the most criminal activity are the Ile de France, the Val D'Oise and the Seine-Et-Marne.

- ☞ Visitors should keep a close eye on confidential business information, as industrial espionage is a problem in Paris.

- ☞ Travel delays may also result from increased security checks imposed by French authorities after a slew of bombings in 1995 and one in December 1996 by Algerian militants. Security has been tightened at airports, Metro and train stations, and border crossings nationwide.

Terrorism: Terrorist activity in Paris has been limited since the bombing campaign by Algeria's Armed Islamic Group (GIA) came to an end in October 1995.

AIRPORTS

Paris is served by Charles de Gaulle Airport (located 14 miles northeast of central Paris) and Orly Airport (9 miles south of central Paris). Both airports maintain 24 hour operations. Charles de Gaulle is the largest airport serving Paris and has two terminals. A free shuttle is available to transfer passengers between terminals. Orly Airport has two terminals, referred to as the Orly-Sud (South) and Orly-Ouest (West).

TRANSPORTATION

There are no specific security problems with public transportation in Paris. There is occasional theft and violence reported on the metro and in railway stations, particularly in the Gare du Nord and Gare de l'Est. Busy metro stations like Chatelet, Les Halles, Barbes-Rochechouert also attract petty thieves. At night, drunks and thieves take up residence in some metro stations. Private transportation or taxis are recommended for maximum safety at night. Taxicabs are readily available throughout the city. Paris is also served by the Metro, which is an extensive subway system, and the RER (Suburban Express Train), which connects with the Metro in many places. Buses run from both airports ever four to seven minutes.

EMERGENCY CONTACTS

Medical: The nationwide ambulance telephone number is 15.

Hospital/Clinics: The American Hospital of Paris, 63 Boulevard Victor Hugo, Neuilly-sur-Seine, T: 4747 5300.

International Association for Medical Assistance to Travellers (IAMAT) Center, 36 Rue du Colisee, Paris, T: 4563 1843.

Police: The Paris police are responsive and professional. The emergency police telephone number is 17.

Fire: The nationwide telephone number to report a fire is 18.

US Government: United States Embassy: 2 Avenue Gabriel, Paris; T: 33-1-4296-1202, 4261-8075.

RIO DE JANEIRO

CITY

Rio de Janeiro (pop. 9.5 million) is known for fine beaches and exciting nightlife, especially in the Copacabana and Ipanema neighborhoods, and its large industrial and financial businesses. The city also has the dubious distinction of having one of the world's highest crime rates, a situation termed "critical" by the US State Department. This is mainly due to a 16 percent unemployment rate, high rates of poverty and rampant drug abuse. The main security concerns for the traveler are random street crime, followed closely by kidnapping. Large amounts of drug trafficking and corruption exacerbate the situation.

CRIME

Random street crime, kidnappings for ransom, drug-related murders and smuggling are all serious problems in Rio. Street crime cannot be avoided simply by staying away from certain areas; caution is advised all over Rio. Although most of the violent crime has been directed at locals, there is a danger of being caught in crossfire. Brazil has a murder rate of 21 per 100,000 people, compared to 10 per 100,000 in the US. Brazil's murder rate has tripled in the past 15 years. Rio's rate is even higher than the national average for Brazil at 70 per 100,000. Most violent crime is committed in the shantytowns which climb the city's hillsides. This fact doubtless contributes to the high number of people hit by stray bullets, 103 in the past two years. In fact, the Italian Circo de Napoli circus had to cancel the rest of its scheduled performances on October 30, 1996 because so many stray bullets were hitting the tents. On the bright side, crimes against tourists are down significantly, as much as 90 percent in Copacabana and Ipanema. The new tourist police force is credited for the drop in crime. Despite the drop in crime and the apparent success of the tourist police, it is still advised to avoid contact with the Rio police due to problems with corruption. There are reports of police planting drugs on foreigners at checkpoints and then extorting money from them to be set free.

Kidnappings

The primary targets of kidnappers are wealthy Brazilians, although several longtime foreign residents and joint venture partners have also been abducted. Family members of businessmen, government officials and sports celebrities are also targets. Multinational personnel are considered secondary targets, especially if they leave themselves in a vulnerable position. The latest multinational kidnapping occurred on 12 June 1996 when an Indian emerald dealer was kidnapped outside his hotel in Rio. A ransom of US $500,000 was demanded, and it is unknown if the man's family was able to secure his release. Most victims are taken when leaving work or home on workdays, with fewer kidnappings occurring on the weekends. Abductions are usually carried out in a very sophisticated manner. The culprits usually are well-organized, well-armed and use paramilitary methods to abduct their victims, giving rise to speculation that corrupt military or civilian police are involved.

AIRPORT

Security at Galeao International Airport (GIG) is not adequate. Security is handled by INFRAERO, a government agency. Airport personnel are poorly paid and drug trafficking is prevalent, both facts which contribute to a significant level of corruption among airport personnel.

RIO DE JANEIRO TIPS

☞ A common tactic for Brazilian thieves is to accost a potential victim and "notice" a spot of some kind on the victim's back. Another tactic used by robbers is to "accidently" spray the target with mustard. In both instances, the target is robbed as the thieves remove the stain.

☞ The areas of Copacabana and Ipanema, while tourist areas, still have higher crime rates than most areas in the US.

TRANSPORTATION

Transportation To/From Airport
The airport is located 15 miles/24 kms north of the city center. Taxis, limousines, airport shuttles and even helicopters are available for transport to the city center. The recommended mode of transportation is by private car arranged through a reputable company. Helicopter service is also an acceptable option. The drive from the airport is between 30 minutes to 1 hour.

Transportation Within Rio
There are problems with all forms of ground transportation in Rio due to the extremely heavy traffic and frequent carjackings and car robberies, especially targeting wealthy-looking individuals stuck in traffic or at red lights.

HOTELS
There are no reported security problems with the Sheraton, the Inter-Continental or the Caesar Plaza.

POLICE
The police department in Rio has been notorious for corruption and violence for many years, but the new police chief seems to have achieved some positive, albeit controversial results. There is now an official policy granting police officers large bonuses for "heroism in the line of duty," which in many cases means engaging in gunbattles with suspects, who are often killed. In fact, according to official figures, 20.5 people per month are killed by the police. This total includes several tragic incidents of police officers shooting innocent suspects and innocent bystanders. Despite the drop in crime and the apparent success of the tourist police, it is still advised to avoid contact with the Rio police due to problems with corruption. There are reports of police planting drugs on foreigners at checkpoints and then extorting money from them to be set free.

EMERGENCY CONTACTS
Medical: IAMAT Center Ipanema, 414 Rue Visconde de Piraja, #802, Rio de Janeiro; T: 294-6343/294-9790; IAMAT Center Copacabana, Avenue Copacabana 534, #308, Rio de Janeiro: T: 255-4706.

Police: The police emergency telephone number is 190. Call 511-5122 for the special tourist police branch.

US Government: US Consulate General, Avenida Presidente Wilson 147, Rio de Janeiro; T: (55-21) 292-7117.

ROME

CITY

Rome (pop. 2.8 million), the Italian capital, remains a tourist center despite its reputation as a mecca for petty thieves. Besides being a popular tourist spot and the seat of Italian government, the city is also a major business center. It is the seat of the supreme pontiff of the Roman Catholic Church (at Vatican City, a sovereign state within Rome). The Tiber, flowing through Rome from north to south, divides the city. On the east bank, the most visible and plentiful remains of classical Rome are located south of Piazza Venezia. Medieval Rome centers to the northwest and along the Tiber. As a cultural center, many of Rome's museums are among the world's greatest. Rome has academies of the fine arts; the oldest music academy in the world; and a state-run University of Rome with an enrollment of 150,000. The city's ancient ruins include the Colosseum, the Catacombs, the Forum, and the Pantheon. Under normal conditions, security conditions in Rome are affected primarily by crime.

CRIME

Most crime in Rome is non-violent. Robberies and pickpocketings are still a serious problem. Most violent crimes are Mafia-related; the Mafia is weaker in Rome than in southern Italy, but its power here has grown in recent years. Nearly 140,000 petty thefts were reported in 1995, most of them committed against tourists. The US Embassy receives at least five calls per day regarding robberies or lost valuables. Thieves are frequently either handbag-snatching youths on motorbikes, gypsy children or drug addicts. Since the beginning of summer 1996, tourists have been followed and then robbed of their Rolex watches. The robberies took place on Via Petralini in the Parioli area, on via Labriola and on Via Nemorense.

Terrorism: Terrorist activity in Rome over the past several years has been minimal.

Protests: Rome witnesses occasional large-scale protests. Such protests often result in travel delays.

AIRPORT

Airport Strikes/Work Stoppages: Strikes and work slowdowns have become the norm at Italian airports. Flight disruptions are almost inevitable during these strikes, particularly when ground crews or air traffic controllers are involved.

ROME TIPS

☞ Sophisticated petty thieves often operate in the city center, especially the Termini Railway Station and the areas around St. Mary Major, the Coliseum, Trastevre, the Prati, Trionfale, Via Emo and Piazza C. Ivour areas.

☞ Be aware that pickpockets are active on the number 64 bus from St. Peter's to the Termini Railway Station are frequently robbed by pickpockets.

☞ Thieves sometimes impersonate police to gain the confidence of travelers. If approached by a police officer, it is prudent to ask to see the officer's identification card.

☞ When changing money, count very specifically the lira you receive. Since you will likely be receiving many thousands of lira, do not allow the money changer to hurry you off before making certain you have the right amount. Many visitors are swindled in this way when changing money.

TRANSPORTATION

Transportation To/From Airport
The airport is located 10 miles/16 kms southeast of the city. Travel time from the airport is about 30 to 40 minutes, depending on traffic. Approved taxis, which are yellow and white, are reasonably safe. It is advisable to avoid using gypsy cabs, as unscrupulous drivers have sometimes robbed their passengers.

Transportation in Rome
There are no specific security problems with public transportation in Rome, although many petty thieves target tourists on public transport, especially buses.

HOTELS

Security and safety measures provided at most upscale hotels in Rome is adequate. There have been no reported security incidents at Rome's Hotel Tziano - Corso Vittoria and Emmanuel II in the past 2 years.

EMERGENCY CONTACTS

Medical: The International Association of Medical Assistance to Travellers (IAMAT) has recognized the following English-speaking hospital in Rome as meeting its professional standards: Balbo Medical Center, 43 Via Balbo, Rome: T: 06-485-775-474-1021.

Police: The Italian police officers receive training similar to that provided to police departments in large U.S. cities. Generally, police responsiveness is adequate. The high incidence of petty theft in Rome has forced the police to develop a full range of services for foreigners, including interpreters, multi-lingual switchboards and telephone lines on which to report stolen credit cards. The nationwide police emergency telephone numbers are 112 (Polizia de Stato) and 113 (Carabinieri).

US Government: United States Embassy, Via Veneto 119/A, Rome; T: (39) (6) 46-741.

SYDNEY

CITY

Sydney (pop. 3.7 million), the biggest city in Australia and capital of New South Wales, stretches almost 60 miles from north to south, and almost 35 miles across. The city is divided into north and south by its harbor (official name is Port Jackson); the areas of greatest interest to visitors, known as the eastern suburbs, are on the southern shore. The area bounded by Chinatown in the south, Harbour Bridge in the north, Darling Harbour to the west, and Kings Cross to the east, has plenty to occupy any visitor for several days. Over the past 50 years the city's Anglo-Irish immigrant population has been enriched by successive waves of Italians, Greeks, Turks, Lebanese, Yogoslavs and, more recently, Southeast Asians. This intermingling of cultures has created a vibrant, cosmopolitan atmosphere in Sydney. The architecturally distinctive Sydney Opera House, opened in 1973, is the Performing Arts Center of Sydney. It sits on promontory extending into the harbor and resembles a series of immense, wind-filled sails. The city is home to the Australia Museum, The Art Gallery of New South Wales, and the Museum of Applied Arts and Sciences. The University of Sydney, the University of New South Wales, and Macquarie University are in Sydney, as is the Mitchell Library, with its extensive collection of original source materials on the history of Australia. The security situation is mainly affected by a low crime rate.

CRIME

The crime rate in Sydney is low, similar to that in other large Australian cities. Sydney's crime rate is lower than most American cities and violent crime is still fairly rare. Rapes occur slightly more frequently in Sydney than in US cities like Los Angeles. However, murders occur 20 times less frequently in Sydney than is Los Angeles. The most common crimes in Sydney are petty theft, burglary and vehicle break-ins, but these are usually carried out without violence.

Bombings: In late October 1996, Sydney's subway was targeted in three bombing attacks, causing damage but no injuries. No one has claimed responsibility for the bombings. The bombs in all three incidents appeared to be home-made and consisted of plastic bottles filled with chemical accelerant or fertilizers.

Demonstrations: Sydney is affected by occasional public demonstrations, most of which end without violence.

AUSTRALIA

SYDNEY TIPS

☞ Places to avoid or use extra caution, especially at night, include Williams Street in Kings Cross, which is the heart of the city's "red light" district, Elizabeth Street near Central Station, and around Redfern Station, as these are high crime areas. The main drag in Kings Cross is sleazy but relatively safe.

☞ Patrons of pubs in the Kings Cross sometimes have been robbed by thieves who render their victims unconscious with drugged beverages.

☞ In late October, 1996, authorities in New Zealand reported that a mail bomb that was received in Wellington went undetected through security inspections in five airports, including Sydney.

AIRPORT

Security at Kingsford Smith Airport (SYD) is adequate. Security at the airport is provided by the Department of Transportation and Communications (DOTC), who are assisted by the Federal Police, the Australian Protective Service, and the State Police. Security personnel conduct round-the-clock patrols.

TRANSPORTATION

Transportation To/From Airport
The airport, which is located 6 miles/9 kms from the city, is served by taxis and buses. Travel time to the city is 20-40 minutes. An Airport Express Bus service runs to sydney's major hotels and operates ever 20-30 minutes.

Transportation Within Sydney
There are no designated security risks in using public transportation in Sydney.

TELEPHONE

To make a call to the U.S. or Canada, dial 00-11-areacode-local number.

AT&T calling card: 1800-881-011 for an AT&T operator;

MCI calling card: 1800-881-100 for an MCI operator;

Sprint calling card: 1800-881-877 for a Sprint operator.

EMERGENCY CONTACTS

Medical: Medical care in Australia is comparable to that in the United States. Urban centers and smaller cities have good hospitals with trained staff. The number for medical emergencies is 000.

The International Association for Medical Assistance to Travelers (IAMAT) has recognized the following facilities as meeting its professional standards: Traveller's Medical and Vaccination Centre, Unit 5, 48 Macquarie Street, T: 891-4850.

Police: The nationwide police emergency telephone number is 000.

U.S. Government: United States Consulate, Park and Elizabeth Streets, 36th Floor, T: (612) 261-9200.

TEL AVIV

CITY

Tel Aviv, a modern city with a population of 140,000, continues to be on alert following several suicide bombing attacks in the past few years. The city, known for its sandy white beaches, is visited by many tourists every year. The police presence in Tel Aviv has been beefed up and there are very tight controls on overall security. There are many checkpoints throughout the city, some of which have caused travel delays. However, daily activities in the city function despite the fear of future terrorist attacks. Security conditions are mainly affected by a threat from terrorism and a moderate level threat from crime.

CRIME

Tel Aviv has a moderate crime rate. Visitors are primarily affected by crimes of opportunity. For the most part, it is safe to walk day or night in Tel Aviv, although one should always be alert to potential criminal activity.

• **Threats against US Interests**: US interests have been threatened by several extremist groups in relation to ongoing international events. The US Embassy has advised American citizens traveling in Israel to exercise greater than usual caution in light of the growing political tensions in the Middle East.

• **Threats against the peace process:** Threats against the peace process continue. Americans are advised to avoid crowded areas, and areas, and avoid travel by buses or waiting at bus stops. The militant Islamic group Hamas continually threatens attack against Israel interests.

AIRPORT

Security standards at Ben Gurion International Airport (LLBG/TLV) are very high and the facility is one of the most well secured airports in the world. The Israel Airport Authority (IAA) is responsible for security at this complex. The IAA security department has total Jurisdiction to enforce security regulations.

• **Transportation to/from Airport:** The airport is located 12 mi./20 km southeast of Tel Aviv. Public buses and taxis are available at the airport. The use of private transportation from a reputable company is recommended. Travel time to Tel Aviv is approximately 30 minutes and to Jerusalem approximately one hour.

TEL AVIV TIPS

☛ Visitors should be aware that buses and bus stops have been targets of militant activity in the past.

☛ When traveling outside of Tel Aviv, visitors should use a reputable tour guide for sightseeing. A local will be very familiar with security conditions and can ensure the visitor does not stray into areas which are potentially dangerous.

☛ While terrorism has always been a concern, there have also been several recent strikes by labor unions, causing some travel delays.

☛ Violence/unrest may increase around these anniversary dates:

♦ November 15 is the 18th anniversary of the declaration of the Palestinian State

♦ November 22 is the 29th anniversary of the adoption of UN Resolution 242

♦ December 9 is the 191 anniversary of the beginning of Intifada

---

• **Aviation Concerns:** The U.S. Federal Aviation Administration has rated Israel to be "in compliance" with international aviation safety standards. It is important to note, however, that Israeli air traffic control has experienced some problems. The large volume of airplanes flying in and out of Ben Gurion has sometimes led to near-misses over Israeli air space. Also, on several occasions in recent years, flights arriving to Ben Guion International Airport have been affected by broadcasts from pirate radio stations that cross air traffic control signals. Pilots have reported difficulties in receiving communications from controllers and the airport has shut down during such times. An additional danger is posed by birds flying near the airport, which have occasionally been sucked into the engines of aircraft. In addition, while terrorism has always been a concern, there have also been several recent strikes by labor unions, causing some travel delays.

• **Transportation in the City:** Travelers should exercise caution when using public transportation, particularly buses, as these have been targets of militant activity in the past. Travelers should arrange for private transportation or use taxis. All taxis inside them major cities are metered, and tipping is not necessary. Self-driving in Israel is considered hazardous.

EMERGENCY CONTACTS

• Medical: Modern medical facilities may be found throughout Israel. The International Association for Medical Assistance to Travelers (IAMAT) has identified the following clinics and multilingual doctors as meeting its professional standards in Tel Aviv: Assuta Hospital: T: 520-1515, 695-1095; Icholav hospital: 6 Weizmann Street; T: 676-7070.

• **Police**: The Israeli National Police are highly trained, very professional and effective. The national police emergency telephone number is 100. The Israeli National Police may also be reached at 02-287-111.

US Government: UNITED STATES EMBASSY, 71 Hayarkon Street, Tel Aviv, T: 972-3-517-4338

TOKYO

CITY

Tokyo (pop. 12 million) is one of the most densely populated cities in the world, but it does not have the problems of crime, pollution and trash that plague other big cities. In fact, as a country, Japan remains one of the safest nations in the world, despite its economic problems. (The country has been experiencing a deep recession for the past four years.) Crime rarely affects foreigners. One problem that visitors often face is the confusing maze of streets, many of which are unnamed or change names frequently. Locals are generally friendly and helpful if asked for directions and many are eager to practice their English. Security conditions are mainly affected by a low crime rate and very infrequent terrorism.

CRIME

Although crime does exist in Tokyo, Westerners are generally left alone. The US Embassy cites less than two dozen reported crimes against Americans a year, consisting mainly of petty thefts and vandalism. Many of the reported crime is related to the Yakuza, or Japanese mafia, who primarily target other gangsters or local people. However, the number of pickpocketings reported in central Tokyo is increasing. Chinese and Korean gangs prowl crowded Tokyo shopping areas.

Terrorism: Tokyo suffered little or no terrorist activity before the March 20, 1995 sarin gas attack in the subway system conducted by the Aum Shinrikyo doomsday cult. However, police found 30-40 grams of super deadly VX gas in a canister buried in a western Tokyo riverbank on December 12, 1996 after a cultist admitted to placing it in hiding there. The cultist was the last fugitive sought from the sarin gas attack. VX gas is significantly more toxic than sarin gas. There may be enough cult members still at large to conduct some form of attack.

Anti-American Sentiment: The rape of a 12 year old girl on September 4, 1995 by three US Marines in Okinawa has become the focus of a national outrage. Two further attacks have reinforced this sentiment. All of these attacks have furthered the cause of those who want to remove the American military from Japan. A recent nonbinding vote showed that 89% of the Japanese people would like to see the number of U.S. bases reduced. Anti-American sentiment runs highest in Okinawa, where 75 percent of the U.S. bases are located. Most people outside of Okinawa, however, do not hold strong anti-American

feelings.

AIRPORT

Security at Narita Airport (NRT) provided by the Tokyo International Airport Authority is adequate.

Transportation To/From Airport
The airport is located 41 miles/66 kms northwest of Tokyo, and is one hour and 45 minutes from downtown by car. Trains, buses, taxis and private cars are readily available for transport from Narita Airport to downtown Tokyo.

Transportation Within Tokyo
Taxis are the recommended mode of transportation in Tokyo; all have meters and they are generally clean and safe. Buses, trains and the subway are also available but may be very crowded at rush hours. It is best to have your destination written down in Japanese so that you can show it to the cab driver if he does not speak English.

HOTEL

No security problems have been reported at the Rihga Royal Hotel, International Hotel, or he Four Seasons Hotel.

EMERGENCY CONTACTS
Medical: Medical facilities in Japan are comparable to those in the US. However,, Japan has a national insurance system and it can be difficult for foreigners not insured in Japan to receive medical care. Some clinics do not require deposits, but insist upon full payment at the time of treatment or require proof of ability to pay beforehand. The International Association of Medical Assistance to Travelers (IAMAT) has identified the following English-speaking facility as meeting its professional standards: Tokyo Adventist Hospital: T: 3392 6151. Ambulance services nationwide are available 24 hours a day at 119.

Police: Local law enforcement is very effective. Police officers are well trained and they have equipment similar to that used by US police departments. Generally, police can be depended upon both to arrive at the scene of an emergency in less than five minutes and to speak English. Police nationwide can be reached 24 hours a day by dialing 110.

US Government: United States Embassy, 10-5 Akasaka 1-Chome, Minato-Ku (107), Tokyo; T (81-3) 224-5000; FAX (81-3) 3505-1862.

TOKYO TIPS

☞ Travelers should exercise caution if venturing to the Kabukicho district, scene of many "adult" entertainment establishments because crimes like murder, prostitution and drug and gun trafficking take place more frequently here than elsewhere in Tokyo.

☞ After dark, it is recommended that women not walk alone in the Azabu section of Tokyo as purse snatchings have taken place there by motorcyclists speeding along the narrow streets.

CHAPTER 19

CONCLUSION

"My goal in life is to unite my avocation with my vocation, as two eyes make one in sight."

Robert Frost

Last year I was invited to Washington, DC to become an advisor to the White House Commission on Aviation Safety and Security. I was asked to consult with committee members as they began addressing the initial recommendations made to President Clinton.

I was told that my background in the airline security business, combined with my current responsibilities involving the corporate side of aviation, provided a well balanced mix of knowledge and objectivity to commercial aviation security.

I told the Commission:

1. We still have not made a conscientious study of the nature and severity of the risks facing the aviation industry. We still expose ourself to unnecessary threats.

2. We cannot assure absolute security for every passenger.

3. Technology alone is not the answer.

4. If we implement the Passive Passenger Profiling System I have recommended, along with high-tech machines, operated by motivated and capable personnel, we will have the capability to focus on the potential threat presented by the selected passenger. This will reduce our vulnerability.

My work with the Commission is expected to be ongoing. In the meantime, the corporate aviation business is thriving. The demands for corporate jets is on the rise, and travel security is a chief concern for many companies.

This country has been good to me and I want to give back more and more to its people. That's why I wrote *The Security Connection*. I feel a compelling need to tell you that you've got to look out for your own safety and security.

The federal government, the airline companies, and the law enforcement community all have roles to play in the war on terrorism...but our individual security roles are as important as theirs.

When all is said and done, we're only as strong as our weakest link. The puzzle is not complete until all the pieces are in place...until each of us does our part.

We can win this war on terrorism if we decide it's important. It's our decision.

I once had a banker ask me, "What's the best investment you can make?" He then replied, "Yourself!"

You can count on yourself. I know that. I've built a business on my banker's advice.

It all comes back to you. It's time now for each of us to build our own "security business"...to secure a better future for ourselves...our families...our communities...our country...and our world. I believe in you. I believe in your family. We're all in this together.